Poetic Epistemologies

––––◄o►––––

Gender and Knowing in Women's Language-Oriented Writing

Megan Simpson

State University of New York Press

Published by
State University of New York Press, Albany

© 2000 State University of New York

For information, address State University of New York Press,
State University Plaza, Albany, N.Y., 12246

Production by Michael Haggett
Marketing by Patrick Durocher

Library of Congress Cataloging-in-Publication Data

Simpson, Megan, 1960–
    Poetic epistemologies : gender and knowing in women's language-
oriented writing / Megan Simpson.
        p.   cm. — (SUNY series in feminist criticism and theory)
    Includes bibliographical references and index.
    ISBN 0-7914-4445-7 (alk. paper). — ISBN 0-7914-4446-5 (pbk. :
alk. paper)
    1. American poetry—20th century—History and criticism.
2. Language and languages in literature.   3. American poetry—Women
authors—History and criticism.   4. Knowledge, Theory of, in
literature.   5. Gender identity in literature.   6. English language—
Sex differences.   7. Feminism and literature—United States—
History—20th century.   8. Women and literature—United States—
History—20th century.   9. Experimental poetry, American—History
and criticism.   I. Title.   II. Series.
PS310.L33S56   2000
811.5099287—dc21   99-37947
                                                                          CIP

10   9   8   7   6   5   4   3   2   1

for my parents

~

Joan Erdmann Simpson
and
Charles Morris Simpson III

Contents

Preface

Among the many women poets who have begun to publish their work in the United States since 1970 are a small but growing number whose innovative, language-oriented writing[1] represents what I find to be some of the most vital and powerful poetry being written today. Though highly individual and distinct from one another in approach, style, and method, what these writers have in common is that their epistemological concerns cannot be separated from the feminist concerns that motivate their projects. What makes this poetry so vital is that by foregrounding the processes of language, "that strange matter in which I'm bound" (Hejinian, *The Cold of Poetry* 120), its writers explore the relations among knowledge, language, and gender, thus (re)uniting art with philosophy, and both with social critique. While their investigations are philosophical in nature, language-oriented women poets write not to espouse already-arrived-at philosophical positions or metaphysical truths, or what Susan Howe refers to as "total systemic circular knowledge" (*Singularities* 28); rather, they write in search of possibility. To this end, these writers enact a variety of playful transgressions in their writing, breaching boundaries between the creative and the analytical, writing and reading, subjectivity and objectivity, one identity and another, male and female, poetry and other genres, and, most important, art and knowledge.

Perhaps in part because their work eludes preestablished categories of genre and stylistic conventions, the writing of these women has been largely ignored by scholars in the fields of feminist criticism and American poetry. A few very notable exceptions include Rachel Blau DuPlessis, whose *The Pink Guitar: Writing as Feminist Practice* includes chapters on Beverly Dahlen and Susan Howe, Lynn Keller, whose *Forms of Expansion: Recent Long Poems by Women* also offers insightful readings of both Howe and Dahlen, and Marjorie Perloff, who has written extensively on Susan Howe and also discusses Lyn Hejinian and Leslie Scalapino among the many other contemporary innovators she treats in *Radical Artifice: Writing Poetry in the Age of Media*. But while several book-length studies of "language poetry" have been published in recent years, including George Hartley's *Textual Politics and the Language Poets*, Linda Reinfeld's *Language Poetry: Writing as Rescue*, and Bob Perelman's *The Marginalization of Poetry: Language Writing and Literary History*, none has focused specifically on women poets. Alicia Ostriker's important contribution, *Stealing the Language: The Emergence of Women's Poetry in America*, does consider women poets exclusively, but almost completely overlooks linguistically innovative writers, and does not treat language-oriented writing at all. In fact, language-oriented poetry by women has been doubly marginalized, avoided by most university and large publishers as well as women's presses and magazines.[2] As a result, an extensive critical assessment of this body of writing is long overdue.

My study focuses on eight American women poets whose work has not previously been brought together in a critical study: Susan Howe, Leslie Scalapino, Lyn Hejinian, Beverly Dahlen, Mei-mei Berssenbrugge, Carla Harryman, Lori Lubeski, and Laura Moriarty. I chose to include these writers in particular because they represent a range of writing styles and philosophical/political perspectives. In addition, they represent different generations: Beverly Dahlen was attending readings by beat and Black Mountain poets in San Francisco before Lori Lubeski was born. Some, such as Susan Howe, Lyn Hejinian, and Leslie Scalapino, are well established in their writing careers, and have been publishing collections of poetry for more than 20 years. Others—Lori Lubeski in particular—have published fewer books and are just beginning to enjoy wider reputations.[3]

Ironically, language-oriented women's writing, one of the most overlooked and obscured bodies of writing in the United States, may be best able to restore to poetry the substance and value we might have thought had been robbed from it. Poetry is neither a luxurious entertainment or pastime, nor a wholly subjective self-expression valuable only to the writer; poetry is a mode of knowing and of exploring the cultural and ideological processes of knowing. In a culture where what counts as knowledge is largely determined by disciplinary norms—the methods and regimes of truth that determine what is science, what is history—the ramifications of women's language-oriented writing are considerable. With the breach of the disciplinary boundaries that determine what passes as legitimate knowledge—a breach that language-oriented writing inherently invites—comes a kind of epistemological permissiveness to acknowledge and validate forms of knowledge and modes of knowing otherwise shrouded or discounted. Though I probably would not have articulated it this way when I first encountered language-oriented women's writing in San Francisco in the mid-1980s, what drew me almost weekly to readings and talks by Leslie Scalapino, Lyn Hejinian, Beverly Dahlen, Laura Moriarty, Carla Harryman, and other women writers at such "alternative" Bay Area literary spaces as New College, Small Press Traffic, New Langton Arts, The LAB, and Intersection for the Arts was the exciting sense of aesthetic and epistemological *possibility* that their poetics incited in me.

Of course for every reading or talk by a woman writer there were three or four by men, and I attended many of these as well, and with interest. But the women language-oriented writers tended to address issues of primary personal interest to me, such as the discursive operations of gender and the attendant relations of power at work in all signifying systems. The opening sense of "free knowing" that I felt in the presence of these writers and their work was certainly also due to the fact that, just when "women's writing" had become a recognized presence in American literature (usually marked by strong autobiographical impulse and transparent representation of women's experience) here was *another* kind of women's writing—indeed, not *one* kind of writing at all, but a variety of writings that had in common the insistence that relationships to language exist that are neither gender-neutral nor determined and fixed by the sex of the author. What a refreshing release from the double-bind by which I had myself felt constricted as a poet: to write with a sense of linguistic and philosophical innovation (and thus "like a man"), or to write autobiographical, confessional verse about my personal experience (and thus "as a woman").

And herein lies the crucial value to feminism of language-oriented women's writing: this work suggests radically imaginative ways that we might examine questions of gender. By suggesting not only that both gender and knowledge are discursively constructed, but that (therefore) knowing is always gendered even as gender itself is a type of discursive knowledge, these writers are able to conduct deeply searching interrogations into how gender functions as an analytical category in the process of knowing. Categories such as "woman," the "feminine," "lesbian," and "mother" can be reinscribed, unhinged, and deconstructed by opening up the processes of the very medium in which they are constructed to begin with: language. If gender is no longer seen as an essential characteristic of a core identity but as relationally and discursively constructed in a social context, a broader range of subject positions might become available for people gendered female and for other "others," allowing, in turn, for greater agency and active participation in the making of meaning and the processes by which knowledge is constructed.

Perhaps one of the more troublesome gendered categories that language-oriented women's writing demystifies is the classification "women's writing." Certainly, this designation has served well to make visible important literary work by women and to identify the subject of much feminist criticism in the United States. But just as "woman," the once-unquestioned subject of feminism, has over the past decade been subject to critiques from within feminism itself, charged with being overly essentialized and essentializing, so "women's writing" and "women's poetry" must yield to equally rigorous reevaluation. The notion that there is *a* type of writing, one poetic mode or set of poetic gestures that can be identified as "women's," tends to render women's writing that does not fit this definition invisible. The fact is that there are many varieties of writing by women in the United States, and many more throughout the world. Taking language-oriented writing by women into account allows us as readers and critics still another means of acknowledging a broader spectrum of writing by women, helping us to avoid pigeonholing any woman writer, whatever her relationship to language. If, in fact, one of the primary goals of feminist criticism is to give critical attention to the work of women writers who might otherwise go unnoticed, feminist readers need to pay considerably more attention to language-oriented writing by women.

Indeed, as feminist critics read more writers who do not fit accepted models of what feminist or "women's" writing is, feminist critical inquiry will become less constrained by its own categories and predetermined literary values. We might begin by revisiting the work of modernist women innovators, as well as contemporary writers, with this in mind. What if we were to regularly include in college literature courses Gertrude Stein's more difficult texts, and not only the occasional more "readable" of her prose works? What if we attended to the role language itself plays in H.D.'s feminist revisionist mythmaking? What if Laura (Riding) Jackson and Mina Loy were to find more than passing mention in courses and critical works on modernist poetry or women's literature? These writers are surely as important today as they were in their own lifetimes, perhaps more so in the context of current issues in feminist criticism and poetics.

As long as language-oriented women's writing is underrepresented in collections of "innovative" or postmodern poetry and virtually excluded from "women's," "feminist," and even supposedly eclectic collections of "contemporary American" poetry, writers such as Susan Howe, Beverly Dahlen, Lyn Hejinian, Lori Lubeski, Mei-mei Berssenbrugge, Leslie Scalapino, Laura Moriarty, and Carla Harryman will continue to be either unknown or dismissed as eccentric at best, pretentious at worst, and essentially unimportant. I agree with Harryman when she insists: "It is important that the art that women produce not be slotted as marginal, privatized, women's writing but that it be articulated dynamically in relation to the discussions already on the table" ("An Interview" 516). Indeed, by reading the work of language-oriented women writers alongside other "women's," "postmodern," "experimental," or merely "American" poetries, we might see that these categories are neither accurate nor useful, but serve rather to limit the ways in which new writing of all kinds might be received and understood.

True, language-oriented women's writing does not lend itself to passive reading methods or reveal itself according to normative values of "clarity." But I hope that this study has implications for further inquiry into language-oriented women's writing and feminist epistemologies—inquiries that do not discount as frivolous or elitist writing that is difficult or different from other women's writing in the United States. Here we might put Gertrude Stein and Mina Loy's advice to good use: If we can discard the "associational habits" and "received opinion" by which we learn to read literature and approach this more difficult writing with a willingness to participate imaginatively in the making of meaning, then we may find that indeed, to answer Lyn Hejinian's question with which I begin chapter 1, there *is* knowledge in poetry.

In chapter 1, "Language-Oriented Feminist Epistemology, and the Case of Lyn Hejinian's Faustienne Poetics," I offer a brief overview of the various intellectual histories and literary traditions out of which women's language-oriented writing has developed, including poststructuralist theories of knowledge and discourse, "language poetry" and feminist language theories. In this context, I introduce my notion of language-oriented feminist epistemologies to account for the connection between the epistemological and feminist concerns of these writers. Then, to illustrate this theory, I discuss the poetic project of Lyn

Hejinian, who most consistently conceives of her own writing project as epistemological. In her most recent and currently developing work, Hejinian explores questions about gender raised by the Western model of the quest for knowledge. Hejinian suggests that because "woman" has been identified with the object of knowledge, or that which is to be known, women writers seeking knowledge can subvert the Western model by taking up the "philosophical quest for uncertainty" ("from *Sleeps*" 42).

Most of the contemporary poets whose work I discuss claim the influence of many male as well as female poets, writers, and thinkers. But their experiments in language and form find special precedent in the work of their early twentieth-century female predecessors, experimenters such as Gertrude Stein, H.D., Mina Loy, and Laura (Riding) Jackson. In chapter 2, I identify the most important questions these poets raised in their work about subjectivity, language, knowledge, and gender, the barriers they breached, the experiments they undertook. Many of their poetic concerns—(Riding) Jackson's interest in language and truth, Stein's experiments in representation, Loy's "crisis in consciousness," and H.D.'s revisionist mythology—carry forward and find continued vitality in the work of contemporary women poets.

The next two chapters focus on specific philosophical issues prevalent in language-oriented writing by women, and in each I draw on the creative and theoretical writings of three poets to illustrate how these concerns are enacted in their work. One tendency that sets these writers apart from many "mainstream" poets and from what is commonly identified in the United States as "women's poetry" is that, rather than claiming the authority of an unmediated transcendental ego ("I"), language-oriented women poets are exploring the very conditions of subjectivity. In chapter 3, "Subjects of Knowledge: Processing Gender and Sexuality," I examine how Beverly Dahlen, Lori Lubeski, and Laura Moriarty "process" gender and sexuality in language as part of this exploration of subjectivity. These writers differ radically in their approaches to these issues. Dahlen's major work, *A Reading*, published in three volumes, is a "reading" of the psychological and cultural "contents" of the writer's unconscious, Freudian and Lacanian psychological discourse, the operations of language, memory, gender, sexuality, and identity. Dahlen puts her "self" into process in this work, which is elliptical, palimpsestically layered, transgressive, self-generating, exceeding itself. She claims to be seeking "forbidden knowledge" in the process. Lori Lubeski focuses on the physical body as a site of contested meanings. Feeling "herself" to be mediated, controlled, catego-

rized by class-, gender-, and sexuality-related biases, Lubeski experiments with fragmentation, incoherence, repetition, and abstraction in
an attempt to resist these oppressions and at the same time give form
to the often extreme emotional and psychic states that comprise personal experience, so that these experiences can, as she puts it, be "re-
seen or re-experienced." In contrast, Laura Moriarty uses lyric poetic
modes to interrogate and deconstruct cultural-literary conventions and
representations—especially conventions of romantic love—that have
participated in the construction of gender and sexuality in Western culture. She is especially interested in the ways she herself as a writing
subject is mediated by these conventions: "Am I that Laura?" she asks
(personal interview).

Chapter 4, "Feminist Phenomenologies: Language as the Horizon
of Encounter," examines how Leslie Scalapino, Mei-mei Berssenbrugge,
and Carla Harryman explore the relationships among knower, knowing, and knowledge. By focusing in their poetry on perception, framing,
spatial relations, memory, and repetition, they suggest that language
plays a significant perceptual and conceptual role in the phenomenological situation; language is always both representative and constitutive of "reality." Despite these similarities, the specific poetic strategies,
styles, and processes the three poets employ differ significantly. Furthermore, each poet offers her own unique alternative to normative or
"patriarchal" phenomenology. These writers enact a variety of feminist
critiques of this tradition, each in her own way and with differing effects. These critiques include the complication of the notion of the transcendental ego, insistence on the relevance of the social and historical
context of the individual's encounter with the world, and the deconstruction of the binarism subjectivity-objectivity. Leslie Scalapino enacts
a kind of perception-in-language that, as in Husserl's model of the subject-world encounter on which modern phenomenology is based, is
both inner- and outer-directed. But Scalapino offers a *feminist* phenomenology by complicating the notion of a transcendental ego in her insistence on the relevance of the social and historical context—including
gender relations and constructions— of the individual's encounter with
the world. Mei-mei Berssenbrugge, on the other hand, describes a more
physical, body-oriented alternative to patriarchal phenomenology. She
describes her poetry as being "about just where the body and word
emerge from each other" (Interview). Her poetic speakers embody
what Iris Marion Young identifies as "feminine existence"—becoming
subjects who possess both transcendence and immanence at once. Carla
Harryman is engaged in what she calls "an aggressive kind of play" or

language game in which she merges genres, subverts writing conventions, and investigates narrative and genre in an attempt to discover and enact "freer" kinds of knowledge and knowing. She is interested in the discourse of power and the marginalization of women, claiming to experience a "gap between my experience and the discourse that's available to me." She wants to "violate forms of knowledge and turn them into something else" in her writing ("An Interview" 526, 532, 527). Her project depends on the insight that language and literary-artistic modes of representation *do* play a definitional role in our encounter with "reality," and her response is to try to change that reality by manipulating the terms of the encounter.

The three writers whose phenomenological concerns are the focus of chapter 4 are also concerned with subjectivity; Scalapino, Berssenbrugge, and Harryman do, in fact, put subjectivity and sexuality into process in language just as do Dahlen, Lubeski, and Moriarty. Likewise, Dahlen, Lubeski, and Moriarty are no less interested in the phenomenological function of language than the writers discussed in chapter 4. In fact, the two issues are so interrelated that it would likely be impossible for a writer to explore one in her work to the exclusion of the other. My decisions regarding which writers to discuss in which chapters are not based on any essential distinctions or similarities among the writers. Writers grouped together within a particular chapter differ stylistically from one another as much as each does from those treated in other chapters, and the philosophical-political similarities among all eight contemporary writers included in this book transcend chapter divisions. Since my purpose has been to draw out the nuances of language-oriented feminist epistemology as embodied in language-oriented writing by women, I chose to organize most chapters around particular philosophical questions rather than according to the careers of individual writers, emphasizing in each chapter only those aspects of each writer's work that has most relevance to the chapter topic. This strategy has also allowed me to avoid certain otherwise inevitable redundancies.

Yet I do dedicate one chapter entirely to one writer in order to show how the various aspects of language-oriented feminist epistemology that I treat separately in chapters 3 and 4 come together in the work of a single writer. In chapter 5, "Textual Truth and Feminist Historiography in the Poetry of Susan Howe," I look at Susan Howe's work to trace how her unique poetic project partakes of all of the dimensions of language-oriented feminist epistemology. Howe's project is so complex and thoroughly realized that adequate treatment of her work requires a full chapter. Howe's intention in her work is to rescue the silenced and "feminized" voices of the past from "the infinite miscalculation of history" (*Singularities* 17), that is, from the ordering forms of traditional narrative history, historical texts, and interpretation. In relation to current debates about history, Howe negotiates between a certain empiricism and a poststructuralist emphasis on textuality. Pursuing truths that cannot be attained by means of rational objective analysis, she foregrounds the materiality of language, so that her writing becomes "a physical event of immediate revelation" (*Birth-mark* 1).

The chapters that follow have been influenced by and depend on recent feminist theory and feminist philosophy as well as poststructuralist language theory and poetics. Some of my most valuable resources, however, are the writers' own poetic theories—theories presented in essays, recorded talks, and published interviews, as well as my own original interviews, conversations, and written exchanges with the writers. I do not view these theoretical works as secondary or subordinate to the poetry, for one of the most significant characteristics of language-oriented writing—by women as well as men—is the interplay and overlap between the theoretical and the creative. Theory is not separate from or commentary on the poetry; rather, poetry and theory are equally vital parts of each writer's continually developing poetic-philosophical project.

This book is intended to offer both an introduction to the work of the individual writers it treats and a deeper appreciation of the philosophical and political implications of language-oriented writing by women in the United States. I am sensitive to the risks of reducing, simplifying, or supplanting the writing that this kind of scholarship necessarily takes. Therefore, I trust that what I say here will encourage readers to seek out and directly experience the writing of these women for whom language becomes an infinite source of possibilities.

Acknowledgments

This book would not be possible without the writers whose work it celebrates; I am deeply grateful to all of them. I am especially obliged to those who gave generously of their time to written exchanges, interviews, and comments on the manuscript: Beverly Dahlen, Carla Harryman, Lyn Hejinian, Lori Lubeski, Laura Moriarty, and Leslie Scalapino. Many others have offered invaluable feedback and encouragement in a variety of forms throughout this project: Ruth Salvaggio, Michael Fischer, Lee Bartlett, Jeannette Riley, Jennie Dear, Peter White, Gary Harrison, Merle Bachman, the three anonymous readers for the State University of New York Press, and especially, Minrose C. Gwin. In addition, I would like to thank Kathleen Fraser for first opening to me the world of women's innovative writing. For reminding me to take time occasionally for more quotidian pleasures and terrestrial pursuits throughout the research and writing of this book, I thank my husband, Tom Hall. And finally, I am indebted to my son Charlie, whose quiet presence during the spring and summer before his birth facilitated the completion of the first full draft of this project, and whose noisier presence since has never been a hindrance.

I also wish to thank the University of New Mexico's Office of Graduate Studies for its Research, Projects, and Travel Grant; the University of New Mexico's Graduate Student Association for its Student Research Allocations grant; the University of New Mexico's Office of Research for the Vice President's Graduate Research Fund grant; and the University of Texas of the Permian Basin's Office of Sponsored Projects.

Carla Harryman, interview, from *A Suite of Poetic Voices: Interviews with Contemporary American Poets,* copyright © 1992 by Manuel Brito, Kadle, by permission of Manuel Brito.

Carla Harryman and Lyn Hejinian, "A Comment on the Wide Road for O," published in *O,* copyright © 1993 by Carla Harryman and Lyn Hejinian, by permission of Carla Harryman and Lyn Hejinian.

Carla Harryman and Lyn Hejinian, "from *The Wide Road,*" published in *Avec,* copyright © 1991 by *Avec,* by permission of *Avec.*

© Lyn Hejinian 1987, 1980. *My Life* (Los Angeles: Sun & Moon Press, 1987). Reprinted by permission of the publisher. © Lyn Hejinian, 1992. *The Cell* (Los Angeles: Sun & Moon Press, 1992). Reprinted by permission of the publisher. © 1978, 1984, 1994 by Lyn Hejinian. *The Cold of Poetry* (Los Angeles: Sun & Moon Press, 1994). Reprinted by permission of the publisher.

Lyn Hejinian, "The Rejection of Closure," from *Writing/Talks,* copyright © 1985 by the Board of Trustees, Southern Illinois University, Southern Illinois University Press, by permission of Southern Illinois University Press.

Lyn Hejinian, "The Person and Description," copyright © 1991 by Lyn Hejinian. "Strangeness," copyright © 1989 by Lyn Hejinian, and "La Faustienne," copyright © 1998 by Lyn Hejinian, all published in *Poetics Journal,* by permission of Lyn Hejinian. Lyn Hejinian, "Barbarism," unpublished manuscript, copyright © 1994 by Lyn Hejinian; "Language and Realism," published in *Temblor,* copyright © 1986 by Lyn Hejinian; "from *Sleeps,*" published in *Black Bread,* copyright © 1993 by Gosling Press, and letters from Lyn Hejinian to Megan Simpson, by permission of Lyn Hejinian.

Susan Howe, *The Nonconformist's Memorial.* Copyright © 1993 by Susan Howe. Reprinted by permission of New Directions Publishing Corporation. Susan Howe, *Frame Structures: Early Poems 1974–1979.* Copyright © 1996 by Susan Howe. Reprinted by permission of New Directions Publishing Corporation.

© Susan Howe, 1990. *The Europe of Trusts* (Los Angeles: Sun & Moon Press, 1990). Reprinted by permission of the publisher.

Susan Howe, "Speaking with Susan Howe" by Janet Ruth Falon, and *"The Difficulties* Interview" by Tom Beckett, both published in *The Difficulties,* copyright © 1989 by Tom Beckett, by permission of Tom Beckett.

Susan Howe, brief excerpts from *Singularities,* copyright © 1990 by Susan Howe, Wesleyan University Press, by permission of University Press of New England.

Susan Howe, "The Poet and the World of Her Influences," copyright © 1993 by Susan Howe, by permission of Susan Howe.

Excerpts from *The Lost Lunar Baedeker* by Mina Loy. Works of Mina Loy copyright © 1996 by the Estate of Mina Loy. Introduction and edition copyright © 1996 by Roger L. Conover. Reprinted by permission of Farrar, Straus & Giroux, Inc.

Lori Lubeski, *attractions cf distractions*, copyright © 1985 by Lori Lubeski, e.g.; *Dissuasion Crowds the Slow Worker*, copyright © 1988 by Lori Lubeski, O Books; *Stamina*, copyright © 1994 by Lori Lubeski, Leave; *Sweet Land*, copyright © by Lori Lubeski, Boron; "from *Shady Lane*," published in *Chain*, copyright © 1995 by Lori Lubeski; "from *You Torture Me*," published in *Abacus*, copyright © 1994 by Lori Lubeski; *Obedient, A body*, published in *lift*, copyright © 1993 by Lori Lubeski; *Flail*, unpublished manuscript, copyright © 1994 by Lori Lubeski; and personal interview with Megan Simpson, copyright © 1994 by Lori Lubeski, by permission of Lori Lubeski.

Lois Oppenheim, "The Field of Poetic Constitution," from *The Existential Coordinates of the Human Condition: Poetic-Epic-Tragic*, copyright © 1984 by D. Reidel Publishing company, with kind permission of Kluwer Academic Publishers and Lois Oppenheim.

Joseph Riddel, "H.D.'s Scene of Writing—Poetry as (and) Analysis," copyright © 1979 by *Studies in the Literary Imagination*, *Studies in the Literary Imagination*, by permission of *Studies in the Literary Imagination*.

Extracts from *The Poems of Laura Riding*, by Laura (Riding) Jackson. Copyright © 1938, 1980. Reprinted by permission of Persea Books, New York, Carcanet Press, Manchester, and the author's Board of Literary Management. In conformity with the late author's wish, her Board of Literary Management asks us to record that, in 1941, Laura (Riding) Jackson renounced, on grounds of linguistic principle, the writing of poetry: she had come to hold that "poetry obstructs general attainment to something better in our linguistic way-of-life than we have."

Leslie Scalapino, *Considering how exaggerated music is*, copyright © 1982 by Leslie Scalapino, North Point; *The Return of Painting, The Pearl, and Onion*, copyright © 1991 by Leslie Scalapino, North Point; *that they were at the beach*, copyright © 1985 by Leslie Scalapino, North Point; *way*, copyright © 1988 by Leslie Scalapino, North Point; "from *Waking Life*," published in *War O/3*, copyright © 1991 by Leslie Scalapino; and written exchange with Megan Simpson, copyright © 1994 by Leslie Scalapino, by permission of Leslie Scalapino.

Leslie Scalapino, "An Interview with Leslie Scalapino" by Edward Foster, published in *Talisman*, copyright © 1990 by *Talisman*, by permission of *Talisman*.

Chapter 1

Language-Oriented Feminist Epistemology, and the Case of Lyn Hejinian

> But let me ask if there is knowledge in poetry . . .
> —Lyn Hejinian, "Oblivion" (*The Cold of Poetry* 195)

"A space that has opened": Gender and Language[1]

Of course language-oriented women writers are not the first or only thinkers to investigate the relationship between gender and language. Language—its limitations and its possibilities—has been of ongoing interest to women writers and feminist theorists. An important moment in the history of feminist theories of writing is occupied by *l'écriture feminine*, or feminine writing, which has helped suggest new possibilities for women writers, possibilities that many language-oriented women writers in the United States have been exploring. Articulated in different ways by French feminist theorists including Julia Kristeva, Hélène Cixous, and Luce Irigaray, notions of feminine writing suggest that women have a problematic relationship to patriarchal discourse (variously described in the theories as "rational," "representational," "symbolic," "coherent," and "fixed"). These theories of feminine writing were developed as part of a broader feminist critique of the structuralist psychoanalysis of Jacques Lacan. According to Lacan's

1

theory of subjectivity, meaning in the symbolic realm of discourse and communication is generated in relation to the primary transcendental signifier, the phallus. Within this model, there is apparently no way for women to exist in the symbolic—in language—except in relation to the male. The so-called French feminists responded variously to Lacan by positing different symbologies for women beyond the phallic— Cixous's "body writing," Irigaray's critique of "specular" economies, Kristeva's "semiotic." By locating the "feminine" elsewhere, feminine writing allows women distinctive voices often disruptive of phallic signification.

Many language-oriented women writers—whether they define their projects as overtly psychological, as does Beverly Dahlen, or whether they are more interested in how socially constructed normative models affect women's relationships to language and knowledge, as is Carla Harryman—share some of the French feminists' ideas about language and gender. The issues they explore in their writing include women's fraught relationship to the symbolic order, the connection between language and power, and the notion of radical aesthetics as ideology critique. While in much of their writing, proponents of l'écriture feminine trace women's problematic relationship to patriarchal discourse to psychological origins, these theorists do not deny that cultural forces are also at play. For them, as well as for many language-oriented women writers, what marks writing as "feminine" is not the gender of the writer, but the qualities of the writing that place it outside the economy of symbolic discourse. But it is important to note that language-oriented women writers share no one unified position on the question of a feminine aesthetic, and often express ambivalence toward the idea of feminine writing. "I am very conflicted over this subject of a feminine or a masculine voice," admits Susan Howe in her interview "Speaking with Susan Howe" (SSH): "I hope poetry that is Poetry contains both voices" (28).

Several recent insightful accounts of the revolutionary potential of linguistically transgressive writing point the direction that my project will take by describing the feminine and feminist implications of experimentation in language. In her article "Women & Language," language-oriented writer Johanna Drucker advocates a further theorizing of the French feminists' Freudian-Lacanian model of sexual identity and language acquisition to include a more thorough consideration of historical and social factors, but accepts their conclusion that women do have a different relationship to language. Drucker argues that language does not structure our experience, but functions to structure our *relationship* to both the real and the imaginary. Therefore, by actively choosing to use language "with a kind of improvisational freedom" (61), to "question the assumption of syntax, the authoritarianism of codes which force the structure of expression into the categorical distinctions of grammatical absolutes," both male and female writers can allow the system of rational symbolic discourse "to be seen not as an inevitable, extant order" but as itself the product of specific linguistic practices (66–67). In this model Drucker defines the "feminine" not as an essence that belongs to biological females, nor as "the product of socially determined situations," but as "a concept which critiques the relation between authority and language in the alignment of the patriarchal power termed 'masculine' with language itself" (57).

And in "Poetic Politics: How the Amazons Took the Acropolis," Jeffner Allen describes what she calls poetic politics—"a commitment to textual action" that she finds common in lesbian and feminist writing (307). Like Drucker's feminine writing, poetic politics effects a kind of "pulverization of 'language proper'" (314) and thereby "takes by surprise, and devastates, patriarchal institutions that would control the distribution of meaning, value, and physical goods against the self-defined interests of each woman" (307). And it is by attending to language itself, its processes of constituting meaning, that this writing is able to have an effect. As Allen puts it, "The poetic are political in the most efficient and ensnaring sense, because it takes place in language . . . writing and action are inseparable" (319). Allen is also careful to insist that poetic politics is not comprised of any one strategy or style, but of many.

Similarly, Rachel Blau DuPlessis's book *The Pink Guitar: Writing as Feminist Practice* is an extended argument for the political viability of language-oriented writing by women. In her opening chapter, "For the Etruscans," DuPlessis explores the notion of a "female aesthetic." Like Drucker with her feminine writing, DuPlessis does not consign the practice of the female aesthetic to biological females only, but instead refers with the term to "any practices available to those groups—nations, genders, sexualities, races, classes—all social practices which wish to criticize, to differentiate from, to overturn the dominant forms of knowing and understanding with which they are saturated" (16). DuPlessis's notion of the female aesthetic, like Drucker's feminine writing, operates as a critique of normative and oppressive discourses. And like Allen, DuPlessis insists that there is "not *a* female aesthetic, not one single constellation of strategies," but rather, "various and possibly contradictory strategies of response and invention shared by women in response to gender experiences" (3, 10).

In her introduction to *Language Unbound: On Experimental Writing by Women*, Nancy Gray also stresses the role that experience plays in experimental writing by women. Where for Allen writing and action are inseparable, for Gray writing and experience are inseparable: "Language and experience become interactive, so that words are not merely symbolic but also experiential—experience itself" (5). Gray warns against equating experimental language uses with *the feminine* (as DuPlessis seems to do). Although such a concept makes experimental writing strategies available to writers of both genders, "feminine" writing by women is read differently than that by men—not as the product of conscious strategy, but as expressions of "a female essence of which she herself is a representative." Avoiding this problem does not require that we treat gender issues separately from the question of experimental writing. In fact, Gray finds that gender is almost inevitably an issue in experimental writing by women: "Insofar as the term *experimental writing* connotes that which does without or makes untenable the assumptions of literary realisms that naturalize cultural ideology to claim it as a Reality, it affords women writers an important means of leaving old gender codes behind and breaking into language as experience, not as representation" (4–5).

By breaking into language as experience, not as representation, language-oriented women writers avoid the trap of striving to represent the feminine through a feminine or female aesthetic. The concept of "the feminine," when it occurs in language-oriented women writers' theories—from Lyn Hejinian's "la faustienne" to Beverly Dahlen's "root of bare breast" that she imagines is revealed in a gap of language (*AR* 11–17 11)—operates not as a fixed essence but rather as Drucker defines the feminine, a "concept which critiques the relation between authority and language" (57). In creative work that is a kind of textual action, language-oriented women writers experience a freedom from preestablished norms, rules, or codes. As Leslie Scalapino puts it, "the process of the writing is an alleviation of the social rigidity" (written exchange). Writing in which language is experience rather than representation might allow an increased agency for both readers and writers (women as well as men who have otherwise felt their own agency to be limited) of such work.

It should not be surprising, then, that so many women poets have become conspicuously language-oriented in their writing. While most of the writers initially associated with "language poetry" were men, a few women—including Lyn Hejinian and Carla Harryman—were involved fairly early.[2] Three poets out of the nine included in Silliman's selection in *Alcheringa* in 1975 were women. Through the 1980s, as the definitions and boundaries of "language poetry" were articulated and refined, contested and denied (by those "outside" the movement as well as those "within"), more and more writing by women continued to appear in the various journals and magazines associated with "language poetry."[3] The number and variety of women poets whose experiments in language and form continue to contribute to the increasingly multifaceted and diverse body of language-oriented writing suggest that linguistic innovation offers many women writers ways to pose questions and suggest possibilities about issues of knowledge, subjectivity, language, and gender that more conventionalized modes of writing might obscure or take for granted.

I focus specifically on women language-oriented writers in this study in order to explore how gender concerns, for these women, contribute to their political-philosophical investigations of language and meaning. What sets American women language-oriented writers apart from their male counterparts is the urgency with which they recognize that the question of how meaning is constituted has particular significant consequences for women. As a result, their writing often explores the role that gender plays in the subject's relationship to language and to knowledge. Certainly such investigations are not conducted only by women writers, or by all women writers. Obviously male writers can and do write language-oriented work, and gender can be of concern to male language-oriented writers as well. And gender is certainly not the only or primary social category of concern to such writers. But, as Rae Armantrout suggests, "[a]s outsiders, women might, in fact, be well-positioned to appreciate the constructedness of the identity which is based on identification and, therefore, to challenge the contemporary poetic convention of the unified Voice" (8–9). DuPlessis offers a more complex and complete model, ascribing to women what she calls an "insider-outsider social status." A woman who "finds she is irreconcilable things: an outsider by her gender position, by her relation to power; may be an insider by her social position, her class" (*Pink* 8). To DuPlessis's duo of gender and class I would add the historically specific social implications of race and sexuality. Still, underlying these theoretical imperatives to limit my study to writing by women is the simple fact that my interest is in women writers. In this sense my project falls within the domain of gynocritics—a term coined by feminist critic Elaine Showalter to refer to the study of women writers and of the history, styles, and structures of writing by women. Showalter defines gynocritics as "historical in orientation; it looks at women's writing as it has actually occurred and tries to define its specific characteristics of language, genre, and literary influence within a cultural network that includes variables of race, class, and nationality" (37). I am looking at language-oriented women writers *as women* and asking what they are doing in their work, why, and how their work speaks to issues of gender.

In particular, most of these poets acknowledge a connection between using language innovatively and their concerns with gender. Beverly Dahlen suggests that "the tradition of the avant-garde is important for women because it's a space that has opened . . . it's a fluid space" (personal interview). Laura Moriarty likewise finds more space in experimental writing, an alternative to the "very masculine" models of writing that were predominant when she began to write in the 1970s, when she "was very interested in a more nurturing kind of writing" (personal interview). Leslie Scalapino acknowledges that her writing is feminist,

> though not as any specific "whole" doctrine known to me. . . . "Centers" as economic and military power exist obviously—and we're articulated by conditions not of our choosing that are creating history—but the place where "one" is created and exists in writing is necessarily elsewhere from this. Because writing alleviates society's rigidity, in fact. The process of the writing is an alleviation of the social rigidity. (Written exchange)

Language-oriented writing also allows one to investigate and expose modes of discourse that serve to marginalize women. Carla Harryman describes this aspect of her project: "Gender is a real concern for me in my writing. . . . I'm very interested in power and the marginalization of women. I'm very interested subjectively in the gap between my experience and the discourse that's available to me—whether it's theoretical, philosophical, or just sort of quotidian media" ("An Interview" 531–32).

Susan Howe shares Harryman's concern with gender and discourse. But Howe's work is historical; her primary intention is to recover the varied female, feminine, and feminized voices of the past, to render audible what she refers to in "*The Difficulties* Interview" (DI) as the "silenced factions" (24) from their "Destiny of calamitous silence" (*Singularities* 25) to which traditional narrative historiography has banished them. Although in one recent interview Howe claims that her own gender is incidental to her writing, for "there's a mystery about poetry that transcends gender" (SSH 28), in another interview she acknowledges a difference that must extend to the conditions under which the poet writes. To Charles Olson's statement "I take SPACE to be the central fact to man born in America"

(11) Howe responds, "I am a woman born in America. I can't take central facts for granted" (DI 21). None of the language-oriented women writers I treat in this study take central facts for granted.

But gender is not the only social category of concern to these writers, nor is their interest in gender traceable to the actual social positions of the writers. For instance, Lori Lubeski and Beverly Dahlen are additionally concerned with sexuality and class. Lubeski is from a working class background and does claim a lesbian identity. But while Dahlen's concern with sexuality is certainly not coincidental to her lesbianism, she has not always lived as a lesbian and she rejects the category itself. Leslie Scalapino, from a white upper-middle-class background, frequently addresses in her writing social injustices related to class and race. In other words, gender is, for most of these writers, one of a network of related axes of difference that their feminist projects address.

Language-Oriented Feminist Epistemology

Despite the diversity among language-oriented women writers and their lack of adherence to any single organized doctrine or method, the eight writers treated here do share a nonconformist, feminist vision and impulse. These writers offer in their work what I call "language-oriented feminist epistemologies"—ways of knowing that take gender into account without essentializing it, and that interrogate the very category of knowledge and the conditions of knowing.

Of course all language-oriented writing, whether feminist or not, is inherently epistemological: the question of how meaning is constituted in language is really a question of how we know what we know. This epistemological function of language, in turn, hinges on a notion of knowledge as inseparable from the social. Such a notion is the basis of Michel Foucault's call "to restore to discourse its character as an event" ("Discourse" 229). And by foregrounding the processes of language, language-oriented writing does treat discourse as an event, suggesting that *how* we know and *what* we know are not distinct categories. Jerome McGann has developed a theory of poetic knowledge that places both poetry and knowledge in the realm of social relations. In *Social Values and Poetic Acts* (*SVPA*) he claims that "what we call knowledge is not a corpus of information but a series of knowing acts that have been and are carried out under particular circumstances" (54), and urges us to conceive of poetry "as a social activity." Poems, in turn, he views as "instances of a kind of social practice carried out through determinate material forms and institutions, and at particular places and times by many different people" (245). A poem is a communicative act, historically situated. Furthermore, poetic knowledge is a function of poetry's performativity. Because "the human world is not made up of 'facts' and/or 'interpretations,' it is made up of *events*" (72), and the poetic is "an event of language" (82), "[p]oems, therefore, should not be conceived of as representations; they are acts of representation" (246). McGann never specifies what he means by "poetry" in these descriptions; presumably all poetry—if it is to be called poetry—functions performatively in a social field, whether its writers and readers acknowledge these facts or not. But whereas "workshop poetry"[4] would seem to depend on obscuring or even denying these characteristics, McGann's theory is particularly applicable to language-oriented writing that calls attention to these epistemological operations, acknowledging that all knowledge is mediated by language, and exploring the implications of this insight.

But as I pointed out in my preface, the epistemological concerns of the women language-oriented writers whose work is my subject cannot be separated from their feminist concerns. Each writer suggests, in her investigations into how meaning is constituted in language, that this question cannot be answered without taking into consideration the question of how the discursive operations of gender participate in the production of knowledge. Although McGann does not address gender per se in his writings on poetics, Joan Scott's gender theory helps show how his theories are conducive to a language-oriented feminist epistemology by revealing gender to be one kind of knowledge that is socially constructed in discourse. Specifically, Scott explains that gender is "the knowledge that establishes meanings for bodily differences" (2). Therefore, "if we attend to the ways in which 'language' constructs meaning we will also be in a position to find gender" (55). Scott's definition of gender "rests on an integral connection between two propositions: gender is a constitutive element of social relationships based on perceived differences between the sexes, and gender is a primary way of signifying relationships of power" (94). In other words, gender functions as a meaning-making mechanism, or a discourse, rather than a fixed biological category. By positing writing as a mode of knowing that continually interrogates its own methods and processes rather than a means to arrive at final conclusions or truths that exist outside the writing, so that "the knowing itself would be new, the news" (Dahlen, *AR 8–10* 133), language-oriented women writers open up to imaginative exploration these social relationships and signifying practices. These writers investigate the social functions of knowledge as well—what Foucault calls each society's "regimes of truth" that determine how knowledge is produced, gets defined, valued, and shared—always taking into account the function that gender plays in these social processes. "No objects, spaces, or boundaries are sacred in themselves" (Harryman, *There Never Was a Rose without a Thorn* 40); gender and language are always interrelated and implicated in knowing. Language-oriented feminist epistemologies begin with the insight that how we know what we know, as well as what counts as "knowledge" in our culture, is *gendered*, and this gendering takes place in—and can therefore be transformed within— language. As such, language-oriented feminist epistemologies are distinct from both positivist and feminist standpoint epistemologies.

Feminist standpoint epistemology, rooted in a historical materialist critique of the sexual division of labor, is not wholly inconsistent with language-oriented feminist epistemology. Certainly they both offer critiques of the normative notions of knowing and knowledge that are based on the Western philosophical traditions of existentialism and phenomenology. They share the view that these supposedly gender-neutral systems of thought are not, after all, gender-neutral. But a closer look at this and some other of the most apparent points of overlap between language-oriented and standpoint feminist epistemologies reveals significant differences. For instance, whereas the feminist standpoint epistemologist would attribute this lack of neutrality to a dominant masculine experience assumed to be normative, a language-oriented woman writer is more likely to suggest in her work that this bias is a function of the way that disciplines maintain their linguistic influence and claims to objectivity by reinforcing gender categories and definitions.

In addition, both standpoint and language-oriented feminist epistemologies are based on the assumption that knowledge claims are always socially situated. But in their analysis of this situatedness, standpoint epistemologists attend to the material conditions of women's lives and pay little attention to the role language and discourse play in the construction of knowledge. Granted, language-oriented women writers' concern with gender and other axes of difference likely do stem from their own gender-, class-, race-, and sexuality-marked experiences in twentieth-century Western culture, but their analysis of that experience as it appears in their writing is never limited to labor divisions or to distinctively "female experience" as such. They focus instead on how gender renders and is rendered in discourse, how gender categories and other marks of difference facilitate the policing of discourse to determine which discourses are available to which people. Feminist standpoint epistemologists, on the other hand, claim that "women's experience" of being oppressed by male dominance defines for them a "standpoint" or perspective from which they are able to gain a more accurate understanding of human relations than males have access to from their positions of dominance. As Sandra Harding and Merrill B. Hintikka put it, "distinctive aspects of women's experience . . . can provide resources for the construction of more representatively human understanding . . . a foundation for a more adequate and truly human epistemology" (x–xi).

Language-oriented women writers make no such claims. To the contrary, their writing suggests that the vision available to those in power is not more partial or less "representatively human" than the vision available to those who experience various forms of oppression. So while standpoint feminist epistemologist Sandra Harding urges her readers to accept "the idea of real knowledge that is socially situated" (50), language-oriented women writers would not make a distinction between "real" knowledge and partial or false knowledge. Language-oriented feminist epistemology posits *all* knowledge as socially situated and discursively constructed. This insight is valuable in a feminist analysis because it can illustrate how gender functions discursively and how socially constructed categories such as gender impose limits on human experience and understanding. Furthermore, a language-oriented feminist epistemologist would perceive power to operate not as a simple dichotomy, as standpoint feminists seem to view it (those in power versus those oppressed by the powerful), but in a more Foucauldian sense, as a constantly changing and multiply located set of complex relations.

As a further point of differentiation, Nancy C. M. Hartsock's proposal "to lay aside the important differences among women across race and class boundaries and instead search for central commonalities" (290) reveals the extent to which a standpoint epistemology, as its name implies, requires some solid ground (natural, universal commonalities among women, for instance) to stand on. Indeed, her description of how the sexual division of labor offers women a different perspective from that of men is steeped in essentialist notions of gender: "The female experience in reproduction represents a unity with nature which goes beyond the proletarian experience of interchange with nature" (293). So while standpoint epistemology operates by identifying "the deeper level or essence [that] both includes and explains the 'surface' or appearance [of sexual/social inequality], and indicates the logic by means of which the appearance inverts and distorts the deeper reality" (Hartsock 285), language-oriented women writers are skeptical of such deep meanings. According to a language-oriented feminist epistemological viewpoint, the surface—discourse—is what structures reality, and understanding how that surface works helps us to see how we are led to believe in deep meanings and essences, such as "feminine experience" or "lesbian desire" or the "self." As I illustrate in chapter 3, Beverly Dahlen's poetic critique of unified subjectivity and fixed definitions of gender and sexuality is based on her suspicion that the power relations in patriarchal social structures that many feminists would most like to change are in fact maintained by and depend on such illusions of deep essence.

To language-oriented women writers, gender, while not the only axis of difference they interrogate, is especially important because it is, to return to Joan Scott, "a primary way of signifying relationships of power" (94).[5] Their writing investigates how gender operates discursively, as an analytical category, not as a perspective of inequality defined by the gender of the knower-writer. One does not have to be a woman or to have had cultural experiences typically associated with women to conduct such an investigation. Language-oriented feminist epistemology is not a *woman-centered* epistemology or a *feminine* epistemology. It is *feminist* because it seeks to disclose and change the operations of power in discourse that have depended on limited and fixed notions of gender and other differences among people.

The modes of inquiry in which these writers engage involve a feminist inquiry into authority. Always indeterminate, open, resisting closure, this writing performs interpretive, expressive, dialogic acts that require both reader and writer to participate in the "untraceable wandering / the meaning of knowing" (Howe, *Singularities* 25)—reader and writer are engaged with language and with one another. Thus, both assume dynamic roles as participants in the making of meaning.

"Night Knowledge": Lyn Hejinian's Faustienne Poetics

"My mortal state, *knowing*, gives
me no guarantee of what
will happen"
So reality is a process
not an identity
—Lyn Hejinian (*The Cell* 105)

That reality is a process, and a person's knowledge of reality is also therefore a process—something experienced rather than something possessed—is a central motivating assumption behind Lyn Hejinian's poetics. Hejinian's many poetic works—open, elliptical, ongoing—demonstrate and explore the epistemological problem of "the real" that we are faced with when we acknowledge that language plays more than a merely descriptive role in our knowledge of the world.[6] Such a perspective, especially if it brings with it a "language-oriented feminist epistemology," as her work does, would seem counter to modes of knowing that value objectivity and certainty and that are bent on the acquisition of knowledge as something existing separate from and prior to the means of acquiring and categorizing that prize. I normally think of this model of knowing as definitive of "Western science." Therefore, I was at first perplexed by Hejinian's correlation of poetic experimentation with scientific experimentation:

> A central figure of the narrative of knowledge, its hero or genius, could easily be Faust. . . . Faustian desire has driven the encyclopedic enterprises which have been undertaken in the name of that quest—the most obvious being Western science. The "scientific method" has dominated not just the laboratory; it has also provided a compelling model for writers who have undertaken a "poetic method" analogous to it. The scientific and poetic methods have analogous rigors, present analogous challenges, and the comparison has been explicit in, for example, the "avant garde realism" that Gertrude Stein got from William James and Flaubert—employing an "experimental method"—"beginning again and again" with patient attention, demanding long and close observation, and so on, bound to an infinite project which opens up before the insatiability of the desire to know and grieves over the brevity of the experience of knowing. ("La Faustienne" 11)

Hejinian's own desire to know, and her grief at the brevity of the experience of knowing, as expressed in her poetic autobiography, *My Life* (*ML*), at first only compounded my puzzlement: "I want to remember more than more than that, more or less as it really happened. It seems that we hardly begin before we are already there" (69). The sense that something is always left out or glossed over in memory—that perfect knowledge of reality (in this case, the past as it "really" was) is impossible—is a recurring, circulating theme of this book-length, nonlinear, poetic work in prose, and is also one source of the work's haunting beauty, the sense I get while reading that each word is strangely charged with a melancholy humor: "Our dog will eat broccoli. Mischief logic; Miss Chief. I would be aloof, dark, indirect and upsetting or I would be a center of patience and material calm. So that later, playing alone, I could imagine myself developing into a tree, and then I yearned to do so with so much desire that it made me shapeless, restless, sleepless, demanding, disagreeable" (*ML* 29). But a closer reading of her critical and poetic works reveals that for Hejinian the significance—and value—of this continually unfulfilled desire for "perfect knowing" lies precisely in its unfulfilledness. Language plays an important role in this desire. Hejinian explains in her essay "The Rejection of Closure" (RC):

> It's in the nature of language to encourage, and in part to justify, such Faustian longings. The notion that language is the means and medium for attaining knowledge, and, concomitantly, power, is old, of course. . . . The . . . position . . . that there is an essential identity between name and thing, that the real nature of a thing is immanent and present in its name, that nouns are numinous . . . suggests that it is possible to find a language which will meet its object with perfect identity. If this were the case, we could, in speaking or in writing, achieve the at-oneness with the universe, at least in its particulars, that is the condition of paradise, or complete and perfect knowing. (281)

In language, then, perfect knowing would be the perfect identity of word and thing. And in *My Life* Hejinian admits to experiencing this linguistic longing as well: "Then cataloguing the travel library I got the mania for panorama which predicts the desire for accurate representation" (58). But language does not mean numinously; in its trajectory from speech to world and back again it marks difference, not identity. In her long poem "The Person," Hejinian writes:

> Realism is an unimaginable ballad: direct speech
> across the trajectory of nature in its trees
> Which word is an object of imitation?
> And in returning differs (*Cold* 179)

This stanza illustrates McGann's adage, which I take as one of the defining features of language-oriented feminist epistemology, that poems are not representations, but *acts* of representation. Individual words cannot be identified with individual things—we cannot tell "which word" is responsible for which meanings, at least not in a one-to-one equation. Language means relationally, associatively, partially, and contextually. The word in world is far flung across a "trajectory of nature"—the field of action and meaning in which it participates, and is changed. "[I]n returning," the word "differs" because meaning and reference are unstable. While these observations about language are by no means unique, the consequences for poetry that Hejinian perceives as a result are remarkable. For therefore, "writing is contextual. It has ethical, phenomenological, cultural, historical, political, etc. contexts which are then also incorporated into its intentions. Work is both influenced and influential" ("The Poet and the World"). These incorporated contexts, then, are the "particular circumstances" under which the "series of knowing acts," which comprise knowledge, according to McGann, are carried out (*SVPA* 54).

And herein lies the epistemological value of writing for Hejinian. Because each act of knowing-in-writing is contextual, it is unique. It cannot be replicated or even repeated. Hejinian points out that this is also the case for Faust's night visions—the scenes distant in time and place on which Faust is able to gaze with the assistance of Mephistopheles—and for Gertrude Stein's writing experiments, both of which knowledge projects serve as departures for Hejinian in her own work. Hejinian sees Stein's project as exemplary of the Faustian model of Western science:

> Gertrude Stein was a great scientific writer, whose writing was about experimentation even as it enacted experiments, and one would place the motivation—the impulse and the method—right in the tradition of Western science, with the one provision that her experiments can't be reproduced.
>
> I think this is ontologically important and the implications have, for me, been exemplary—she had a strong sense of the uniqueness of absolutely anything while at the same time seeing that that uniqueness always depended on (because it was derived from) the ever-changing relationships which serve as the context and pretext for anything's existence. (Letter 1/22/95)

But what finally sets both Stein and Faust apart from the concept of Western science that seems so at odds with the kind of free knowing and radically open experimentation that defines Hejinian's writing project is that they both acknowledge that context, including language, is constitutive of all knowing. Since what we know and how we know can never be separated from the *process of knowing*, objective, final knowledge—scientific certainty—can never be secured. Some uncertainty or doubt will always remain. Indeed, the epistemological significance of Faust, Stein, and Hejinian's projects is dependent on this insight. Hejinian explains: "I've learned from Stein (from her method) that knowledge may sometimes produce certainty but that it may often produce uncertainty. Doubt (now dignified by a lot of postmodern philosophical attention) is central to Stein's project. I, of course, don't mean tentativeness, nor even self-doubt, but rather an awareness of incompleteness and perpetual or recurrent newness" (Letter 1/22/95). Hejinian finds a positive value in this uncertainty—and in the awareness of it. Of course if context is always constitutive of knowledge, then this same doubt or uncertainty is a quality of all Western science. And indeed, a scientific result has to be repeatedly verified. The difference is that rather than attempting to eradicate doubt by seeking ever greater objectivity, Hejinian hones in on it, exploring and pursuing the epistemological implications of doubt. Although Hejinian identifies the Faustian "desire that is stirred by language" as "androgynous" because it "seems to be located . . . within language" (RC 283), rather than in the gendered language user, her poetic explorations of the doubt that this inevitably unfulfilled desire continually produces do seem to take gender into account—including problems of gender important to feminist thought—and to offer solutions, greater freedoms, ways of knowing that can be called feminist, if not explicitly gendered. "But who," Hejinian asks, "is Faust's female counterpart. Who is La Faustienne?" ("La Faustienne" 12). In her exploration of uncertainty, Hejinian suggests a faustienne poetics and epistemology—a way of knowing already implicit in the Western scientific method, but whose implications have yet to be fully explored, much less validated.

By aligning the poetic with the scientific, Hejinian is not advocating the kind of poetry objected to by the New Critics, poems with paraphrasable and extractable meanings that can be submitted to a scientific analysis. But neither is she arguing that the only truth poetry can approximate is the truth of subjective personal experience, as the most widely published American poetry of the 1970s insisted. For Hejinian, as for McGann, poetry is able to investigate truth by investigating "the relation of language and truth." In her writing, "the question of poetry's truth . . . gets . . . engaged as an epistemological self-interrogation" (McGann, *Black Riders* 123, 136). Hejinian's self-interrogation focuses on the experimental *method* rather than its results in order to attend to the role that language plays in both method and outcome, including the significance of doubt in the process.

Hejinian's poetics take the process, context, and materials of the knowing situation into account as components of the knowing itself, rather than trying to separate knowledge (as a product) from the process of "acquiring" it. As is the case for all the writers I discuss in the following chapters, knowing is for Hejinian something experienced, not something claimed, staked-out, possessed. Language, of course, is one of the more significantly material components of the epistemological situation, and Hejinian's writing highlights the constitutive role language plays in how we know and what we know by maintaining a continual state of uncertainty. Thus, her project serves as introduction to the different ways in which Leslie Scalapino, Mei-mei Berssenbrugge, and Carla Harryman explore the phenomenological function of language that I examine in chapter 4. Among Hejinian's works, *My Life*, both as a whole and in its individual passages, serves as an excellent example of Hejinian's sense that process and context—and hence, language—are inseparable from what we say we "know."

My Life unfolds within a formal structure that actually allows the work to remain open and open-ended because the form is both arbitrary and externally imposed; it is not presented as "organic" or the inevitable outcome of the writing's "content." First completed in 1978 when Hejinian was 37 years old, *My Life* was comprised of 37 sections, each containing 37 sentences. The revised edition, which Hejinian produced eight years later, now has 45 sections, 45 sentences in each. The sentences and sections represent units of consciousness—instances of perception, memory, awareness or description of which one's "life" is inevitably constructed. The work continually enacts the interplay between past and present in which any autobiography takes part by presenting details and events not in order of their chronological occurrence in history, but in the order in which they are remembered, even triggering each other associatively: "Sticky finger licking chicken. Cliches and lamentation. We were floating the logic in a rushing medium" (78). The rushing medium is language itself, and submitting to its playful processes allows a more encompassing kind of realism than that which insists that language is merely descriptive, external to the experiences it describes. As a result, Hejinian's sentences describe not only experiences, but a person's experiencing of those experiences. "The synchronous keeps its reversible logic, and in this it resembles psychology, or the logic of a person" (44). The synchronous is more real than chronology because it allows for a broader spectrum of reality—not just the objects a person describes in language, but the language as well, its processes, and the person's own consciousness.

Hejinian continually reminds herself and her readers that in autobiography, a life is constructed in language and is itself a writing process: "I pushed my thumb to make a lever of the blunt spoon, he took up the palette knife and ships came out of the blue, I hit the space bar" (32). For Hejinian, gaining access to the reality of one's life depends on taking account of language as an active partner, for "What follows a strict chronology has no memory. For me, they must exist, the contents of that absent reality, the objects and occasions which now I reconsidered" (13). One of the work's most compelling effects is the sense of dual consciousness that results when reality is comprised of objects, mind, *and* language, functioning together in the present, and therefore not referable to chronology or a fixed "past."

A significant component of the nonlinear progression of *My Life* is its repetitions. Certain key phrases recur throughout the text, but in ever-shifting contexts, so that the resulting loops and overlays serve a generative function. Here are three of the many recurrences of one such repeating phrase: "As for we who 'love to be astonished,' my heartbeats shook the bed" (22). "As for we who 'love to be astonished,' every Sears smells the same" (34). "As for we who 'love to be astonished,' she pretends she is a blacksmith" (36–37). The phrase is different each time it recurs because the context—in this case, the main clause that the repeated modifying phrase introduces—is different, unique, unreproducible; "Hence, repetitions, free from all ambition" (7). Hejinian's readers who love to be astonished are continually rewarded by the perpetual newness of her text and its meanings.

That *My Life* is a work composed in sentences is notable for the emphasis placed on the relationship between the sentences. Hejinian does not disrupt syntax within sentences, some of which contain conventionally embedded phrases and clauses: "At the circus men were selling live chameleons which wore tiny collars and were attached to red and yellow ribbons that one could pin to one's dress or shirt as a living jewel" (30). And though some of the units punctuated as sentences are fragments, these tend to be syntactically complete constituents, such as noun phrases—"A common act, the swing of the leg" (70)—or prepositional phrases: "Between plow and prow" (65). The subtle disorienting effect of the writing, then, results from disjunction between rather than within these syntactic units. Here, again, Hejinian is intentionally exploring the epistemological potential of uncertainty. "One of the results of this compositional technique," Hejinian explains,

> building a work out of discrete units, is the creation of sizeable gaps between the units. The reader (and I can also say the writer) has to overleap the period, and cover the distance to the next sentence. But, meanwhile, what remains in the gaps, so to speak, remains crucial and informative. Part of the reading occurs as the recovery of that information (focus backward) and the discovery of newly structured ideas (focus forward). (RC 274)

This interactive reading process that the text initiates, then, ensures that "Utterances are made intelligible because of differentiating features, features which are activated by the exigencies of the moment and context of the utterance" (RC 276). And a significant component of this context is the subject—reader and/or writer—who is always mediated, acting through and dependent on the operations of language that construct a variety of shifting and often gendered subject positions the subject might occupy.

Hejinian resists what she describes in her essay "The Person and Description" (P&D) as the "existential premise . . . of some core reality at the heart of our sense of being" and this notions's attendant conception of "the work of art as an expression uttered in the artist's 'own voice,' issuing from an inner, fundamental, sincere, essential, irreducible, consistent self, an identity which is unique and separable from all other human identities—an independent, undemonstrable, but sensible entity" (166). As I mentioned in the preface, this rejection of essential being is common in women's language-oriented writing, and Hejinian's investigation of the conditions of subjectivity is just one of a number of such inquiries. In chapter 3, I consider three very different versions of this critique offered by Beverly Dahlen, Lori Lubeski, and Laura Moriarty. In Hejinian's critique, she offers in place of the existential notion of an essential self, *the person*—an active, knowing subject mediated by the person's relations to experience—including language—and her consciousness of those relations:

> Certainly I have an experience of being in position, at a time and place . . . but this position is temporary . . . I have no experience of being except in position.

All my observations are made from within the matrix of possibly infinite contingencies and contextualities.
This sense of contingency is ultimately intrinsic to my experience of the self, as a relationship rather than an existence, whose exercise of the possibilities (including consciousness) of its conditions
and occasions constitutes a person. (P&D 167)

Hejinian's "person," in fact, has much in common with Julia Kristeva's
"subject-in-process" in that the person's condition of plurality and of
being in flux is a function of its being a speaking subject, speaking (or
writing) in language always marked by a quality of uncertainty. For
Kristeva this uncertainty exposes a semiotic "disposition" in language,
what she describes as "a distinctive mark, trace, index . . . a *distinctiveness* admitting of an uncertain and indeterminate articulation because it
does not yet refer . . . to a signified object for thetic consciousness" (133).
Hejinian perceives a similar tension in language and describes it in remarkably similar terms:

The point is that there's a very generative struggle between the two
impulses. On the one hand, for the writer, faced with the world of
meaning and the intention or hope to make something meaningful
out of it, there is an urge to identify, locate, be comprehensive, have
content. On the other hand, there is the, to me, endlessly obvious
observation that no single thing ever holds it all, or even adequately
comes to say what it was I thought I could really get to this time . . .
It's like this yearning from one to the other and back again. This is
why I used that word desire. (RC 291)

The person, suspended in an interminable state of desire in language,
becomes "not an entity but a dynamic. There is no self undefiled by
experience, no self unmediated in the epistemological situation, but a
person instead" (P&D 167). *My Life*, as one would expect of an autobiography, is riddled with first-person assertions and observations; "I" is
one of the most frequently used words in the work. But in Hejinian's
writing, the "I" is disunified and rendered slightly incoherent by this
very process of "recollection," which demands that "I" exist in at least
two places and two times simultaneously. To tell of my past or my
"self" coherently demands that "I" occupy a third position neither here
nor there, now nor then, subject nor object. She does not attempt to conceal or mend the rifts in the narrative that result. Hejinian shows what

happens when the speaker of one's "own" life does not weave the fiction of an essential continuous self, but instead acknowledges that "My life is as permeable constructedness" (*ML* 93):

> I am looking for a little hand mirror. The summer evenings saw window shoppers in a reflecting system, man with merchandise agog. It is hard to turn away from moving water. All summer I worked as a mountain guide and behind me hiked a group of girls giggling in descent of a president. He made me nervous as soon as he began offering a special discount. But the work is probably a good deal wiser than the horny old doctor he was. I wrote my name in every one of his books. A name trimmed with colored ribbons. (*ML* 53)

The overlapping of past and present observations, discontinuity from one sentence to the next, and shifts in point of view, show the person to be constantly moving, dividing from herself both temporally and spatially. The person is here engaged in what Hejinian calls "radical introspection"—a kind of consciousness of consciousness that "newly delineates and constantly shifts the boundary between subject and object. It establishes the relationship between self and other, between body and mind, and then transgresses the borders it has established" (P&D 170).

Hejinian explores the process and implications of radical introspection most directly in "The Person," comprised of 28 short sections or individual poems, each of which is also entitled "The Person." This repetition invites the reader to see each section as commenting on every other section of the poem, as well as pointing to "our contemporary experience of being a person—a zone" ("La Faustienne" 11). Also, each new section offers in its title—"The Person"—an answer to the question posed in the first stanza of the first section of the series:

> Is there a name
> for the imploding series
> "consciousness of consciousness"
> Realism and depth perception
> The audacious science of the thought
> of poetry (*Cold* 143)

Because "there is no outside/position" for the person to occupy, no place outside of experience or of the language used to "describe" one's experience, a person is constantly mediated by language, and her sense of experience—both her sensations and the "sense" she makes of them—are constituted in language:

> A person is clinging
> with the monotony of generosity
> In the sentence is the sense-impression
> Jealousy of perception is a grammar
> The appearance of the person in nature (*Cold* 156–57)

To be aware of the mediating function language plays in a person's reality is to perceive the person "in nature"—that is, *in language*. The person (subject) and the world (object) are, in these relations, constantly shifting and realigning themselves vis-à-vis one another; the positions they occupy as subject-object are anything but stable and fixed: "The real appears before us every second," but yet "the world is relevant / as the medium of recognition." The person is "making constant adjustments" (*Cold* 168) and the state of radical introspection allows the person to perform these adjustments while being aware of them:

> I feel
> my brain
> At first I didn't fasten
>
> this feeling to words
> Adorable Subject-Object
> A moment of intense orientation
> as it swings (*Cold* 174)

Hejinian finds the possibilities for literature suggested by this "contemporary experience of being a person"—freed from the certainties of essential selfhood—to be both epistemologically rich and liberating. "The sense of independence must now include a sense of interdependence, where it hasn't been replaced by it, and, in writing, interest in free expression may be giving way to interest in free knowing" ("La Faustienne" 11).

The feminist implications of "free knowing" in writing become apparent when a woman, no longer conceived of as a self but as a person, is therefore no longer bound to occupy the object position to which the Western model of knowing has relegated her. How meaning is constituted in language does have significant consequences for women.

Hejinian explains: "Description, whether it is intentional or the result of merely ambient ideology, bounds a person's life, whether narrowly or broadly. In another sense it likewise bounds a person, and this is, for example, a central (perhaps the classic) issue for feminism, which recognizes that traditionally women are often described but they have very seldom been the describers" (P&D 169). But the person—plural, shifting, mediated, and implicated in the knowing situation— has increased freedoms to cross this boundary between describer and described. Such a move facilitates other crossings as well, between self and other, one and several. Writing in a state of "radical introspection," the person can explore other subjectivities, including shared subjectivities.

The fluidity of subjectivity is a central concern for Hejinian and Carla Harryman in their ongoing collaborative work, *The Wide Road*. Written in the first-person plural, this hybrid piece—part verse, part prose—explores the erotic tendencies of language by describing heterosexual female erotic fantasies. The narrative incorporates and indeed finds momentum in the uncertainties that result, revealing the extent to which more normative, subject-object descriptions are dependent on the notion of coherent selfhood and the belief in "natural" a priori gender categories. In a passage where the plural speaker approaches a sleeping figure, apparently a man, the question of who is whom becomes central, but its lack of resolution is what is most crucial for the narrative: "Bending over the bed we insert a finger into the small cave formed by the lightly curled hand. Is it the hand of one sleeper or the hand of two sleepers? Our bed seems fully occupied. But who is company? Is it peaceful in the bedroom. Will we scare what sleeps if what sleeps wakes?" ("from *The Wide Road*" 26). In an introductory comment on their project, Hejinian and Harryman specify the liberating implications of this collaboration:

> We were "we," meanwhile, for several reasons. First, it allowed us to have more than the usual number of body parts. Second, we were determined to adventure across normal boundaries, or to blur them at the very least. The identification of "we" allowed us easily to include each other in the work all the time and to identify with each other continuously. This provided us with unusual liberty and power. ("A Comment" 83)

This shared subjectivity Hejinian and Harryman create in writing shows how both selfhood and gender are discursively constructed, and so can be otherwise constructed. Furthermore, by adventuring "across normal boundaries," this writing redescribes gender as not being subject to fixed boundaries, but rather, as Joan Scott understands it: socially constructed in discourse, or as Judith Butler would say, continually "performed." This writing takes part in a language-oriented feminist epistemology by redescribing—in a lively spirit of play—the relations of power that gender signifies.

Hejinian's realism is facilitated by this transgression of subject-object boundaries, a transgression that is further explored in a technique she calls "description." Hejinian claims that "the very incapacity of language to match the world allows it to do service as a medium of differentiation. . . . While failing in the attempt to match the world, we discover structure, distinction, the integrity and separateness of things" (RC 285). This differentiation in language is what Hejinian terms "description," and to a great extent, a faustienne poetics is a poetics of description. But Hejinian clarifies in her essay "Strangeness" that by "description" she does not "mean after-the-fact realism, with its emphasis on the world described . . . nor do I want to focus on an organizing subjectivity; nor, finally, am I securing the term to a theory of language." Rather, description is "a method of invention and or composition" (32). Description, then, serves an epistemological function as a process through which the world is both discovered and invented. Understood as "a special way of writing" in which, as Hejinian puts it in her essay on Stein, "Language and Realism" (L&R), "The realism of the means—the materiality of the poetic language, for example—is a precise manifestation of the artist's attention to the alien particularity of the subject matter" (130); description does not render the objects of the world less real but more so. The objects of the world are called into being, put into place where we can see them more directly, by description, which is aware of its own methods of representation and the constitutive role these processes play in what a person sees when she perceives anything in the world, such as, say, the sky:

> Described, the corresponding sky
> in circumstantial detail goes up
> as if having yielded—blue
> seems to yield to our gaze—
> having as its object something unknown but
>   conscious (*Cold* 179)

In this stanza it seems as if the sky is launched upward to its place by the very gaze that sees it there. Both the sky and the gaze, as well as the gazing person's experience of knowing, are at the same time called into being by this very description. Individual perceptions and events— both "objects" of the world—take on a heightened reality when seen as unique, unrepeatable knowing situations—knowing that is never complete, never coherent, never part A or B of a closed cause-effect relation, for among "the great sequences / of incompleteness,"

> The trees rustle in the wind
> and suck in the rain suppressing sound
> and then release it
> In discontinuity, distinction (*Cold* 144)

In this stanza the rain, the rustle in the wind, the release—these details are isolated and displaced from a context of narrative or logic that would give them rhetorical design and meaning. The meaning, then, of Hejinian's description, depends on a broader and more immediate context: that of the describing act itself.

In order to keep this process of description forefront in her writing, Hejinian relies on metonymy and avoids the kind of metaphor that emphasizes equivalency or simple substitution, functioning to clarify something otherwise imperfectly known.[7] This skepticism toward metaphoric equivalencies can be traced to Hejinian's belief in the generative possibilities suggested by language's inability to perfectly match the world. As she writes in *My Life*, "If words matched their things we'd be imprisoned within walls of symmetry" (70). Like many observations about language, memory, and perception that occur throughout *My Life*, this statement is both part of the work and a comment on the work it is part of. In *My Life*, words do not match their things. Instead, things and words pile up, juxtapose, resonate, and assert their interminable difference: "The sudden brief early morning breeze, the first indication of a day's palpability, stays high in the trees, while flashing silver and green the leaves flutter, a bird sweeps from one branch to another, the indistinct shadows lift off the crumpled weeds, smoke rises from the gravel quarry—all this is metonymy" (*ML* 59). The openness of the metonymic text, its perpetual newness and refusal to settle into closed equivalencies, offers both reader and writer opportunities for experience and knowing that a text ruled by the logic of metaphor suppresses: "In the metaphor, life is landscape, and living it is a journey, for which one is provided with a limited amount of time" (*ML* 83). As David Jarraway so aptly puts it in an essay on *My Life*: ". . . it is the substitutive property of metaphor in its singular *direc-*

tion toward equivalence and ultimate identity which betrays the processual character of generative textuality and, along the way, its responsiveness to time, place, and circumstance. The distributive agency of metonymy, on the other hand . . . remains faithful to the openness of textual production . . ." (330). Metonymy, then, is more true than metaphor to Hejinian's sense that writing is always contextual, for metonymy continually acknowledges context, the very conditions that render untenable the perfect replacement which metaphor seeks to achieve.

Proceeding by way of metonymy and not following a strict chronology in terms of the order in which events "happened," *My Life* is an excellent example of Hejinian's poetry of description. Each individual memory, observation, or statement—as well as the repetitions that are not, after all, repetitious—marks a further differentiation. Not only is the speaking subject "a shard, signifying isolation," but each thing described by that "I" is a "separate fragment taken under scrutiny" (*ML* 52). In this kind of poetic description, each sentence—or, in the case of Hejinian's verse poems, each line or phrase—is as descriptive of itself as it is of whatever is its supposed object. Hejinian explains the connection between perception and description:

> The ontological and epistemological problem of our knowledge of experience is, to my mind, inseparable from the problem of description.
> An evolving poetics of description is simultaneously and synonymously a poetics of scrutiny. It is description that raises scrutiny to consciousness, and in arguing for this I am proposing a poetry of consciousness. ("Strangeness" 44)

Description, then, is the process of perception in language. And when scrutiny is raised to consciousness in writing, that writing is phenomenological—an enactment in language of the complex relations among perceiver, perception, perceived—as these relationships are constituted in language. When Hejinian asks in a poem, "Is there a spectral sentence? a spectator one?" ("La Faustienne" 21), she implies that a linguistic unit can both see and be seen, suggesting that language is not merely a medium of representation but also an interactive participant in the meaning-making process. Hejinian conceives of language as essentially epistemological: "Vocabulary and grammar are themselves an intense examination of the world and of our perceptual relations within the experience of it. . . . Description then is apprehension" (L&R 33). By "apprehension," of course, Hejinian means mental perception: not just to see, but to grasp, to understand. Description *is* a kind of knowing.

When writing explores the gaps and uncertainty in meaning and representation that mark the limits of language, as Hejinian's writing does through description, the world is not so much discovered as called into being, created. Knowledge is made, not merely acquired or gathered. This distinction seems to be central to Hejinian's notion of what might comprise a faustienne poetics, setting it apart from the Faustian project. Where Faust is "one who knows by acquiring knowledge," la faustienne—though perhaps rather a method than an identity—is one who knows "by making it" ("La Faustienne" 10). The Faust legend is not the only tale of knowledge Hejinian considers in her piece "La Faustienne." Of equal interest to her is *The Arabian Nights*, in which the heroine, Scheherazade, tells a series of interlinking, digressive tales to her would-be murderer, Shahryar, thus keeping him in a state of epistemological suspense from one night until the next. He does not kill her because she is his source of knowledge, promises to fulfill his faustian desire. Scheherazade thus has a very different relationship to knowledge than does Faust. "Where Faust sells his soul for knowledge, Scheherazade saves hers by offering it," explains Hejinian ("La Faustienne" 27). In exploring this difference in her poetry, Hejinian explores the function that gender plays in the social valuing of knowledge.

That knowing takes place in the night in both the Faust legend and *The Arabian Nights* is significant for Hejinian, and she examines the implications of such knowing in the dark in her poetic work *The Book of a Thousand Eyes*, a series of poems that explore the question of knowledge, uncertainty, and faustienne poetics more directly than any previous work. Hejinian describes her intentions with this work:

> *The Book of a Thousand Eyes* is a night work, in that my interest is in the processes of assimilation and assessment that take place in the figurative dark and silence of night, where opposites as such can't exist because they always coexist. I have wanted, so to speak, to write in the dark, when the mind must accept the world it witnesses by day and out of all data assemble meaning. The writing would do so—assemble (a Faustian project) and, in its way, make knowledge (the work of La Faustienne). ("La Faustienne" 20)

When writing is directed at making rather than acquiring knowledge, especially while exploring the sleeplike state that is emblematic for Hejinian of epistemological uncertainty, and hence possibility, language is freed to play a more exploratory and creative role. In fact, language's epistemological role as constitutive of knowledge is inherently highlighted in such a writing situation, as this final stanza of one of the poems from *The Book of a Thousand Eyes* illustrates: "Because we are not innocent of our sentences we go to bed / The bed shows with utter clarity how sentences in saying something make something / Sentences in bed are not describers, they are instigators" ("La Faustienne" 21). Of course, Hejinian is being doubly playful here by pointing to the sexual implications of bedroom talk. The speaker in this poem is also "not afraid to look nor afraid to be seen in/the dark" because she senses the positive value of uncertainty that the dark represents and presents to language and its "users." The bed as well as the dark, sex, dreams, and sleep are examples of what Hejinian thinks of as "border zones." The border, Hejinian clarifies,

> is not an edge along the fringe of society and experience but rather their very middle—their between; it names the condition of doubt and encounter which being foreign to a situation (which may be life itself) provokes—a condition which is simultaneously an impasse and a passage, limbo and transit zone, with checkpoints and bureaus of exchange, a meeting place and a realm of confusion. ("Barbarism")

By entering these border zones in her poetry, Hejinian hopes to accomplish in writing the same kind of epistemological work that she feels takes place in dreams: "processing information, comparing experiences, taking new data into account, making sense. . . . Dreams serve as an active . . . border between the sleeping person and that same person awake. They are, in this sense, not a place but a dynamic ("Barbarism"). Hejinian considers this kind of dynamic even as she enacts it in writing:

> Sleep constitutes experience delivered.
> But that won't be music. Nor lies.
> Association is clearly the best means
>   for shifting
> to a waking world with its status of law
> and assonance.
>   Each sleep is an apple
> in a metonymic world then and waking remains
> recurrent. It gives us the memory
> that *this* activity requires, a broken sequence
>   of second recognitions
> which slipping by become themselves. ("from *Sleeps*" 44)[8]

In this example the recognitions that take place in sleep "become themselves"—act as the sentences do in the preceding example, as instigators. Through association and metonymy, language enters a border zone and shifts from one side to the other, achieves a state of epistemological efficacy that is only possible in such a zone of uncertainty, where the dynamic relationship between experience and language can *make* knowledge. The person, of course—the reader as well as the writer—is, to return again to the first example from *The Book of a Thousand Eyes*, "not innocent" of her sentences. The person is implicated in what is instigated.

In her essay "Barbarism," Hejinian describes the person who writes such border-zone poetry as an agent of change, plumbing the dark of uncertainty for a new kind of knowledge, night knowledge, faustienne knowledge. Explaining that the term "barbarism" has its roots in the Greek *barbaros*, meaning foreign or "not speaking the same language," Hejinian appropriates the term as a positive value for difference, strangeness, for border zone poetry.

> This poet-barbarian . . . is not a weirdo but rather a rigorously attentive observer and active participant in the interminable newness of poetic language, a language which generates an array of logics capable, in turn, of generating and responding to encounters and experience. . . . It is the logics of these new connections which provide poetry with its enormous mobility and its transformative strategies. ("Barbarism")

These transformative strategies are what Hejinian proposes in response to Adorno's famous claim that after Auschwitz, to write poetry is an act of barbarism. In a letter Hejinian explains that what she wants to do is understand Adorno's pronouncement "not necessarily as a prohibition" but "as a behest" (Letter 8/4–5/95). Barbarism, she feels, "is precisely the task of poetry: *not to speak the same language as Auschwitz*. Poetry after Auschwitz must indeed be barbarian; it must be foreign to the cultures that produce atrocities. As a result, the poet must assume a barbarian position, taking a creative, analytic, and often oppositional stance, occupying (and being occupied by) foreignness . . . ("Barbarism"). This political imperative that drives Hejinian's poetic project marks a final important distinction between faustienne and faustian knowing, and a final crucial characteristic of Hejinian's language-oriented feminist epistemology. Faust, as Hejinian points out, "considers himself, by the terms of his pact with the devil and through the authority of his imagination, to be beyond considerations of good and evil. . . . This is a terrain that 'pure science' sometimes claims, but at least with Goethe's Faust it is also a claim of 'pure art'" ("La Faustienne" 12). But la faustienne would not make such a claim, because for her all knowing and all writings are contextual—and that context includes ethics. In fact, in her response to a question about her relationship to other women writers, Hejinian identifies the "intersection between ethics and aesthetics" as a defining feature of the otherwise hard to categorize mutual concerns of the community of women writers she feels a part of:

> My sense of a gender community . . . is quite a strong component of my thinking about contemporary writing. I think there are currents of sympathy and even interdependence between my work and that of . . . [many language-oriented women writers]. Perhaps what we have in common is a sense that our gender is a part of our aesthetic dynamic—a motivating force, rather than a static definition. . . . Historically, of course, essential kinds of ethical work . . . have been undertaken by women; perhaps the difference now is that women have no doubt as to the efficacy and urgency of such work. (Letter 1/25/95)

By conceiving of gender as "a motivating force," Hejinian takes gender into account without essentializing it, while still finding a place for women writers to act as agents of change. Hejinian's poetics insists that the most powerful knowledge in poetry is made, not found; we can transform the world and ourselves by participating in the open and dynamic production of shared knowledge. Thus, Hejinian offers as the final of four "morals" in "A Fable," one of the few titled poems that comprise *The Book of a Thousand Eyes*, the prediction that "Various women writers will take up the philosophical quest for uncertainty" ("from *Sleeps*" 42). In the chapters that follow, I examine the different ways some language-oriented women writers in this century have already taken up this quest, where uncertainty is understood as a questioning of normative and potentially limiting categories of knowledge and modes of knowing. Hejinian's notion of a faustienne poetics finds evocative echoes in the various language-oriented feminist epistemologies articulated in the projects of these writers.

Chapter 2

"Come, words, away": Modernist Women's Invitations to Innovation[1]

Contemporary language-oriented writers are by no means the first in U.S. literary history to investigate the philosophical and ideological implications of language and the role it plays in how meaning is constituted. And this group does not include the first women to carry out such poetic experiments, or the first to do so from a feminist perspective. Indeed, the early part of the twentieth century saw some of the most radical linguistic and formal innovation ever undertaken by U.S. women writers, and poets such as Laura (Riding) Jackson, Gertrude Stein, Mina Loy, and Hilda Doolittle (H.D.) set some precedence for the aesthetic-philosophical experiments undertaken by their younger compatriots.

It should be no surprise that many women writers experimented with language during the modernist period in American literature. Radical linguistic experimentation is one of the benchmarks of U.S. and British modernist writing in any genre and by writers of both genders. Indeed, many of the tendencies identified in chapter 1 as characteristic of language-oriented writing are fully consistent with certain major trends in English-language writing throughout the first third of the twentieth century. Modernist writers' intense interest in language is indicative of the deeper epistemological concerns with which many writers became preoccupied in the early decades of the century. Especially in the face of the social and political upheaval brought on by World War

I, many writers, according to L. S. Dembo, sought to "transcend the rational and chronological apprehension of history" that seemed to fail to account adequately for modern reality and turned instead to art as "a medium for 'knowing' the world in its 'essentiality,' for apprehending things as they are" (1–5). Furthermore, as Michael H. Levenson notes, all of the various developments and "displacements" in modernist thought and literature "are linked by a commitment to *immediacy* . . . to a directly present reality" (116–17) so that modernist linguistic innovations were based on "the primacy of individual perception" (78). Although many women modernists did share in these interests in perception, immediate reality, and art (writing) as a mode of knowing, what I identify in this chapter as language-oriented writing, as practiced by some early and mid-twentieth-century women writers, is not adequately described by these tendencies alone. Recent feminist scholarship in the field of literary modernism offers some valuable context for this distinction between women's language-oriented writing and modernist literature in general.

Some feminist critics argue that what we know as literary modernism has been constructed as masculine by its canonized male practitioners and theorists as well as its critics. As a result, they believe that we need to rethink the parameters and definitions of modernism to account for the vast numbers of women writers who were as active and as instrumental in the developments in modernist literature as the famous male modernists were. But in their rereadings of modernism, some feminists are reinforcing binary constructions by not allowing women an interest in or faculty with language. As Bonnie Kime Scott points out in the introduction to her anthology of modernist writing, *The Gender of Modernism*, some feminist critics who are concerned with recovering the work of so-called nonexperimental women modernist writers tend to view linguistic experimentation itself as a masculine phenomena: "The 'experimental, audience challenging, and language-focused' writing that used to be regarded as modernism becomes for some [feminist critics] a gendered subcategory—'early male modernism' . . . for example, or 'masculinist modernism'" (4). But as Nancy Gray notes, linguistic innovation is not inherently or irretrievably masculinist: "Writers sought word-forms for human consciousness, dispensed with linearity of plot and time, and created voices and styles that interrogated the very foundations of what constitutes meaning, perception, self-in-the-world, and art. Such innovations are potentially well suited to dispensing with fictional Woman and investigating a/any woman as herself" (16). I agree with Gray, and would go a step further to observe that writers (women and men) engage in linguistic experimentation for wildly different reasons. Just as not all literary experimentation results in language-oriented writing, not all experimentation serves patriarchal interests. As Shari Benstock observes in an article on American expatriate women writers of the twenties,[2] many male modernists experimented with language "in *reaction* to a collapse in cultural values, taking as [their] defense the ironic mode," while other modernists, including many women writers, "were interested in cultural symbols and norms as subjects under analysis, writing a literature that exposed the operations of these cultural norms as they were present *in* language" (14). Such projects often involved equally radical experimentation with language.

Modernist writers who fit Benstock's latter category are those who understood that their epistemological investigations into language, perception, and reality also had ideological implications. These writers sought in their work to reveal rather than "to conceal the production of what we understand as reality" (Gray 21). Riding, Stein, Loy, and H.D. are such writers. In a variety of ways their writing projects anticipate the late twentieth-century language-oriented women's writing I discuss in other chapters. Rather than attempting to reassert logocentric control over a reality fragmented by the social and political upheavals of the early part of the century as well as contemporary developments in the disciplines of science, psychology, and philosophy by evoking "an historic density and a depth of literary allusions" as Randa Dubnick describes the linguistic innovation of Joyce, Pound, and Eliot (115), these women modernists tested the limits of language, form, and genre in order to investigate the role that language plays in knowing, and in the cultural construction and validation of certain forms of knowledge. Writing was for each of them an open process, an active engagement with language, in which the reader is invited to participate fully. And although these writers assumed differing positions in relation to feminism, they all implicate gender as one of the crucial sites of their investigations in language and directly or indirectly suggest feminist language-oriented epistemologies in their writing projects. It is this interest in gender, informed by the writers' own experiences as gendered subjects, that distinguishes feminist modernism from modernist experimentation in general. By exploring some specifics of these four modernists' projects, I hope to give some sense of the range and variety of the language-oriented experiments they undertook, as well as to identify significant points of contact between the early-twentieth-century innovators and their late twentieth-century counterparts.

Laura Riding's Lifelong Project with Language

> Between the word and the world lie
> Fading eternities of soon.
> —Laura (Riding) Jackson, "Echoes"
> (*The Poems of Laura Riding* 74)

I begin with Laura (Riding) Jackson in part because her poetic project might at first seem to be as far removed from the notion of writing as a mode of knowing, much less a social process, as a writer's project can be. Her tightly crafted, self-contained poems, fraught with ambiguity and complexity won her the admiration of the Fugitives, a group of American southern poet-critics whose members included Allen Tate, John Crowe Ransom, and Robert Penn Warren—the future New Critics. In 1924 they awarded their annual Nashville Prize for Poetry to (Riding) Jackson, who remains the only woman ever welcomed as a member of the Fugitives. While the alliance was short-lived, it is noteworthy that certain poetic values and methods of close textual analysis later articulated in William Empson's *Seven Types of Ambiguity* (1930) and still later championed by the New Critics can be traced to (Riding) Jackson's own poetic theories and intense interest in the meaning of words. She shared her ideas eagerly with the Fugitives, and made them public in *A Survey of Modernist Poetry* (1927), which she coauthored with Robert Graves.

Indeed, many of the ideas expressed in *A Survey* do seem inconsistent with the concerns of language-oriented writers. How can a poem explore the processes of language, of knowing, or remain open to genuine interaction with the reader if "the poem has the character of a creature by itself"? (118). Further arguments against classifying (Riding) Jackson as language-oriented might be implied by the fact that she stopped writing poetry in the middle of her life because she had come to the conclusion that it was not possible to attain truth in poetry. A belief in such an absolute as "truth," much less the desire that poetry should reveal it, certainly seems antithetical to the aims of language-oriented writing, which seeks to examine how meaning (including anything one might call "truth") is constituted in language. Yet, it seems to me that (Riding) Jackson's poetic technique as exhibited throughout her poems collected in *The Poems of Laura Riding* (*PLR*), her convictions, her pursuit of truth, and even her abandonment of poetry all partake of a single lifelong project *with language* "to explore the possible in knowledge," as she puts it ("Engaging" 14).

Concerned that words had become "worn meaning-thin from bold use, timid use" (*Telling* 23), (Riding) Jackson wanted to restore to language what she considered to be its inherent vitality. For (Riding) Jackson, words were "live, organically logical apparatus" ("Word-Play" 241); therefore, (Riding) Jackson attempted to use words "to mean what they mean" ("Exchange" 206), unambiguously—not arbitrarily, not according to context or convention, but according to their "rational" meanings. As Joyce Piell Wexler observes, "Riding wanted to destroy the personal associations of words to make language a medium for the universal" (59). For (Riding) Jackson, a word's meaning inhered in its unique ability to define human experience, "the experience of knowledge and understanding of existence" ("Engaging" 6). Such "experience of ourselves" allows us the "fullness of participation in the human reality" (*Telling* 119). Language's potential to be truthful does not depend for (Riding) Jackson on its ability to refer to external reality; rather, as the living embodiment of human thought, words can enact "the clarity of full-minded occupation of the immediately existent" ("Engaging" 6). (Riding) Jackson believed that human beings are by nature thinking beings, beings-in-language, and to know ourselves, we must know the language in which our thoughts are embodied. But by "embodied," I do not mean to imply that (Riding) Jackson conceived of a static equivalency between word and idea. For (Riding) Jackson did consider language to be a *living* process.

(Riding) Jackson is as attentive in her poetry as she is in her essays and theoretical writings to the process of how words mean. Ben Friedlander notes that in (Riding) Jackson's poems, "words record the struggle to construct meaning as well as meaning itself. Words express *thinking*, not just thought" (39). The struggle to construct meaning as well as the extent to which the individual human subject as a language user is constructed in that struggle is the subject of (Riding) Jackson's poem "Disclaimer of the Person":

> What am I?
> I am what I say.
> Who am I?
> I am I who say.
> Where is now?
> Now is where I am.
> Where am I?
> I am in what I say.
> What do I say?
> I say myself. (*PLR* 230)

Although the language here is playful in its almost childlike riddling, (Riding) Jackson is not joyfully celebrating the free play of language. Her awareness of how meaning, and especially identity, is constituted in language—her sense of how both are formed and reformed in the moment, so that such meanings are not fixed but indeterminate and often temporary—underscores her insistence that poets should use words responsibly, according "To earthy right of meaning," constantly guarding against language's capacity for sensual deception and duplicity (*PLR* 235). In order to do this, a writer must use words in their most denotative, literal, nonmetaphorical and nonsymbolic capacity. The "immediately existent" that (Riding) Jackson seeks to make evident in her poetry is intellectual, not sensual experience, accounting in part for her avoidance of imagery. In her poem "Come, Words, Away," she articulates her continual attempt to purify language by wresting it away from the sensual, "away to where / The meaning is not thickened / With the voice's fretting substance"; away from artistic metaphor (even as she uses metaphor to make this point); "away to miracle / More natural than written art. / You are surely somewhat devils"; away from the pride of poets, "That was an alien vanity, / A rash startling and a preening" (135); away from the known: "Come, words, away, / And tell with me a story here, / Forgetting what's been said already" (*PLR* 134–35).

(Riding) Jackson was aware that "what's been said already" about "Woman" in Western culture has been especially damaging to women. Near the end of her poetic career, (Riding) Jackson wrote a number of poems tracing the connections she perceived between cultural ideals of femininity and linguistic imagery, suggesting that women's freedom from objectification depends on their freedom from actual as well as linguistic adornment. In "Divestment of Beauty," (Riding) Jackson implores men to notice (intellectually) women's inherent beauty ("wisdom") and not to be deceived by their (the men's) own "stilted vision":

> Forswear the imbecile
> Theology of loveliness,
> Be no more doctor in antiquities—
> Chimeras of the future
> In archaic daze embalmed—
>
> And grow to later youth,
> Felling the patriarchal leer
> That it lie reft of all obscenities

While she and she, she, she, disclose
The recondite familiar to your candour. (*PLR* 267)

(Riding) Jackson's association of the poetic image with the male gaze is consistent with Shari Benstock's assessment that "the discovery . . . that language held the power to create meanings . . . was the founding premise of imagism, where form and substance were intimately and irrevocably joined through the image, through language" ("Beyond" 15). The image offered the poet a method of maintaining control over "his" reality as well as a safe distinguishing distance between "himself" and all that is *other*. As a woman, (Riding) Jackson was especially sensitive to the ways that patriarchal discourse could define and control women.

Such a consciousness, as well as (Riding) Jackson's poems that address this issue, would today unquestionably be called feminist. But (Riding) Jackson vehemently rejected this term to describe herself or her project, and advised women not to participate in the feminist movement. (Riding) Jackson's position offers valuable insight into the deep connections she perceived between gender and writing, and the crucial role that gender played for her in "language's capability of supporting the mind in its effort of attaining to complete embracing of the knowable and understandable" ("Engaging" 17). (Riding) Jackson was critical of "the new feminist insistence on having everything that men have" (*The Word "Woman"* 195) because she felt that advantageous gender differences would be lost or obscured in such a battle, and what (Riding) Jackson believed to be women's unique abilities to perceive truth and unify experience were for her a function of difference. According to (Riding) Jackson's view, unlike men, women possess "the force of kindship," which prepares them in turn "to pass beyond kindship to oneship (to eternal humanship)." (*Telling* 46). (Riding) Jackson believed that women's perspectives are more comprehensive than men's because, whereas a man's identity is determined by his professional or public actions, women view the "whole universe" as "an indoor place," an extension of woman's stable domestic realm where she is apparently defined not by what she does but what she is: "a fixed being, unchangeable" (*The Word "Woman"* 62, 68).[3]

Certainly the essentialist leanings of (Riding) Jackson's views about gender difference will make many contemporary feminists uneasy. But her essentialism is tempered with a dose of constructivism, for she felt that it was important for women to resist and cast off the male-defined conception of woman's difference in order to discover for themselves their essential difference as a powerful unifying force that such culturally imposed constructions serve to conceal or disguise. "She must, indeed, take over from man his sense of her difference and make it articulate" (*The Word "Woman"* 79). But whether (Riding) Jackson conceived of gender differences as biologically essential, culturally constructed, or both,[4] (Riding) Jackson's concerns about gender play an important part in her writing project and her ideas about language. Most significantly, her sense of her own capabilities and function as a writer was inseparable from her sense of self as a woman and as a poet. "As a poet," she explains, wittily quoting back Geoffrey Grigson's questionnaire words at the start of her response, "I am distinguished from ordinary men, first, in that I am a woman; second, in that as a woman I am actively and minutely aware of the fundamental distinctions in life . . . which as a poet it is my function to organize into unities" ("Enquiry" 3–5).

But for (Riding) Jackson, poetry proved an unworthy genre in which to perform this profound operation. In 1939, at 38 years old, Laura (Riding) Jackson stopped writing poetry. Yet her move away from poetry represents not an end to (Riding) Jackson's project with language, but merely the next phase in her profound commitment to that project. "My consciousness of words . . . led me into poetry, and led me out of it," she later explained ("The Road" 71). In 1972 (Riding) Jackson published her most important prose work, *The Telling*, in which she both explains her rejection of poetry 30 years earlier and attempts to enact a more "truthful" linguistic practice than what she felt was possible in poetry. She had come to the conclusion that in poetry, "humanly perfect word-use" was impossible because poetry's aesthetic concerns are incompatible with the truthtelling function of language (*PLR* 416). Significantly, then, (Riding) Jackson's earlier call to divest women of artificial beauty is not unrelated to her own eventual divestment from poetry. As she writes in *The Telling*, "Poetry no less than other institutions of authority has its power-using, authority-imposing, devices. They are obscured in its charms: indeed, the charms may be said to be the devices!" (66). Here, (Riding) Jackson seems to be resisting the limiting conventions of the genre as it had been culturally and historically defined, as inherently figurative, metaphorical language use. And because poetry's social value was therefore perceived to be precisely a function of its indirect meaning, "[p]oets live bedazzled by the ideal beauty of their professional role" (*Telling* 65).

(Riding) Jackson gave up on verse, but not on language. Her shift to prose seems to indicate less a move away from poetry than a move to a different kind of poetry, what Stephen Fredman identifies as "poet's prose," which became a major trend in mid- and late-twentieth-century writing in the United States. Seen this way, (Riding) Jackson's rejection of verse distinguishes her as one of the first writers to react to the "crisis in verse" that, according to Fredman, drove poets to prose forms in order "to interrogate the realm of truth, rather than merely to present an aesthetic object" (Fredman 7–8). (Riding) Jackson, though committed "to the truth-possibilities of language" ("Exchange" 214), claims never to have conceived of language as identical to truth ("Exchange" 197). For (Riding) Jackson truth is not an absolute or Platonic ideal, fixed and static, located prior or external to language, but it is "the missing story of ourselves"—located in the act of language (*Telling* 9). (Riding) Jackson believes that truth can only be found, and only in language, in company with other humans, her "companions in being" (*Telling* 97), readers who, rather than passive receivers of a poet's monologic message, are "equal companions in poetry" (*PLR* 411). It is no wonder she found poetry (as she understood the genre) not up to the task, and opted for looser, more open prose forms, for how could such a meeting of companions as she envisioned take place within the bounds of a "creature by itself"?

Jerome McGann finds in (Riding) Jackson's views an important political implication. He explains that "for Riding truth is a 'telling,' an enactment"—"an interactive event . . . for language is a social practice" (*BR* 126, 125). These values, implied by (Riding) Jackson's reasons for ceasing to write poems, are shared by many contemporary language-oriented writers, and many of (Riding) Jackson's objections to poetry are echoed, forty years later, in the "language poets'" rejection of so-called workshop poetry. McGann goes on to suggest that if (Riding) Jackson had accepted language's materiality as an inherent property of language, rather than viewing it as a perversion of language performed by poets, she might have granted her own project more success in its pursuit of truth:

> In the contemporary scene, poetry is once again placed at the center of language by an argument that has constructed a theory and practice of "poetry" out of key elements of Riding's ideal of "prose." The argument grounds itself in an understanding of language as the practice of the forms of arbitrary signification. All aspects of language (or writing) are materialized (that is, they are approached through Jack Spicer's triad of morphemics, phonemics, and graphemics). Indeed, author and audience are themselves exposed as functions of language, coded beings and sets of activities. When "poetry" is seen as the linguistic mode that calls attention to the activities of these codes, its truth-telling power appears in a new

way. The physique and apparitions of poetry do not become, as they were for Riding, truth's obstacles and distractions. They become, rather, truth's own "tellings" and eventualities. (*BR* 140)

Indeed, the materiality of language becomes the key to its truth-telling capabilities for poet Susan Howe, whose project is as driven by a concern for truth as (Riding) Jackson's was, as I will show in chapter 5. But (Riding) Jackson's abiding dis-ease with language's materiality made her skeptical not only of poets who courted language's sensuousity, but even perhaps ironically, in light of McGann's observations, of those who were interested in critically investigating language's materiality.

Inside Language as Language with Gertrude Stein

> To tell it all in a sentence is not what I wish to do I wish to
> tell it all in a sentence what they may make it do. . . .
> A sentence is their wedding.
> —Gertrude Stein (*How to Write* 123)

Gertrude Stein had such an interest, and though (Riding) Jackson admired Stein's work for a short time, late in (Riding) Jackson's life and long after she had stopped writing poetry, she condemned Stein for using words "as inert artistic material" ("Word-Play" 241), not seeing Stein's writing as every bit the active, social process that (Riding) Jackson herself valued in language. Of course the writings of Gertrude Stein have always been problematic for readers and critics, whether they approach her work predisposed toward repudiating it as "mere nonsense" or toward rescuing it from those who would repudiate it. Two approaches to recovering (by explaining) Stein's work that are common in recent Stein scholarship accurately conceive of Stein's writing as being about language and its relation to the "real," but seem to fail to take into account that for Stein writing was a mode of knowing. The first explanation posits that Stein does not use language to represent "the world" external to the written composition itself, but merely as inert matter like a painter's oils or a sculptor's stone (precisely for which (Riding) Jackson condemned Stein). By radically disrupting normative syntax and punctuation, so goes the explanation, Stein is able to resist the communicative function of language and show that words do not inevitably mean, but can be—*are*—objects in themselves.[5] Virtually any entry in

Stein's poetic sequence *Tender Buttons* (*TB*) can be used to illustrate this linguistic materiality, such as this excerpt from the section "Food":

SINGLE FISH.

Single fish single fish single fish egg-plant single fish sight.
A sweet win and not less noisy than saddle and more plough-ing and nearly well painted by little things so.
Please shade it a play. It is necessary and beside the large sort is puff.
Every way oakly, please prune it near. It is so found.
It is not the same. (50)

The physical and sensual characteristics of the word "fish," the repetition of the sounds [s], [f], and [š] in the first line, and the grammatically complete but semantically absurd sentence units that make up the rest of the composition do heighten our awareness of language-as-such. But if we limit our awareness of language to the notion that words are material entities, we are left with no way of really reading Stein. In fact, once we understand this basic idea, there's no need to *read* Stein at all, for we have gotten the point—the same point she seems to make over and over again, from one word composition to the next.

The second explanation of Stein's language use argues that Stein does not forego representation of reality in her writing, but rather, she uses language to resist patriarchal meaning and instead represent some aspect of "the feminine"—conceived of as either presymbolic *jouissance* or a coded-but-decipherable representation of lesbian love and domesticity. Marianne DeKoven offers a thorough and convincing analysis of "feminine" language in *Tender Buttons*, describing the text as an "irreducibly multiple, fragmented, open-ended articulation of lexical meaning" (76). DeKoven acknowledges that "[a]s gestures toward content, the subtitles of *Tender Buttons* make as well as mock meaning" (79), suggesting that Stein might be exploring the meaning-making processes of language. But by privileging the writing's "erotic celebration" of departure from meaning, DeKoven is claiming a representational function for Stein's language, representing "the feminine" as nonrational, irreducible (16). *Tender Buttons* offers a myriad of examples to support the encoded lesbianism theory as well,[6] beginning with the title of the work, itself an instance of the clitoral imagery which, according to Paula Bennett, has nestled in poetry by women for centuries.[7] Other examples are less subtle, such as Stein's assertion in "LUNCH" "that necessity is a silk under wear. That is best wet" (48–49).

The difficulty with such readings of Stein that locate textual meaning in secret encodings is that Stein's language, although not seen as purely material, is conceived of as purely transparent. The point of such readings is that Stein's language *refers*—not without difficulty, because as readers we must resist the patriarchal reading models that have been passed down to us in order to interpret the language, but refers nonetheless—not only to a world external to the text, but to a specialized and privileged feminine reality. Thus, the ultimate transparency of the at-first-apparently-not-transparent language becomes its most prized quality. This reading necessitates that we look *through* language, avoid seeing it *as* language.

Jane Palatini Bowers avoids this pitfall by placing emphasis on language as language, suggesting that "a more useful approach to [*Tender Buttons*] . . . is to ask not what it is about, but what it is doing" (85). For Stein, language is neither pure matter nor purely referential—words both *are* and *mean*. In an interview with Robert Bartlett Haas conducted just months before her death in 1946, Stein recounts her discovery in the process of writing *Tender Buttons* that language is never purely material:

> I took individual words and thought about them until I got their weight and volume complete and put them next to another word, and at the same time I found out very soon that there is no such thing as putting them together without sense. . . . I made innumerable efforts to make words write without sense and found it impossible. Any human being putting down words had to make sense of them. ("Transatlantic" 18)

The point is that even when words are manifest as objects in themselves, they still *do* inevitably mean. Stein's writing is neither "about" anything, nor is it nonsensically about "nothing"; it is a direct encounter *with* language, language *as* language, both material and meaningful.

And so when we read Stein we encounter both language and our own encounter with language, which together make up the process by which meaning is constituted. Lyn Hejinian suggests that Stein saw language as "an order of reality itself and not a mere mediating medium" so that "it is possible and even likely that one can have a confrontation with a phrase that is as significant as a confrontation with a tree, chair, cone, dog" and so on (L&R 129). But how can one have a "confrontation" with a phrase? The term "confrontation" implies action from both parties—the phrase *and* the reader or writer. To confront a phrase is not to receive or even extract its message, but to engage in a lived relation. The activity that characterizes these lived relations is essentially phenomenological—a perceptual act in which knowers apprehend their own processes of perception as well as the worldly phenomena they intend thereby to know. What Stein shows us by investigating this process as it takes place in writing-reading is that language is a participant in the phenomenological situation. Stein wanted to foreground the role that language plays in the perceptual experiences through which one comes to "know" the world. She explains in "Poetry and Grammar" that language "should force itself upon you, make you know yourself knowing it" (*Lectures* 221).

Stein's interest in the experimental painters of her day—including Matisse, Cezanne, and Picasso—stemmed from her insight that these Cubists were investigating the same problems of representation and perception in their visual work that she was pursuing in her language compositions. She felt a special affinity with Picasso, with whom she freely discussed these ideas. The two created portraits of one another, and both portraits represent not their ostensible subjects so much as the process of representation itself.

> At Picasso's studio Stein saw that daily for ninety days, Picasso stared at the same object (herself) and painted again and again the same image (her portrait). Yet, every day this image changed. Her vision of her portrait would have been like a palimpsest, her mind's eye retaining previous images that Picasso had erased. Gertrude Stein witnessed Picasso's portrait of her recording the process of its own creation. (Bowers 61–62)

Stein's method of verbal portraiture similarly depends on a synchronic conception of time so that the various discrete moments of perception that make up the layered palimpsestic view coexist in a continual ongoing present. The effect is not of a collage of static perceptions, but a field of simultaneous action. Stein uses a number of techniques to create this constant motion, including a heavy reliance on present participles and gerunds (to suggest ongoing actions), and repetition. Both techniques are evident in Stein's portrait of Picasso, as this excerpt shows: "This one was one who was working. This one was one being one having something being coming out of him. This one was one going on having something come out of him. This one was one going on working. This one was one whom some were following. This one was one who was working (*Selected Writings* 334)". The repetition takes place on a number of levels: among individual words, phrases, and grammatical patterns. In fact, the repetition is so ubiquitous that what stands out is not the repeated elements, but the variations—the points at which a repeated element does not identically replicate the previous occurrence. It is these slight variations and irregularities that lend credence to Stein's at first absurd-sounding claim, a claim she makes again and again in her essay "Portraits and Repetition," that she does not repeat:

> Each time that I said the somebody whose portrait I was writing was something that something was just that much different from what I had just said that somebody was and little by little in this way a whole portrait came into being, a portrait that was not description and that was made by each time, and I did a great many times, say it, that somebody was something, each time there was a difference just a difference enough so that it could go on and be a present something. (*Lectures* 177)

Repetition requires memory, and memory requires that there be a past. In Stein's writing there is no past—only the continual present moment. Hence, there can be no repetition: "anything one is remembering is a repetition, but existing as a human being, that is being listening and hearing is never repetition" (Lectures 179).

Stein's portrait of Picasso is not merely "about" perception and representation but itself contextualizes and creates both. In it she is using her medium, language, to actually produce and reproduce these processes in some of the same ways that the Cubist painters use their medium, paint. As Allegra Stewart observes, "Gertrude Stein devoted a great deal more attention to her medium, considered in itself, than writers ordinarily do. . . . The *word*, then, is parallel to the *eye*, as a twin theme. Along with the power derived from vision, she is thinking of the powers, and developments, of words" (79). But since she was quite aware that one of the inherent qualities of her medium is that it is never inert, Stein did not try to mimic the visual effects achieved by artists with paint, but intended instead to explore language's function *as language*. Note how very nonvisual, nonimagistic, and simply nondescriptive the language is in her portrait of Picasso. Stein discovered that language functions as a perceptual medium without imitating the effects of visual perception: "I became more and more excited about how words which were the words that make whatever I looked at look like itself were not the words that had in them any quality of description," she writes in "Portraits and Repetition" (*Lectures* 191). Language functions perceptually, Stein discovered, not by presenting visual images to the reader, but by operating as the point of contact between the human subject (the knower) and the world (the known). The meaning-making process of this contact—knowledge—takes place in language. We become aware of this function of language only when we consider language in its materiality as well as its referentiality.

By heightening her own and her readers' awareness of language in all its immediate, lived reality, Stein hoped to restore to poetry its capacity to provoke knowing, which she imagined it once had before the operations of words themselves were rendered invisible by people's associational habits that develop from knowing "anything's name for so long," as she puts it in "Poetry and Grammar." Such habits dull one's sense of "the thing being alive" as well as the awareness of being oneself a participant in the perceptual process (*Lectures* 237). Stein discovered in poetry a way to challenge these habits and the passivity they foster. In "*Narration* Lecture 2" Stein distinguishes prose and poetry according to their purposes: prose functions as telling *about* while poetry functions—or should function—as being *with*. She writes:

> Prose was more and more telling how anything happened if any one had anything to say about what happened how anything was known if any one had anything to say about how anything was known, and poetry poetry tried to remain with knowing anything and knowing its name, gradually it came to really not knowing but really only knowing its name and that is at last what poetry became. (113)

As readers, we remain *with* knowing as long as we remain *in* language, engaged in a continuous confrontation with language, a confrontation that implicates the words, their relation to each other, the referential possibilities of the words, both singly and in combination, and the reader's own (knowing) participation in the meeting (meaning). "Rooms," the series of prose paragraphs that comprise the third section of *Tender Buttons*, begins with an imperative that advises the reader to be attentive to this entire field of simultaneous action and not to rely on learned reading habits that assume language to be transparent and meaning to be central, fixed, or more important than the process of the encounter itself:

> Act so that there is no use in a centre. A wide action is not a width. A preparation is given to the ones preparing. They do not eat who mention silver and sweet. There was an occupation.

> A whole centre and a border make hanging a way of dressing.
> This which is not why there is a voice is the remains of an offering.
> There was no rental. (63)

Syntactically, the words add up to sentences. But semantically, the sentences do not add up to any final meaning. This is not to say that the language is meaningless; on the contrary, because the writing is without closure, meaning is continually *in process*. Words and sentences combine and recombine for the reader, who is never merely a passive observer of linguistic phenomena, but a full partner in the process. Stein explains her intention: "To tell it all in a sentence is not what I wish to do I wish to tell it all in a sentence what they may make it do. . . . A sentence is their wedding" (*How to Write* 123).

Several contemporary readers of Stein appreciate that her work invites—indeed, insists on—active participation from them as readers. But at the same time it should come as no surprise that this quality is precisely what has turned readers and critics away from Stein's work, certainly in her own day but even among contemporary readers, for her writing challenges not only normative reading habits but the literary "values" such habits depend on: clarity, unproblematized reference, linearity, decodable meaning. But those who find Stein's work to be quite readable not in spite of, but *because of* the absence of these qualities seem to feel liberated from the imperative toward mastery implicit in the traditional model of literary interpretation, and that model's implication that until a reader attains such mastery, she is bound in subordination to the writer, the text, and the text's implicit meaning, all of which have mastery over her. In her reading of *Tender Buttons*, Bowers welcomes that the text's "intimacy comes from our being involved directly in the making of the text" (104). And Gray feels that Stein's words "invite me in and let me choose my own part in the composition" (46). Linda S. Watts finds that Stein empowers her reader "by displacing the reader's faith in writers as authorities, narratives as absolute doctrines, and interpretations as rituals of tribute and affirmation" (3). Stein was herself aware of the implications for the reader of writing in which, like a Cezanne painting, "each part is as important as the whole," for, she explains, "[a]fter all, to me one human being is as important as another human being" ("Transatlantic" 15–16).

This nonhierarchical stance Stein takes toward her readers has been, and I think rightly, identified by some critics and readers as a feminist impulse in Stein's language project. Harriet Scott Chessman convincingly articulates this position:

Stein's feminism . . . infuses her modernist form with a concern for the exposure and transformation of all hierarchies, particularly those of gender. Central to this revision of hierarchy is a poetics of dialogue, where dialogue presents an alternative to the possibility of patriarchal authoritarianism implicit in monologue, reliant upon the privileging of one voice, one narrator, or one significance. (3)

Chessman continues:

Informing my own approach to Stein's writings is a belief in the feminism implicit in her "invitation" to a new kind of reading. . . . urging us toward an open-ended and speculative responsiveness to her writing, resisting traditional critical claims to objectivity and closure, and allowing ample room for subjectivity. . . . Stein makes it difficult to master her writing or to enter into a relationship with the writing that could even figure mastery as a possibility. (8)

Gray postulates the liberating effects of Stein's writing slightly differently, but like Chessman cites the increased access to language and meaning, and to one's own processes of knowing that Stein's writing affords, as the primary feminist values in her project: "Stein's remarkable freedom ungenders our access to language, uncodes our relationships with words, and teaches us to pay attention" (5). As a result, "Stein's words offer . . . consistent resistance to the cultural codes of meaning [which] makes her work especially relevant to a feminist theorization of an ungendered access to language" (63). Watts advances a similar argument: "Rather than creating an autonomous or separatist language, Stein reclaims existing language by creating oppositional strategies to the hierarchy and patriarchy encoded within that language" (3). But Stein's relevance to any feminist theory of language and gender has also been challenged by some feminist critics who find Stein's attitudes and behavior inconsistent with feminist goals. As Shari Benstock explains in *Women of the Left Bank*,

although an important woman in twentieth-century literature and culture, she remained absolutely uninterested in supporting the work of other women or even in acknowledging herself as one of them. As a lesbian, her relationship with Alice Toklas duplicated the imbalance apparent in many heterosexual unions to the extent that Natalie Barney was shocked on feminist grounds by Stein's treatment of Toklas. (18)

But it is precisely these kinds of behavior that indicate the extent to which Stein felt the special problems of gender identity in relation to writing and language and philosophical investigations. Rather than claiming special gender-related powers for women writers as (Riding) Jackson did, Stein reacted to patriarchal culture by claiming for herself "the powers of manhood" that this culture guaranteed (Benstock, *Women* 11).

My interest, however, lies not so much in Stein's "feminism" or lack thereof, but in the significance of her language experiments to contemporary language-oriented women writers in their feminist projects. Stein's work has been of interest to "language writers" of both genders since that group's early theorizing in the 1970s, because of her sense of the role that language plays in how meaning is constituted, and her particular interest in the sentence as a building block of meaning that prefigures some experiments by "language-writers."[8] Nearly all of the writers whose work I discuss in this study consider Stein to be an enabling presence. Laura Moriarty claims that Stein is "very important to [her]—a very generating kind of writer" and her investigation of repeated forms and phrases betrays a Stein-like fascination with perception and representation (personal interview). Leslie Scalapino has been particularly interested in Stein's portraiture and what those experiments suggest about writing, perception, and time. Stein "taught me something about writing plays," Scalapino acknowledges. "Her notion of writing being the time that it is has bearing . . . on . . . issues of narrative suggesting to me writing as movements, sole actions which can be seen as such in the writing's structure" (written exchange). My understanding of Scalapino's writing project as phenomenological, which I detail in chapter 4, rests on her demonstration of writing as taking place in a continual present tense, so that the writing does not represent, but as in Stein's work, is itself the action, action rich with simultaneous and multiple possibilities. Lori Lubeski also values Stein for the possibilities her work opens up, especially in undermining our learned reading (perceptual/associational) habits: "Stein . . . really intrigued me by showing that things are not what they seem to be. She makes a statement and it's not what we expected. There can't be anything more enlightening than having one's expectations broken down. . . . there's that whole possibility in what she does" (personal interview). As I shall show in chapter 3, Lubeski is a writer concerned in her own work with finding nonhierarchical and ungendered relations to language along the lines of those which Nancy Gray identifies in Stein's writing.

But of all the contemporary writers whose work I consider here, Lyn Hejinian's project intersects the most significantly with that of Stein, as my discussion of Hejinian's work in chapter 1 evidences. Not only has Hejinian written and delivered talks on Stein, but she continues to read and learn from Stein's work. Although Hejinian is careful to problematize the notion of "influence," explaining that "[i]t's hard for me to sort what I've learned solely from Stein's writing from what I might always have had (actually or potentially) in mind" as well as "from what I've learned from . . . my immediate peers" (letter 1/22/95), Hejinian's deeply felt appreciation for Stein's writing project offers evidence that despite the multiple erasures and misreadings and marginalizations that the work of modernist women innovators has been subject to, this writing is vital and relevant to a perhaps small but devoted readership that not inconsequentially includes contemporary women innovators.

"From stepping-stone to stone of creative explorations": Mina Loy's Deconstruction of Femininity[9]

> The word made flesh
> and feeding upon itself
> with erudite fangs
> The sanguine
> introspection of the womb
> —Mina Loy, "Joyce's Ulysses" (89)

Stein was also appreciated by a small—very small—number of her own contemporaries, including poet Mina Loy, who understood Stein's project and shared her interest in language as language—as both material and referential. And Stein recognized Loy's rare ability to depart from conventional reading habits that prevented and continue to prevent so many readers from fully appreciating Stein's writing. "Mina Loy . . . was able to understand without the commas," writes Stein. "She always has been able to understand" (*Autobiography* 132). And in a short poem entitled "Gertrude Stein," Loy dubs her "Curie/of the laboratory/of vocabulary" whose purpose is "to extract/a radium of the word" (94). A radium is not an inherent meaning or essence, or inert matter, but a luminescence—highly unstable, active and interactive. Loy understood Stein so well because their poetic projects had much in common. Both writers were deeply involved in the visual arts—Loy not as a patroness of modern art as was Stein, but as an artist herself[10]—and like Stein, she investigated some of the same problems of perception and representation explored by modern painters in her experiments with language. But most significantly, Loy also conceived of language as action and of reading and writing as dynamic interactive processes. She understood language to be the medium in which we come to know anything—ourselves as well as the world. But it seems that Loy's poetic experiments were motivated by a more overtly feminist consciousness than either Stein's or (Riding) Jackson's, and her investigations into language and gender imply that linguistic freedom and sexual freedom are closely connected.

In Loy's poems, though every bit as carefully "honed" and crafted as any by (Riding) Jackson, she enacts a *process* of inquiry into how we know rather than presenting a beautiful aesthetic *product*. As a result, her poems often lack the traditional poetic values of internal consistency and coherence. But as Carolyn Burke explains, "in order to pursue her epistemological concerns, she risks imperfection" ("Mina Loy's 'Love Songs'" 45). Indeed, what Loy recognized as language's inherent "imperfection," in the sense of the impermanence and multiplicity of meanings it creates, is precisely what made writing such a viable genre in which to pursue her epistemological concerns—much as Lyn Hejinian is motivated by epistemological uncertainty. Loy explored the conditions and limits of what she dubs "perceptive consciousness" in her poetic essay and first American-published written work, "Aphorisms on Futurism," by foregrounding the phenomenological situation in her poetry (152). But Loy's interest in perception, rather than leading her away from linguistic concerns, everywhere informs her poetics, a poetics characterized by a keen awareness of how language functions in the constitution of meaning. Loy began to publish her poetry around 1914, and by 1918 Ezra Pound recognized Loy's interest in language and paid her what was for him quite a compliment, announcing that she wrote "logopoeia or poetry that is akin to nothing but language, which is a dance of the intelligence among words and ideas and modification of ideas and characters" (57).

But in Loy's poetry of words and ideas, it is the painterly way she uses imagery—juxtaposing disparate, often visual, images, and interjecting abstract observations—that keeps the reader's attention on the level of language. Loy's poem "Parturition," perhaps the first poem in English to describe the experience of giving birth from a woman's perspective, offers an example of this effect:

Have I not
Somewhere
Scrutinized
A dead white feathered moth
Laying eggs?
A moment
Being realization
Can
Vitalized by cosmic initiation
Furnish an adequate apology
For the objective
Agglomeration of activities
Of a life.
LIFE
A leap with nature
Into the essence
Of unpredicted Maternity
Against my thigh
Touch of infinitesimal motion
Scarcely perceptible
Undulation
Warmth   moisture (6)

Throughout the entire five-page poem, from which these lines are but a short excerpt, both space and time are distorted by the "circle of pain / Exceeding its boundaries in every direction" of which the speaker has become the "centre" (4). The sensation of simultaneity that I feel while reading this poem would seem to be a function of this altered consciousness. But significantly, Loy creates this simultaneity formally rather than thematically through painterly collage and linguistic, imagistic, and even typographical experimentation. Like Stein, Loy conceives of poems as fields of action, which distinguishes her mode of imagism from Pound's pre-Vorticist theory of the image as a complex but static presentation, the product of "the poet-sculptor's forceful mental imprint upon matter." Burke observes that in contrast, "Loy, a trained artist, knew that images were inherently unreliable and no more numinous with meaning than anything else. She also knew that images could dissolve, shatter, break into their components, fade out, or prove unrecognizable from different angles of vision" ("Mina Loy's 'Love Songs'" 39–40). Remember that (Riding) Jackson, too, felt that images were unreliable, deceptive in their aesthetic enhancement. I cannot help but think that (Riding) Jackson might not have abandoned poetry, but instead found in it a way to deconstruct the deceptions to which she objected, had she shared Loy's insight that the unreliability of the image is as much a function of language itself as the use to which poets put language.

This dynamism and constant movement in Loy's poetry may be traced in part to the influence of Italian Futurism, especially the literary theories of Filippo Marinetti (Koudis 56–57). Certainly Marinetti's insistence that poetry should be a continuous flow of image on image is consistent with Loy's belief that language and consciousness are closely linked. In "Aphorisms on Futurism" she lays out the fundamental guiding principle of her poetics: the conviction that modern humans were facing a "crisis in consciousness" (151), brought on by an inability to perceive immediate reality because their perceptive faculties had been clouded by received opinion—"the turbid stream of accepted facts" (150)—and the cultural debris that fills our subconscious—"that rubbish heap of race-tradition" (152). From Loy's perspective, these normative values have the same effect as the normative "associational habits" that Stein objected to: they limit our access to language as a way of knowing. For Loy, the way to break out of such perceptual prisons is linguistic experimentation. Only by breaking free of literary tradition and imagining new linguistic forms will humans be able to achieve new states of consciousness. For "form hurtling against itself is thrown beyond the synopsis of vision" so that the perceiver is forced to adjust how she "sees," to look further, and to participate more fully in the process of knowing (149). "[I]t is the new form . . . that moulds consciousness to the necessary amplitude for holding it" (151). Simply put, Loy believed that new ways of using language would lead to new ways of knowing that would penetrate and thwart culturally imposed definitions of knowledge and facilitate self-realization.

An important aspect of Loy's language-oriented feminist epistemology is her configuration of knowledge itself as a process of perception rather than as a set of truths to be finally arrived at, for "CONSCIOUSNESS has no climax"(151). Thus, Loy sought a condition of perpetual novelty in her writing, advising that "THE Futurist . . . must spring from stepping-stone to stone of creative explorations" (150). Loy was especially sensitive to how women in her culture could benefit from such creative exploration in language, and her own poetic innovations, including her dynamic imagism, are inseparable from the feminist concerns that inform her entire writing project. As Burke puts it, in Loy's writing, modernism and feminism "converge" ("The New Poetry" 38).

Sharing both (Riding) Jackson's and Stein's rejection of activist feminism's immediate goal of economic and political equality between men and women, Loy's writing outlines a more deconstructive approach to gender-based inequality, changing not laws but consciousness. Loy's "Feminist Manifesto" targets the "social code," society's "theoretical valuation" of women as unimportant, and the reductive thinking that divides "women into two classes *the mistress, & the mother*" as women's most dangerous modern enemies (153–54). Before women can be economically and politically free, Loy believed they must be psychically and sexually free from patriarchal institutions such as marriage and conceptual constructs such as romantic love and virginity. Most important, in order to avoid the binary thinking that designates "woman" as the negative term in the man-woman opposition, women should not define their identities in relation to men.[11] "Leave off looking to men to find out what you are *not*," Loy advises women. Instead, "seek within yourselves to find out what you *are*" (154). In her poetry, Loy employs the deconstructive method she theorizes in the "Manifesto" by foregrounding language: she both reveals the role language plays in the construction of gender categories and social conventions and shatters these constructions with her fragmented images and jarring linguistic configurations.

In some of Loy's most powerful poems she deconstructs the cultural conventions that constitute the ideal of romantic love, including the institution of marriage, and the constricting and damaging definitions of femininity these conventions perpetuate. In "The Effectual Marriage or the Insipid Narrative of Gina and Miovanni," Loy offers a portrait of a woman, Gina, trapped in the role of the wife in a conventional marriage: "Being an incipience   a correlative /an instigation of the reaction of man / From the palpable to the transcendent" (36). Gina's options are limited as much by her own received knowledge, the conventional (cultural) "wisdom" that says that marriage is the surest way for women to find fulfillment through love, as she is by her husband Miovanni, who "so kindly kept her" in the kitchen "among his pots and pans" (36). Loy's most famous poetic sequence "Songs to Joannes" is markedly less satirical in tone than "The Effectual Marriage," probably because its theme of bitter disappointment in romantic love is based on Loy's own particularly painful experience of a failed love affair. The 34-part sequence begins with a challenge to the

notion that love, transcendent and eternal, has the power to genuinely
elevate lovers to a "superhuman" condition:

> Spawn   of   Fantasies
> Silting the appraisable
> Pig Cupid   his rosy snout
> Rooting erotic garbage
> "Once upon a time"
> Pulls a weed   white star-topped
> Among wild oats   sown in mucous-membrane (53)

Love is here revealed to be not only the product of human fantasy, but
also a cultural fiction, a fairy tale that exists not in real time but in the
narrative convention, once upon a time. And love, here embodied as
"Pig Cupid," is anything but transcendent, "Rooting erotic garbage."
The poem's closing section is comprised of a single line which drives
this point home and deconstructs, by revealing its "truth" as textually
constituted, "Love— — — the preeminent litterateur" (68). Throughout
the poem the speaker's tone is often angry, resentful for having herself
fallen prey to the illusion that love is anything other than "the impact of
lighted bodies / Knocking sparks off each other / In chaos" (59). Loy
sees the convention of romantic love as one of the old forms that needs
to be deconstructed in order for women (and men as well) to achieve
new forms of consciousness.

Loy also suggests in her writing that neither gender nor subjectivity are fixed, permanent, or essential, but, as what Burke calls "conceptual and perceptual constructs" (images), are themselves subject to
dispersal and reformation ("Without Commas" 50). In "Parturition"
Loy points to this aspect of gender by introducing the "fashionable por-
trait-painter" on his way to a woman's apartment where he will, as portrait painters are wont to do, construct her image (5). Loy juxtaposes his
view of women as generally frivolous and insignificant playthings, expressed in the song he sings on his way up the stairs—"All the girls are
nice/Whether they wear their hair in curls/Or—"—to the speaker's
own experience of being a particular woman in a particular moment:

> He is running up-stairs
>
> I am climbing a distorted mountain of agony
> Incidentally with the exhaustion of control

> I reach the summit
> And gradually subside into anticipation of
> Repose
> Which never comes
> For another mountain is growing up
> Which   goaded by the unavoidable
> I must traverse
> Traversing myself (5)

The speaker seems to experience femininity as intense, powerful, transformative (and she is not paying any attention to her hair). But more important, she does not cast this particular gender-related experience as definitive of essential femininity. ("All the girls" are *not* climbing mountains of pain.) Rather, it is this particular process of consciousness, of knowing herself in the world, through which the speaker constructs her identity, an identity subject to the internal fragmentation implied by self-traversal.

In "Three Moments in Paris," Loy comments even more overtly on the constructedness of gender. The first of the three "moments," written in first person from the perspective of a woman addressing her male companion, begins "Though you had never possessed me / I had belonged to you since the beginning of time" (15). The poem explores the implications of this observation that people are not identical with the gender constructions they—wittingly or not—inhabit. Significantly, this poem illustrates the extent to which gender is a concern for Loy not in addition to her interest in knowing, but as an integral part of her epistemological concerns. Loy brings attention in her deconstruction of gender in this poem to questions of knowledge—what constitutes it and who has access to it. Loy suggests that what is normally valued as knowledge—abstract thought and the contentious assertion of the theories such thought produces—is also normally thought of as the special domain of men:

> As your indisputable male voice   roared
> Through my brain and my body
> Arguing dynamic decomposition
> Of which I was understanding nothing (15)

By inhabiting the binary poles of this gendered opposition in which male is to female as mind is to body, the lovers in this poem are hopelessly separated not only from themselves, but from each other, so that the woman experiences the man's voice as "the thunder of alien gods" (15). Loy's satire extends to the cultural ideals of femininity that associate women with the natural, material realm of the body and its functions.

The poem's third "moment" describes (in third person) two prostitutes passing a shop window. The thrice-repeated line "All the virgin eyes in the world are made of glass" suggests that virginity is itself man-made, so to speak (17). In allowing themselves to be identified according to gender roles constructed for them by men, especially roles that define them as commodities such as wives or virgins, women are deprived of the ability to perceive—that is, to exist in the world as knowing, acting subjects. Still, Loy is not attempting to supplant male-created fictions with feminine "truths" or the masculine subjectivity that asserts these fictions with an authentic female subjectivity. Instead, according to her understanding that certain "truths" such as these are culturally sanctioned literary constructions, Loy chooses the same deconstructive strategy that Margaret Homans in her book *Women Writers and Poetic Identity* ascribes to Emily Dickinson, to "embrace and exploit language's inherent fictiveness" (217).

In fact, many of Homans's insights into why subjectivity is such a concern for nineteenth-century women poets seem equally applicable to women poets of the early twentieth century. Homans's argument offers an apt introduction to Loy's investigation of the very conditions of subjectivity in "Songs to Joannes." If "the major literary tradition normatively identifies the figure of the poet as masculine, and voice as a masculine property," Homans asks, "How does the consciousness of being a woman affect the workings of the poetic imagination?" (3). This question is especially pressing in light of Homans's observation that in nineteenth-century Romantic poetry this masculine subject represents as feminine all that he—as the speaking subject—is not. Being cast in the role of the "other" and precluded from possessing subjectivities of their own, argues Homans, women poets attempted "to forge a self out of the materials of otherness" (12). But because women poets were thus made painfully aware that centrist conceptions of self as manifested in traditional male-produced poetry are linguistically created gestures of domination, they often resisted simply duplicating this gesture in their own writing, opting instead to take subjectivity itself "as the necessary subject" of poetry (34). Indeed, Homans's analysis of Dickinson's poetic exploration of female subjectivity might also illuminate Loy's project, especially in light of Loy's views on feminism. Homans writes: "It will not do simply to perform a poor imitation of the masculine 'I' for the sake of asserting equality, because true equality is inconceivable within the conceptual framework of dualism" (218).

So, though I agree with Virginia Koudis that Loy "strives not for 'escape from the self' but for self-realization" (139), I am also convinced by Carolyn Burke's assessment that "Loy's own exactness of mind would not allow her to assume that the self was an unchanging, bounded entity with a fixed perspective" ("Supposed" 138). The "I" in Loy's "Songs for Joannes" is very much a fragmented self, a perceiving "eye" as Burke observes, "aware of the dispersal of perception in space and conscious of the self as if from a great distance as well as from within" ("Supposed" 138). I also find Burke's comment salient that Julia Kristeva's theory of subjectivity is more useful in reading Loy than are feminist theories of identity politics. For Loy's idea of the "crisis in consciousness" that I have described, when explored from a female perspective as in "Songs to Joannes," resembles nothing so much as Kristeva's notion of the "subject-in-process." What Kristeva calls "poetic language" is that which is both disrupted and disruptive, for in it the "semiotic" element of language continually unsettles the meanings which the symbolic element of language is continually attempting to assert. As a result, the speaking subject of such language is herself disrupted and in flux, a subject-in-process. Similarly, the form that consciousness takes, as Loy insisted in her "Aphorisms on Futurism," is determined by the linguistic forms it apprehends.

In the case of "Songs," Loy presents a speaking subject whose self-identity is transient—"I bring the nascent virginity of / —Myself for the moment" (58)— and in flux:

> The procreative truth of Me
> Petered out
> In pestilent
> Tear drops (62)

The subject is subject, as it were, to the perceptual language in which it (she) is constructed, variously "With steel eyes" or "From slit eyes" or with "Impossible eyes" (63–64), depending on the degree to which perception is affected by the contesting constructions of gender and sex-roles that the lovers in the poem must continually navigate at their own peril—certainly at the peril of any sense of self-unity or coherence they may expect or desire.[12] The possibilities for so- called authentic selfhood are even slimmer for the woman in this construction of heterosexual romantic love in which her very existence—the

> synthetic
> Whiteness
> Of my
> Emergence

—depends on being constructed (seen) by the male gaze: "And I am burnt quite white / In the climacteric / Withdrawal of your sun" (64). Loy's poetic project is largely motivated and defined by these inquiries into subjectivity and how it is constituted in relation to gender.

Until very recently, Loy's poetry has been on the whole less available, and the subject of fewer critical studies than that of Stein, (Riding) Jackson, or H.D., so it comes as no surprise that even the writers whose work Loy's experiments anticipate seldom mention her as an important "influence" or enabler.[13] Nonetheless, Loy's deconstruction of gender as a socially constructed category allies her with many contemporary language-oriented women writers who see similar connections between gender constructions and women's subjectivity. Two contemporary writers in particular share Loy's interest in literary and cultural conventions, suggesting the same kinds of connections that Loy did between such conventions (and the linguistic forms they foster) and consciousness. Laura Moriarty is especially concerned with the conventions of romantic love and adventure, and explores her own experiences as a gendered subject in relation to these literary traditions. A very different writer, Carla Harryman, intentionally violates normative literary conventions in an attempt to allow access to kinds of knowledge and experience that have been systematically devalued and even suppressed in our culture (often these are forms of social knowledge and experience particular to women), so that, in turn, we might imagine a freer and more just world. Harryman's project, including how she describes her own intentions, is remarkably similar to Loy's. But Harryman's writing, marked by her interest in genre and narrative, scarcely if at all resembles Loy's dynamic word-based fragmented lyric. This difference is significant, for what links the various writers treated in this study—both modernist and contemporary—is not any fixed set of stylistic or aesthetic practices, but rather a political-philosophical disposition that prompts them to formulate in their poetic projects language-oriented feminist epistemologies.

Slipping the Knot of Language: Realism and Indeterminacy for H.D.

> *we know no rule*
> *of procedure,*
>
> *we are voyagers, discoverers*
> *of the not-known*
> —H.D. (*Collected Poems* 543)

Mina Loy and H.D. represent cases in point. Of course none of the writers treated in this study presents the unproblematized fully present speaking subject of Western masculine humanist thought in their poetry, but the particular problems that women face regarding subjectivity take an especially predominant place in the projects of both Mina Loy and H.D., as aesthetically disparate as these two projects are. Like Loy, H.D. was concerned with the intersection of gender and subjectivity, and writing was for her a way of exploring these categories, as well as the role that language plays in their construction. In addition, H.D. resisted and deconstructed culturally prescribed definitions of the feminine from a feminist perspective. H.D. explored the creative process as a kind of self-analysis, taking into account the symbolic meanings of gender at work in constructing her own subjectivity as a woman in the context of the Western patriarchal culture she sought to deconstruct and reconstruct.

It is H.D.'s reconstructionist impulse that many feminist critics have zeroed in on in their enthusiastic praise of her poetry and prose. H.D.'s long poem written late in her life, *Helen in Egypt* (*HE*), is a particularly clear example of the revisionist mythmaking these critics value. In it, H.D. retells the story of the Trojan War from the point of view of Helen, effectively assigning authority and subjectivity to the female character who in traditional versions of this story has occupied the object position as the emblem of love and beauty as well as the symbol of death and destruction—a role assigned to her by masculine conceptions of female sexuality. H.D.'s earlier long poem *Trilogy*, written out of her experience of the blitzes in London where she remained throughout the second world war with her close friend and lover, Winifred Bryher,[14] explores other myths (the story of Isis, the New Testament) in a similar investigation of how gender has been inscribed in western culture. Rachel Blau DuPlessis summarizes H.D.'s revisionist project in her book *H.D.: The Career of that Struggle*:

> In *Trilogy*, as later in *Helen* . . . H.D. poses some building-block stories of Western civilization; the Trojan War, the Christian belief system, the quest narrative and its end in social regeneration and individual integration. By reinterpreting the women in these stories, she calls the authority of each tale into question. Her assumption of gender authority in the rescripting of these tales opens the narratives first by showing what they said in their deepest crevasses about women's psyche and social place, then by inventing a female perspective always implied, but never articulated, and finally by, as Robert Duncan has indicated, offering "female revelation." (86)

Susan Stanford Friedman, Susan Gubar, and Alicia Ostriker all share DuPlessis's view of H.D.'s writing project, and in addition argue that H.D.'s articulation of female perspective in her revisionist mythmaking is an integral part of her own quest for "authentic selfhood." Friedman emphasizes H.D.'s "rediscovery and creation of a women's mythology" as the key to Helen's (and H.D's own) identity as a woman ("Creating" 374). In a perspective consistent with Homans's assessment of the special identity problems that confront women poets, Gubar sees H.D.'s quest for identity as one woman writer's "struggle against entrapment within male literary conventions" (299). In her book *Stealing the Language*, Ostriker devotes one-quarter of her chapter on revisionist mythology (one of the five thematic motifs that she identifies as characteristic of women's poetry in the United States) to a discussion of H.D.'s work. Ostriker ascribes more universal implications to H.D.'s revisionist project; about *Helen in Egypt*, she concludes that it "is first of all personal, one woman's quest epitomizing the struggle of Everywoman" (228). Although this analysis of H.D.'s project occurs in a book entitled *Stealing the Language*, Ostriker's reading is not finally about language at all. In fact, of the four critics I have just mentioned, only DuPlessis acknowledges the extent of H.D.'s engagement with language. Many feminist readings of H.D.'s revisionist mythmaking tend to downplay or even overlook the role this concern plays in her revisionist project.

Certainly H.D. was seeking to discover or even *re*cover the feminine in cultural knowledge, myth, religion, and philosophy, but I do not believe that we can adequately understand how she went about doing this in her writing without taking into account her attention to language and her sense that all knowledge—whether personal, spiritual or cultural—is discursively constituted. In her revisionist mythmaking H.D. insisted that writing must be the site of transforming the knowledge contained and concealed within patriarchal/traditional histories, religions, and myths. Therefore, for H.D., writing is always also reading: "I tell and re-tell the story/to find the answer" (*HE* 87). This method of retelling, as well as the attention she gives to the ways "woman" has been inscribed in the stories she retells, make H.D.'s project well-suited to palimpsest, a kind of writing-over-of previous texts that allows the overwritten texts still to be legible. Earlier in this chapter, I described as palimpsestic Gertrude Stein's phenomenological writing in which the act of perception is always as much a part of the representation as the object being represented. H.D.'s similar suspicion that meaning never resides fully beyond the meaning-making processes of language itself—that "Beyond the Zenophiles of this world there is another Zenophile, beyond the Heliodoras another Heliodora, beyond the dank, hot and withering roses, other roses" (*Notes* 35)—caused her to view all writing as palimpsestic, and she experimented with a variety of textual layering methods in her own works.

Thus, just as Loy does not supplant male fictions with female truths in her poetic deconstruction of gender roles, H.D. does not replace patriarchal myths with equally self-contained women's versions in her revisionist mythmaking. Instead she overlays telling on retelling so that elements from multiple versions are simultaneously present in the text. In *Helen in Egypt*, for example, H.D. does not supplant the version of the Trojan War story that "we all know," in which Helen is present in Troy as the obvious cause of the war, with the version Euripides tells in his *The Trojan Women* in which, according to H.D.'s prose introduction to the first section of Book One of *Helen in Egypt*, "Helen was never in Troy. She had been transposed or translated from Greece into Egypt. Helen of Troy was a phantom, substituted for the real Helen, by jealous deities" (*HE* 1). H.D. does not reverse this substitution; rather, H.D.'s Helen is comprised of both Helens. "She is both phantom and reality" (*HE* 3). As a result, the language of H.D.'s text

> lifts and falls,
> conceals, reveals,
>
> (the actual
> and the apparent veil) (*HE* 112).

Thus, the traditional myth is disrupted and its accepted meanings unfixed, especially its normative and restricting definition of "woman," revealed as a function of ideological discourse, discourse always in struggle with other discourses—a struggle represented in H.D.'s poem by layers of the palimpsest. DuPlessis finds in H.D.'s palimpsests a kind of Kristevan poetic language in which the contesting discourses are associated with the symbolic and the semiotic functions of language: "The 'symbolic order' is thus affiliated with the political and social power of dominant discourses. The 'semiotic' with the marginal, and with subversion, critique, weakening of the permutations of dominance. Both are social" (*Pink* 86). Understood this way, H.D.'s use of palimpsest marks her poetic practice as specifically feminist and deconstructive.

But H.D.'s works are not only palimpsests of cultural texts and word meanings; they are self-palimpsestic—continually writing and overwriting themselves. Considering H.D.'s works in relation to one another, each poem, novel, and essay by H.D. seems to take part in a larger, unfolding work that is her lifelong written palimpsest. Her three earliest collections of poetry seem all of a piece, and her three autobiographical novels written during World War I—*Paint It To-Day*, *Asphodel*, and *Bid Me to Live*—all rework the same experiences, in effect overwriting one another. H.D.'s "Writing on the Wall," an essaylike prose memoir of her analysis with Freud, covers the same material as her poem "Advent." These works are published together under the title *Tribute to Freud*. Such palimpsestic relationships abound among H.D.'s works. But individual texts by H.D. are also often internally self-referential, constructing readings of themselves, overwriting the writing which is itself already an overwriting of the other texts it reads. The poem *Trilogy*, then, is not only a palimpsestic overwriting of St. John's The Book of Revelation as well as other texts such as the Cabala; it also overwrites itself. In the first part of, "The Walls Do Not Fall," H.D. offers on one level a reading of the events of the war, the "ruin everywhere" caused by the bombing of London (*Collected* 509), the "*zrr-hiss, / lightning in a not-known, / unregistered dimension*" (*Collected* 542). And on another level H.D. is "reading" this very act of writing, in terms of the role that writing plays in keeping the walls from falling, as it were, by ensuring with its "indelible ink of the palimpsest/of past misadventure" that history will not be forgotten. Life will continue as long as writing continues, this poem implies, for "it bears healing: / or evoking the dead, it brings life to the living" (*Collected* 512). It is significant, then, that the poem ends by *opening* rather than closing, opening into the uncertainty that is a function of writing that explores rather than solves the problems it addresses:

we know no rule
of procedure,

we are voyagers, discoverers
of the not-known,

the unrecorded;
we have no map;

possibly we will reach haven,
heaven. (*Collected* 543)

Commenting on these final stanzas, Joseph Riddel observes that this section of *Trilogy* ". . . ends in commitment, not reconciliation. The walls endure not because the poet has read the writing there, but because she has committed herself to continue the writing, the voyage. . . . the poem has become a process or act of discovery. . . . a generative act. And thus it has become a poem about itself: both the writing-on-the-wall and the analysis" ("H.D. and the Poetics" 467–68).

By continually acting as reader in (and of) her own writing, H.D. is performing the same modernist—and feminist—gesture enacted differently by all four of the writers I treat in this chapter—in effect undermining her own authority as "author" and inviting her readers—also doubly engaged in reading/writing—to participate more freely in the texts. Bruce Campbell explains his sense of this process in his reading of H.D.'s *Hermetic Definitions*, which H.D. wrote late in her life and in which she poses the question, "Why must I write?"

> Language . . . veils and unveils its mysteries to eyes intent on following clues. And this is exactly what H.D. does: her poem offers a series of readings. . . . So, on one level . . . the poem is a reader's and deals with the entanglements of language. Why write? Because we are already involved in language and, perhaps, only through writing can language become a process with a goal. Its goal is reality: H.D. offers a reality realized *through* language. ("H.D.'s 'Hermetic Definitions'" 27)

Campbell's idea that reality is the goal of language in H.D.'s writing reminds me of Lyn Hejinian's observation about Gertrude Stein's writing that in reading it, one can have an encounter with a phrase. The reality, in both cases, is our own entanglement in language. Even if we could

extricate ourselves from language in our consideration of very real phenomena—a table in a room, a human relationship, an air raid, the relative powerlessness of women in society—the depth of our knowledge of
these things, and of their realness, would be greater if we also considered the role that language plays in our own perception as well as in constituting the cultural and psychological meanings that all objects, events,
and situations carry. H.D.'s interest in the "reality" of language is precisely what characterizes her writing as language-oriented. In fact,
Joseph Riddel's comment that "The Walls Do Not Fall" "is a poem about
its own medium, language, and the world encompassed by language
which is at once open and closed," seems to describe not only this one
poem, but H.D.'s lifelong poetic project with language ("H.D. and the
Poetics" 469).

H.D. emphasizes the "reality" of language not only through textual
palimpsest, but also by foregrounding and problematizing reference
and interpretation, or—to return to the phrase I used at the beginning of
this chapter in describing (Riding) Jackson's and Stein's poetics—by investigating language *as language*. As a result, although H.D. is often
identified as the quintessential, even original, imagist, the poet whose
work was most instrumental in Pound's articulation of imagist poetics
and his promotion of those ideas in the United States, "imagism" as it
appears in H.D.'s work does not neatly fit Pound's early criteria for
imagism. Just as Mina Loy's images are more active than a mere "direct
presentation of the thing," instead always on the brink of dissolving
into other (equally unreliable) images, so H.D.'s images, as Robert Duncan puts it, "set things into movement . . . as if each knot that bound the
whole . . . was knot but also slipping-of-the-knot" (48). But whereas
Burke finds Loy's images not to be "numinous with meaning," I believe
that the "slippage" in H.D.'s images is precisely a function of her deep
sense of the unrecoverable numinousness of language. It is not that language does not mean or cannot mean, but the opposite: language
means endlessly, multiply, palimpsestically, and therefore signs can
never be fully or finally read. Though arrived at quite differently, H.D.'s
insight is similar to Gertrude Stein's that language cannot *not* mean,
and its meanings are not always subject to the writer's control or intentions. This is in part because words do not simply mean but also *are*.

But for H.D. (and this thinking sets her apart from both Loy and
Stein, while resembling in some ways (Riding) Jackson's philosophy of
language), words *are* because language partakes of a spiritual realism.
H.D.'s sense that language always contains some hidden mystery or indeterminacy, so that the power and value of the direct image is that it

can be used "as a means of evoking other and vaguer images,"[15] may be attributable to H.D.'s own well-documented interest in the occult, hermeticism, and alchemy.[16] If H.D. thought of herself as the visionary that Robert Duncan considers her to have been, then she must have seen it as her office to preserve indeterminacy. But H.D.'s inclination toward mysticism is not inconsistent with her orientation toward language. In fact, H.D.'s sense of the numinousity of language, evidenced in what Duncan calls her "spiritual poetry,"[17] is precisely what brings her attention, and her readers', to the operations of language itself. For even if "by prayer, spell, / litany, incantation," words "become, as they once were, / personified messengers" (*Collected* 529), we do not always get the messenger we expect; the language knot slips, and the poetic image is neither stable nor static:

> So Saint Michael,
> regent of the planet Mercury,
>
> is not absent
> when we summon the other Angels,
>
> another candle appears
> on the high–altar,
>
> it burns with a potent flame
> but quivers
>
> and quickens and darkens
> and quickens again (*Collected* 567–568)

H.D.'s fascination with the problems of signification permeates her poetry, which is rich with "jottings on a margin, / indecipherable palimpsest scribbled over," unreadable signs, codes, unhatchable words (*Collected* 533). In *Trilogy* the wanderers/poets "know each other / by secret symbols" (*Collected* 521) and the secrecy itself, not the revealed meaning, is what makes of poetry

> the rare intangible thread
> that binds all humanity
>
> to ancient wisdom
> to antiquity (*Collected* 523).

H.D. unravels this rare thread by tracing etymological as well as ana-
grammatic relationships at work within individual words.

> now polish the crucible
> and set the jet of flame
>
> under, till *marah-mar*
> are melted, fuse and join
>
> and change and alter,
> mer, mere, mère, mater, Maia, Mary,
>
> Star of the Sea,
> Mother. (*Collected* 552)

Marina Camboni remarks on this example of H.D.'s linguistic alchemy:
"By connecting new and old, derived and root words, H.D. puts together archaeology and myth, history and language: whole ranges of
words are therefore embedded one in the other till no word stands by
and for itself" (105). Interpretation is thus deferred indefinitely by such
metonymic chains of signification—the movement of language itself.
H.D. theorizes this plenitudinous activity of language in her autobiographical novel *Bid Me to Live*, in the passages describing the protagonist Julia's experiences of translating Greek, a task with which H.D. was
herself quite familiar:

> The words themselves held inner words, she thought. If you look at
> a word long enough, this particular twist, its magic angle, would
> lead somewhere. . . . She brooded over each word, as if to hatch it.
> Then she tried to forget each word, for "translations" enough ex-
> isted and she was no scholar. She did not want to "know" Greek in
> that sense. She was like one blind, reading the texture of incised let-
> ters, rejoicing like one blind who knows an inner light, a reality that
> the outer eye cannot grasp. She was arrogant and she was intrinsi-
> cally humble before this discovery. Her own. (162–63)

Julia's discovery—significantly "her own"—is that words cannot be
"hatched." Just as the "language poets" have subsequently argued,
H.D. here suggests that words are not vehicles containing extractable
meanings. The "inner light" in each word may be understood as its

hidden meaning, but only if we understand that hidden meaning to be the discovery of the inherent quality of language that complicates the very notion of hidden meanings. In her poetic images, H.D. wanted to open the word to the operations of language that make it meaningful, "to watch its faint / heart-beat, pulse beat / as it quivers" (*Collected* 555). and not to overlook these operations by settling for any fixed meaning.

H.D.'s account of her extraordinary vision of picture-writing appearing (as if projected from her own consciousness) on a hotel wall at Corfu in 1920, an account written 20 years later in "Writing on the Wall," offers another example of how the value of the sign, for H.D., lies in its very indeterminacy. Rather than seeking definitive meanings or translations of the signs as Freud had during H.D.'s analysis with him in 1933, H.D. emphasizes the multiplicity of available readings of the images and the impossibility of fixing on any one final meaning. Her comments about two of the six hieroglyphlike images that appeared in succession on the wall are particularly telling. About the third image to form, a circle with three lines supporting its base, she writes, "The tripod, we know, was the symbol of prophecy, prophetic utterance that or occult or hidden knowledge; the Priestess or Pythoness of Delphi sat on the tripod while she pronounced her verse couplets, the famous Delphic utterances which it was said could be read two ways" (*Tribute* 51). Significantly, H.D. interprets this image as the sign of indeterminacy itself, referring not to an external signified, but to another process of signification in which reading is similarly problematized—the Delphic oracles. The fifth image, which H.D. names Nike, "is a moving-picture and fortunately she moves swiftly" (*Tribute* 55); this physical movement of the material signifier H.D. takes to be a symbolic manifestation of the unfixability of signs in general. And this may be why she attaches a special significance to this figure as representing signification itself, even claiming it as her own personal signifier-as-signifier: "Nike, Victory seemed to be the clue, seemed to by my own especial sign or part of my hieroglyph" (*Tribute* 56).

H.D.'s lifelong interpretive quest was premised on her sense of language as "some common deep sea of unrecorded knowledge" that the writer/reader could dive into (*Palimpsest* 255). It is perhaps ironic that what sustains such a project is also what determines it can never end: the numinousity of language. The rich sense of presence implicit for H.D. in the unreadable sign is precisely a function of the textuality of its meaning. As Riddel points out, whatever knowledge H.D. is investigating in her palimpsestic texts and etymologies—psychology, history, the ancient mysteries—"the primordial text or event is already literary, already cultural" ("H.D.'s Scene" 43). H.D.'s writing purveys the postmodern view of language on which her project also depends— that there is no nontextual origin on which meaning finally rests. Even H.D.'s poetic images indicate this textuality. Riddel continues: "a 'presentation' which precedes 'representation' . . is the grounding of poetry in its own textual complications—in the double movement of a text that tries at the same time to maintain the illusion of its fidelity to an external event or to nature and to falsify the event, thus marking its textuality. The Image in this sense is an analytical scene" ("H.D.'s Scene" 43). This double movement as Riddel theorizes it seems to be the same quality Duncan describes as the knot that both slips and is tied in H.D.'s images. Each image is an enactment of the textuality of all images, an analysis of the ways in which presentation is always necessarily representation.

But how do the palimpsests, indeterminacy, and self-referential textuality in H.D.'s writing add up to an investigation of subjectivity? Just as writing was for H.D. a process of discovery and self-analysis as interminable as Freud's notion of psychoanalysis and coextensive with life itself ("Write or die," she writes in *Hermetic Definitions* [7]), so Helen as she appears in *Helen in Egypt* is identified with writing (not eros or death) right from the start: "She herself is the writing" (23). And if "she" (H.D.? Woman? Helen?) is the writing, then all the qualities of that writing define her subjectivity. She is also not only without nontextual origin, but is indeterminate, self-referential, never finally whole, always a reading of herself, a layering of readings of herself—in short: a palimpsest. And this is how H.D.'s language-oriented writing complicates and resists Susan Stanford Friedman's notion that H.D.'s revisionist mythmaking effects "the metamorphosis of the woman as 'other' to authentic selfhood" ("Creating" 374).

What H.D. brings to her writing as a woman writer-reader of the cultural inscriptions of "woman," is precisely what she brings to her analysis with Freud (a process in which she participated as both text and reader): "the already doubled figure of the woman/translator/ poet—hence the woman as the body of the text, neither presence nor absence, but the sign of the sign" (Riddel, "H.D.'s Scene" 51). In fact, it seems likely that H.D.'s interest in palimpsest, her double act of reading the world and reading her own reading of the world, is well suited to, and may have developed out of, her investigations of gender and her own subjectivity as a woman poet. DuPlessis explains how the conditions of such an investigation are right for inviting the self-reflexive stance of writing that is a reading of the very text it produces that H.D. takes in her poems: "Reading the sign of the woman, reading signs generated around women, reading the presence of the sign, woman, in our culture, means reading a situation of being read" (*Pink* 97). Thus, the poet herself is at stake in the text, being as much a part of it as its creator. And we find in H.D.'s female characters this same doubled, self-reflexive stance as they attempt to read the hieroglyphs of themselves, including the texts in which they themselves have been culturally inscribed as women.

H.D.'s Helen epitomizes her conception of the female subject. That Helen is always in two geographical locations at once—in Greece and Egypt, "together yet separate"—is only the surface fracture of her deeper fragmentation. She is also struggling to "study and decipher / the indecipherable Amen-script" (*HE* 22) at the same time that "she herself is the writing" (23). Therefore, like the speaker in Loy's "Parturition," H.D.'s poetic speakers are inevitably subjects-in-process, speakers of a language necessarily disrupted by the palimpsestic interplay of the symbolic and the semiotic. Paul Smith reads these plenitudinous subjects as evidence of a positive feminist strategy on H.D.'s part, and not as the symptom of patriarchally imposed alienation to be overcome through unification into authentic female selves. "Instead of trying to establish a kind of rival identity and self-possession with which to confront the male," Smith writes, "H.D. attempts metonymically to unfold a series of overlapping and unfixed identities that will respond to her desire" (34). Helen's identity is not just fragmented or doubled, but infinite, a name containing the seeds of its own metonymic projection: "Helen—Helen—Helen— / there was always another and another and another; / the rose has many petals" (*HE* 194). As a subject-in-process, the reader/writer (H.D., Helen) guarantees that the writing will not stop, the walls will not fall, and the woman will not be silenced in a binary system of gender oppositions. Helen's plural subjectivity threatens, by overspilling, the very system of fixed identities on which gender categories also depend. That Helen is unfixable implies that she (who herself is the writing) is uncontainable by the economy in which the female's value is determined by the male gaze. H.D. was certainly aware of the unsettling power such a female subject-in-process possesses. Her Achilles reacts with fear and confusion to Helen's plurality. When he recognizes her in Egypt as the same woman he had seen on the ramparts in Troy, even as she tries to conceal her face with charcoal from a burned stick, he demands of her:

> What sort of enchantment is this?
> what art will you wield with a fagot?
> are you Hecate? are you a witch?
>
> a vulture, a hieroglyph,
> the sign or the name of a goddess?
> what sort of goddess is this? (*HE* 16)

His inability to "read" Helen throws him into a sort of identity crisis, what Jeanne Larsen identifies as an instance of "male ego-anxiety" (93): "where are we? who are you? / where is this desolate coast? / who am I?   am I a ghost?" (*HE* 16). In her prose introduction to this section of the poem, H.D. dubs Achilles "Greece-incarnate, the hero-god" (*HE* 15). Larsen's Freudian diagnosis extends, then, to the Western patriarchy H.D. intends for Achilles to represent. His attempt to strangle Helen "with his fingers' remorseless steel" represents that culture's impulse to discursively contain and control, to "fix," female identity (*HE* 17).

H.D.'s indeterminate palimpsests with their metonymic chains of hieroglyph and signification in which the female subject is "hardly decent," always in-process, are important elements of H.D.'s language-oriented feminist epistemology (*Collected* 590). She theorizes this epistemology in her poetic prose essay, *Notes on Thought and Vision*, where she describes the "over-mind," a particular state of perceptual consciousness. The over-mind, like the palimpsestic text and palimpsestic self, is marked by plurality. She explains that "the over-mind is a lens. I should say more exactly . . . two lenses. When these lenses are properly adjusted, focused, they bring the world of vision into consciousness. The two work separately, perceive separately, yet make one picture" (23). Significantly, not only is the perceiving consciousness fragmented or doubled, but the fragmentation itself is linked for H.D. to the female body. "I first realized this state of consciousness in my head. I visualize it just as well, now, centered in the love-region of the body or placed like a foetus in the body," she explains (19). Then, in a remarkable prelude to Irigaray's notion of the feminine as fluid (not in opposition to but in excess of masculine "solids"), H.D. describes the over-mind "like water, transparent, fluid yet with definite body . . . . It is like a closed sea-plant, jelly-fish or anemone" (18–19). She also anticipates the questions her own metaphors beg about gender and this doubled perception:

> Is it easier for a woman to attain this state of consciousness than for a man?
> Are these jelly-fish states of consciousness interchangeable? Should we be able to think with the womb and feel with the brain?
> May this consciousness be centered entirely in the brain or entirely in the womb or corresponding love-region of a man's body? (20)

H.D. leaves these questions unanswered. But just the fact that she raises such questions about gender and knowing, both directly, as here in *Notes on Thought and Vision*, and implicitly, as throughout *Trilogy* and *Helen in Egypt*, is significant. By assuming this questioning stance and then pursuing the questions by exploring the operations of language itself, H.D. establishes a feminist language-oriented epistemology in her writing.

I agree with Ostriker that H.D. intuits in her work "a kind of knowledge, softly but firmly opposed to the world of rationalism and violence" ("No Rule" 344). But just as Loy's "crisis in consciousness" precludes the viability (and desirability) of a unified and coherent, authentic female voice, H.D.'s "over-mind," imagined as a heightened (rather than inhibited or limited) state of consciousness, does not suggest this opposition will come in the articulation of a unified "I" with a fixed perspective. H.D. makes clear in her description of "the veiled Goddess" who appears in *Trilogy* that the knowledge this female deity represents is not containable as any whole doctrine, equal-but-opposite to male knowledge:

> she is not-fear, she is not-war
> but she is no symbolic figure
>
> of peace, charity, chastity, goodness,
> faith, hope, reward;
>
> she is not Justice with eyes
> blindfolded like Love's (*Collected* 570)

H.D.'s palimpsestic method and interest in problems of reading indicate instead a language-oriented way of knowing, which as DuPlessis describes it, "counters Freud's 'materialist epistemology' [rational, scientific method], not by opposition but by a dialogic movement of incorporation and transcending" (*Career* 89). Such dialogic movement is present in all of H.D.'s texts, not only where she is countering Freud. H.D.'s feminist language-oriented epistemology does not oppose masculine epistemology, but exceeds it, shatters the binary structure on which notions of "female" versus "male" ways of knowing depend.

In the first place, H.D.'s configuration of the phenomenological situation is much messier than that described by early twentieth-century male philosophers in their attempts to discover a method of investigating phenomena that would be free of the doubts and errors inherent in naturalism. According to Edmund Husserl's phenomenology, theorized just after World War I, the knower always exists prior to and outside of the world and its phenomena that he seeks to know. His perception must thus be both inner-directed, toward his own perceiving consciousness, and outer-directed, toward the world external to his consciousness. But as Adalaide Morris points out in her analysis of how the concept of projection informs H.D.'s poetic technique, "inner" and "outer" are not wholly or consistently distinct realms for H.D.: "From the verb . . . *to throw forward*, projection is the thrust that bridges two worlds. It is the movement across a borderline: between the mind and the wall, between the brain and the page, between inner and outer, between me and you, between stages of being, across dimensions of time and space" (275). Thus, H.D.'s phenomenology differs from that of Husserl and his followers in intent, for like Stein, H.D. wishes to preserve rather than avoid doubt by enacting a kind of perpetual newness in her writing. This H.D. accomplishes not by fragmenting syntax and defamiliarizing common nouns as does Stein, but by continually posing questions. *Helen in Egypt* seems especially driven by clusters of questions that evoke multiple layers of the palimpsest of which all phenomena are comprised for H.D.: "Agamemnon? Menelaus? Odysseus?" (87); "where have you been? what brought you here? / what kept you there in the cold?" (156);

> was Achilles my Minotaur?
> a dream? a dream within a dream?
> a dream beyond Lethe?

> Crete? (189)

By means of questions such as these, referring always to textual uncertainties, H.D. complicates the boundaries between items in Morris's litany and at the same time implicates language as a crucial element in the phenomenological situation.

In addition, such boundary-breaching seems an inevitable consequence of perceiving with the "over-mind" as H.D. describes it, a perceptual consciousness marked at its core with the breaching of the most essential binary opposition in Western thought: body/mind. Although in one sense H.D. seems to reinforce this opposition by assigning each its own "lens," that both body and mind are conceived of as perceptual faculties and that they work together as equally important parts of a single consciousness seems quite contrary to normative distinctions between the mind as perceptual and abstract, the body as sensual and material. H.D.'s Helen seems to experience this messy phenomenology in her quest for knowledge:

> my mind goes on,
> spinning the infinite thread;
>
> surely, I crossed the threshold,
> I passed through the temple-gate,
> I crossed a frontier and stepped
>
> on the gold-burning sands of Egypt;
> then why do I lie here and wonder,
> and try to unravel the tangle
>
> that no man can ever un-knot? (*HE* 309)

As this last line suggests, H.D. shares with Stein, (Riding) Jackson, and Loy the belief that knowing is a never-ending process of engagement with language that cannot adequately be extricated from that process or contained in product form as "knowledge." And in this emphasis on process lies H.D.'s most effective transgression of binaries, for rather than opposing masculine myths with feminine or feminist truths, H.D.'s writing deconstructs phallogocentric literary history by exploring the excesses of language that make all truths suspect. According to Jeanne Larsen, in signs bearing "multiple and shifting significances," H.D. recognized "the means for a deconstruction of myths central to the Western patriarchal tradition and the model for a new understanding of the nature and possibilities of language itself." Larsen understands this process in H.D.'s writing to represent "a search for a language that bases its authority outside the hegemony of the *patrius sermo*" (88). Even when H.D. represents this new language with unmistakably female imagery, such as the *"delicate sea-shell"* given to Helen by Achilles's mother Thetis, *"a simple spiral-shell"* that *"may tell a tale more ancient than these mysteries"* (*HE* 118), such imagery is inseparable in H.D.'s work from her focus on language itself. The spiral of the shell certainly also represents the various language-oriented techniques H.D. employs, such as the metonymy operating in H.D.'s writing "as resistance to the fixity of male discourse" (Smith 333).

Finally, H.D.'s project is marked by a number of related paradoxes that continue to operate in the poetics of several contemporary language-oriented writers. The most crucial of these paradoxes lies in the relationship between textuality and knowledge that H.D.'s writing suggests: she is both questing for knowledge through writing and insisting, by this very method of the quest itself, that all meaning (and hence all knowledge) is ultimately textual. (As I discuss in the final chapter, a similar tension between reality and textuality lies at the heart of Susan Howe's poetic project—a project which, like H.D.'s, conducts a reading of history and myth in order to recover the feminine.) But H.D. shows how this paradox is precisely what gives writing its value and power, even or especially in times of war when people tend to see poetry as a peacetime luxury, a waste of time and energy that could be devoted to more pressing concerns:

> But we fight for life,
> we fight, they say, for breath,
>
> so what good are your scribblings?
> this—we take them with us
>
> beyond death . . . (*Collected* 518–19)

Thus, it is the paradox itself that enables H.D.'s own writing and ensures that her project is interminable—the writing will never stop.

Beverly Dahlen, whose own three-volume-to-date poetic sequence, *A Reading*, is similarly interminable (as I detail in chapter 3) understands the self-referentiality and repetition throughout H.D's work as that work's own generative method: "H.D.'s repeating was of that order which found the seeds of thought in these correspondences, these appearances by which or through which she seems to have *grown* her work" ("Homonymous" 9). The organicism implied by Dahlen's metaphor may at first seem inconsistent with the indeterminacy and epistemological focus I have been emphasizing in H.D.'s writing, but I think it is appropriate because it points to another aspect of the paradox I just mentioned. H.D.'s resistance to closure imparts a continuous, all-of-a-piece quality to her writing on the one hand, and a sense of unbounded fragmentation, of always becoming and never arriving at wholeness, on the other.

Such resistance to closure is itself a common characteristic of the writing projects of both modernist and contemporary language-oriented women writers, a resistance I take as emblematic of the questioning, exploratory impulse that guides these various projects. Even Laura (Riding) Jackson, as prescriptive and compulsory as her theories about language and truth seem to be, rejected poetry for being too restrictive, for not permitting the truths in language to emerge through the exploratory, dialogic process she felt was necessary. Stein also wanted her readers to participate in the meaning-making process of her writing, but her desire to defamiliarize words and free them from any preestablished meanings is certainly incompatible with (Riding) Jackson's wish to reduce words to their single "rational" meanings. And while H.D.'s sense that words hold some hidden inner truth at first seems consistent with (Riding) Jackson's view, H.D.'s spiritual realism is incommensurate with (Riding) Jackson's rationalism, not to mention Stein's scientific approach to language and Loy's aesthetic-perceptual dynamism. Loy tends to court the very sensuousity in her experiments with imagery that (Riding) Jackson shuns. But the differences among these women's projects—even or especially the irreconcilable differences—are as important as the similarities. These differences are significant not despite, but *because* all four writers were exploring the same territory in their work, asking the same questions about the intersections among language, meaning, and gender. And these are the same questions and differences that inform the projects currently taken on by language-oriented women writers in the United States.

The nature of the alliances these related interests suggest between modernist and contemporary American women writers, however, cannot be pinned down or summed up as any single or coherent phenomena of influence or literary history, "maternal," feminist, or otherwise. The eight contemporary language-oriented writers I treat in this study claim a wide range of influences, including male writers and nonliterary practitioners such as artists and philosophers. And though most of these contemporary writers consider one or more of the modernist women I discuss in this chapter to be important to them, the reasons they cite for this importance are not always related to gender. As Lyn

Hejinian puts it, "my first and on-going relationship with the writings of . . . Stein . . . H.D. [and others] . . . was not a gender-conscious one. . . . In other words, I had ungendered enthusiasm" (Letter 1/25/95). Susan Howe is more overtly conscious of gender as she considers her most important predecessors, but it seems not to be the biological genders of the writers that matter to her so much as gender as a quality in language, or a function of discourse. She explains: "I hope that I am working in an eccentric twentieth-century American tradition that embraces among others Duncan, Olson, Williams, Stevens, H.D. and Hart Crane. Seven poets move in puzzling ways through the ruins of our violent patriarchal history . . . Six men and one woman" (DI 18). Yet at the same time, Howe acknowledges the extreme importance to her own literary practice of three biologically female writers of the recent past— Dickinson, Woolf, and Stein: "In fact these women were and are great innovators. We haven't yet caught up to them. I can't conceive of twentieth century writing without them" (SSH 35).

Howe's statement is provocative. I likewise cannot conceive of poetry in the United States as the vital force that I think it is without the women writers of the early twentieth century who conducted significant epistemological investigations into gender, language, and knowing, or the women who conduct these experiments today. Together these writers comprise a literary tradition of women language-oriented writers. But I caution myself as well as my readers against any generalizing about these modernist women writers that my use of the term "tradition" might invite, for such generalizing would be counter to my purpose. What I hope my analysis of the writing of (Riding) Jackson, Stein, Loy, and H.D. in this chapter suggests is that language-oriented writing by women stands in significant ways outside of both twentieth-century traditions it also most nearly belongs to: avant-garde and feminist writing. Even when recognized as important modernist innovators in their own time, the early twentieth-century women writers' concerns with gender tended to be overlooked or ignored. Carolyn Burke explains, for instance, that "Pound's sponsorship of their poetry because of its intelligence . . . is notable precisely because he seems to have ignored the fact that they were intelligent *women*, whose 'logopoeia' was as gender-conscious as his own was gender-blind. . . . Pound was sure that 'intelligence' was coded 'masculine,' and for this reason, gender as an aspect of modernist poetics never suggested itself" (Introduction 234). Ironically, it may be a similar coding of "intelligence" as "masculine" that has prevented these writers from receiving much critical appreciation from feminist critics and readers.[18] Their epistemological interests in language in combination with their marginal interest in overt political activism would seem, perhaps, to align them too closely with masculine aspects of the avant-garde, itself often coded *as* masculine by many feminists. Yet as Susan Stanford Friedman points out, modernist women writers'

> distrust of political activism may be part of a larger gender-based pattern that includes writers like . . . Gertrude Stein . . . Different in degree, extent, and explicitness, these women nonetheless expressed a progressive politics originating in an exploration of the power structures underlying the personal. The private domain of the individual self in relationship to others, the scene of women's very confinement, served as the point of political origins. ("Modernism" 94)

So in spite of—and because of—this double-marginalization to which both early and late twentieth-century women innovators have been subject, language-oriented writing by women represents not only a tradition with a history, but a continuing, expanding force in American literature. In my analysis of contemporary language-oriented women writers in the following chapters, readers will hear echoes of (Riding) Jackson, Stein, Loy, and H.D.—echoes at times distant or subtle, at times resoundingly clear, but always evocative, indicative of the many ways language-oriented women writers enrich and inform one another's work.

Chapter 3

Subjects of Knowledge:
Processing Gender and Sexuality

The question of what constitutes knowledge and knowing cannot be separated completely from the question of what constitutes a knower. Taking subjectivity itself "as the necessary subject of poetry" (Homans 34), as did Mina Loy and H.D., continues to be one of the more notable shared tendencies among contemporary language-oriented women writers. Language-oriented writers of both genders are inevitably concerned with subjectivity, for when a writer foregrounds the processes of language in order to investigate how meaning is constituted in language, subjectivity emerges as a significant site of discursively constructed meanings. But in language-oriented writing by women whose concerns with language and knowing extend to the role the sex-and-gender system plays in constructing social relationships and organizing and legitimizing knowledge, it becomes apparent that gendered subjectivity is discursively constituted.

In this chapter I look at the projects of three language-oriented women writers—Beverly Dahlen, Lori Lubeski, and Laura Moriarty—who explore the conditions of subjectivity in their writing by processing gender and sexuality in language. By "processing in language" I mean that these writers investigate by entering into and engaging the discursive processes by which subjectivity, gender, and sexuality are constructed. This writing subjects these social categories to a critique that

79

reveals them to be, like the writing itself, "a process of contextual experience" (Gray 5). As I discussed in chapter 1 regarding Lyn Hejinian's faustienne poetics, writing that posits knowing as contextual and as taking place in the processes of language necessarily posits a subject that is—and does.

By writing in open, exploratory forms and refusing to represent the writing subject as a transcendental ego or self with a fixed or essential gender and sexuality, all three writers I discuss in this chapter suggest that since subjectivity, gender, and sexuality are discursively constructed, they can be discursively dismantled and reconstructed—in the processes of language. Rejecting the notion of unified essential subjectivity, these writers are aware, as was Foucault, that this "prevailing theory of the subject . . . contribute[s] to . . . normalizing power . . . [and] renders us particularly susceptible to the operations of normalizing power" because of the unified subject's "demand for unitary morality" (Diamond and Quinby xii). If "[s]ubjective identities are processes of differentiation and distinction," which insight Joan Scott attributes to the French feminists, then they are in fact "highly unstable." Rather than suppressing "ambiguities . . . in order to ensure . . . coherence," Dahlen, Lubeski, and Moriarty—though in very different ways—explore the ambiguities that disrupt fixed notions of gendered identity and keep gender as well as subjectivity continually *in process* (J. Scott 38).

Processing subjectivity, sexuality, and gender in language also necessarily involves processing one's writing "self." For all three writers, "the writing subject is herself the site of discursive struggle" (Weedon 5). For Dahlen, putting her writing self into process means engaging in a potentially interminable project of writing-as-analysis. This is a project in which, as for H.D., "she herself is the writing"—continually defining, redefining, and deconstructing her "self" in the constitutive processes of language itself. For Lubeski, processing the self means experimenting with fragmentation, incoherence, repetition, and abstraction in an attempt to give form to the often extreme emotional and psychic states that comprise her own experiences, so that these experiences, as she puts it, can be "re-seen or re-experienced" (personal interview). Moriarty takes a less psychological approach than Dahlen, and a less personal focus than Lubeski, processing her "self" by interrogating and deconstructing the cultural and literary conventions that have participated in the construction of gender and sexuality in Western culture. She is especially interested in the ways she herself as a writing subject is mediated by these conventions. These three writers, then, are remarkably different in their emphases and methods of processing subjectivity and sexuality; their projects represent no single unified, fully theorized, or articulated "position" on language, subjectivity, and gender or the exact role these play in the production of knowledge. What Nancy Gray says about the experimental women writers she treats in her book *Language Unbound* applies equally to the three writers I treat here: "Each has made sentences suited to her needs, using her own processes of knowing. Each is completely herself" (2).

But before turning to the particular projects of these individual writers, I would like to address one final, perhaps central, theoretical component of their poetic explorations of the discursive construction of subjectivity: the question of how subjectivity, gender, and sexuality are interconnected as they are constituted in language. My analysis of these writers' different projects is informed by the work of two contemporary feminist theorists who address the question of how gender, sexuality, and subjectivity are related—Judith Butler and Elizabeth Meese. Of course the relatedness of these terms begins with the poststructuralist observation that neither subjectivity, gender, nor sexuality are natural or fixed categories; all are subject to and constructed by discursive processes and institutional practices. But more important, these categories are not constructed in isolation from one another. In *Gender Trouble*, Judith Butler convincingly argues that "*regulatory practices* of gender formation and division constitute identity, the internal coherence of the subject" and that "'identity' is assured through the stabilizing concepts of sex, gender, and sexuality" (17). In fact, she continues, "the very notion of the subject [is] intelligible only through its appearance as gendered" (33). As I shall illustrate shortly, Dahlen and Lubeski both present themselves as writing subjects who fit Butler's description of "those 'incoherent' or 'discontinuous' gendered beings who appear to be persons but who fail to conform to the gendered norms of cultural intelligibility by which persons are defined" (17). All three writers affirm Butler's suggestion that, like subjectivity, "woman itself is a term in process, a becoming . . . an ongoing discursive practice . . . open to intervention and resignification" (33).

In her book *(Sem)erotics*, Elizabeth Meese theorizes what she terms "lesbian : writing." The colon, placed equidistant between the two words of the term, is especially important for how it keeps "lesbian" and "writing" in shifting relation to each other. "Lesbian : writing" is both "the 'lesbian' who is writing and the 'writing' that is lesbian" (xvii). And Meese's colon puts *process* into the definition, so that the lesbian *is* (equals, is comprised of) the writing, and vice-versa. Quite simply, and at the risk of oversimplifying, "lesbian : writing" is a processing of subjectivity and sexuality in language.

In suggesting that Dahlen, Lubeski, and Moriarty enact versions of Meese's "lesbian : writing," I am not claiming a necessary link between their language-oriented writing and the sexual preferences they articulate in their lives. For as a group, they represent no single or stable category of sexuality. Moriarty considers herself to be heterosexual, Lubeski has always claimed a lesbian identity, and Dahlen rejects labels such as "quote gay unquote life. The word is almost meaningless; it just doesn't hold the varieties of human experience" (personal interview). Similarly, for Meese, the word "lesbian" is not a fixed category of being or desire, but rather, refers to a site of meaning-in-process, where the story of the self and of the other is "always being solved or written—made and unmade every day" (18). Thus, "lesbian : writing" is also an ongoing processing of the self in language: "I am always writing, describing 'the lesbian' as an il-licit (unreadable, *illisible*, or unwritable) woman, whose meaning I am constantly called upon to (re)produce)" (15). Language, in "lesbian : writing," does not transparently represent a prior reality or experience—neither the subject's body nor its sexuality exist separately from the language that describes and inscribes bodily experience: "Language is not 'outside' me, except in the way that skin is 'outside' the body. No skin, no body. The body is already in(side) language" (14). Therefore, Meese's notion of "lesbian : writing" emphasizes the interrelatedness of language, subjectivity, and sexuality.

"Lesbian : writing" creates a writing subject in the process of writing, and that written/writing subject is lesbian in that it occupies a position outside the law of phallogocentric discourse. Just as Hejinian's faustienne poetics depends on the insight that language cannot achieve a state of perfect knowing or meaning, so the viability and value of Meese's "lesbian : writing" relies on the "gaps, the 'holes,' or the 'spaces'" (10) that result from "language's inability to control and to determine itself perfectly or completely." Through these gaps, "the lesbian slips in" (9), bringing with her "the space for writing" in which to "re-invent language to write a new identity" (13). But this "new identity" is not of the fixed or essential variety; rather, it partakes of the incoherence and discontinuity that mark Butler's unintelligible subjects. By foregoing perfect knowing in language and the notion of unified subjectivity that comes with it—as seductive and reassuring as these concepts can be—all three writers partake of a quest in writing similar to Hejinian's: to explore uncertainty and the new possibilities for knowledge that present themselves when assumptions of universality and objectivity are put into doubt.

Beverly Dahlen

> the future fields into which I write are unimaginable. I do not
> know, any more than you do, what is around me, nor how far
> to go, nor precisely what I leave behind.
> —Beverly Dahlen (*A Reading 8–10* 59)

Beverly Dahlen's major poetic work, *A Reading* (*AR*), is a performance of exploration and discovery in which the writing functions as
a reading of the author's life, self, unconscious, relationship to language, and the cultural knowledge that informs and partakes in the
construction of all of these.[1] She is especially interested, as was H.D.,
in how gender has been inscribed in Western culture and how she, as
a writing subject who is gendered "female," is mediated by these cultural definitions. Modeled after Freud's method of free association in
psychoanalysis, a process which is "potentially unending,"[2] *A Reading* offers itself as "the interminable reading. the infinite analysis"
(*AR 1–7* 17).

A Reading, published to date in three volumes, comprises a total of
seventeen sections. Each untitled section, further divided into untitled
subsections, is dated and geographically located according to when and
where it was written. Though Dahlen began the project in 1978 with "a
stricture about not editing, and [she] tried not to edit in the process of
writing" (personal interview), most sections in the second and third
volumes have two dates: the date of the original writing and a revision
date. Various thematic groupings and clusters are apparent throughout
the work. Section one, for instance, seems to center on questions of
space and time, while section five focuses more on myth and religion.
Certain themes continue throughout all sections, most notably commentary on language itself and speculation about gender and language.
But these themes appear to be the outgrowth of the free associational
method Dahlen employs rather than any preconceived formal design.
This method renders a text delightful to read for its perpetual novelty
and associational leaps:

> then he asked the listeners. then he heard them out. put out.
> then put out with his eyes. the relation to the object. the social
> relations of books to each other. that was an outburst, she decided.
> she moves back and forth among the petunias. that indicates slight
> eye movement. or this rapid. fire. couch yourself in the nineteenth
> century sentence. what is needed is a foil. (*AR 11–17* 84)

A Reading is written in prose and verse, in sentences which, though punctuated with periods, do not always begin with capital letters and frequently lack grammatical completion. Furthermore, because "there is nothing in the unconscious which corresponds to *no*" (*AR 1–7* 42–3),[3] *A Reading* is all inclusive, admitting memory, dreams, myth, autobiography, allusions to Charles Olson, H.D., Freud, Lacan, Kristeva, and others. These various discourses and "sources," in turn, overlap and comment on one another, creating an elliptical, palimpsestic text, both self-generating and exceeding itself.

Dahlen's subject-in-process is also a woman-in-process: "this interminable work is women's work, it is never done, it is there again and again. I live here, an unreconstructed housewife" (*AR 1–7* 102). The speaker's subjectivity and gender are in process because she "lives" *here*—in the process of the writing itself. As it was for H.D. in her interminable continuous palimpsests, for Dahlen, the writing subject—she herself—is the writing, "her manuscripts dribbling along the spine of the desk" (*AR 8–10* 88).

Ostensibly free of formal design and conscious intention beyond Dahlen's commitment to "find out what I'm going to write" each day (personal interview), *A Reading* is, like Hejinian's *The Book of a Thousand Eyes*, a kind of writing in the dark in which "writing face downward we have no view of the terrain" (*AR 8–10* 59). This is at times a frightening proposition, but Dahlen presses on, "writing scared, running with it" (*AR 1–7* 73). Free association allows the writer's consciousness to step back so that language itself steps up, becomes the generative agent in the writing: "these are words, one at a time. a step. one at a time. learning to walk, I fell down the backstairs, skinning my nose" (*AR 1–7* 23). The writer's task, in a project such as this, is not to employ craft or create beautiful forms or find the right words; rather, she has only to come into contact with language, for "touching a word it spreads like a stain in every direction" (*AR 11–17* 19). Commenting on *A Reading*, Dahlen suggests that this kind of self-generative writing with its never-ending metonymic chains of association is well suited to an investigation of the unconscious:

> In this way we say that *word* presentations are representations of *thing* presentations—i.e., the unconscious is known through its derivative representations. . . . Invoking a metonymy which was already a metaphor, the word itself, any word, a representation, a replacement, a substitution for some thing, any thing, which was not there, naming backwards, following it forward back and forth from nothing to nothing. ("Forbidden" 17)

Dahlen's sense of language as endlessly meaningful (i.e., generative) and yet interminably indecipherable renders her project quite similar to H.D.'s. Both writers, of course, are working out of Freud's theory of the unconscious. Rachel Blau DuPlessis explains how Dahlen's use of "[t]he Freudian secret H.D. knew too" in allowing language itself to become the active agent makes *A Reading* a reading: "Not to propose, but to have the work propose through her, her job being patience. Receptivity. Silence. Fearlessness. Permission. That is—her job is to claim a praxis. Not 'writing' exactly, but transmissions, being a wire, being wired (we say) and making writing. Making marks to read" (*Pink* 115). Dahlen's own conception of how language does what it does—or what, exactly, it does do, is never clear or certain. Throughout the work, she variously describes language as "a pattern, an archaic heritage" (*AR 8–10* 120), "not a code" (*AR 1–7* 32) and "constitutional" (*AR 8–10* 96), but it has for her material presence, a thingy weight in the world that is stubbornly real, as her humorous biological metaphors in this passage illustrate: "if the word does not arise it will fall back, the thing itself, it will fall again into that ocean where it is not biodegradable. it is not truly broken up into its constituent parts. it is a hunk of something indigestible" (*AR 11–17* 58). What language is *not*, in this work whose primary method of composition is free association, is seamlessly symbolic, coherent, or controlled.

Fitting Julia Kristeva's description of "poetic language," Dahlen's writing in *A Reading* "posits its own process as an undecidable process between sense and nonsense . . . between the symbolic and the semiotic" (135). According to Kristeva, the symbolic—associated with logos and reason—is one of two primary functions that operate within language. It does not account for all of language's operations, for also at work in language is the semiotic, "a distinctive mark, trace, index, the premonitory sign, the proof, engraved mark, imprint—in short, a *distinctiveness* admitting of an uncertain and indeterminate articulation because it does not yet refer . . . or no longer refers . . . to a signified object for a thetic consciousness." The speaking subject of such discourse in which the semiotic constantly disrupts the symbolic, Kristeva continues, "in order to tally with its heterogeneity, must be . . . a questionable *subject-in-process*" (135). The speaking (writing/reading) subject in *A Reading* is shown to be in a constant process of construction—indeterminate, interminable, fluid and multiple—indeed, a series of overlapping and unfixed identities, much like H.D.'s Helen in *Helen in Egypt*.

Dahlen had already read and thought a great deal about Kristeva's theories of subjectivity by the time she began work on *A Reading*. She explains: "I was very convinced by a lot of the French feminists who had reclaimed Freud and I always felt at odds with the American feminists who did not claim Freud or who cast Freud as the enemy" (personal interview). But Dahlen's acceptance of the French feminists' psychoanalytic theory is itself grounded in her own experience. She explains why she does not write coherent formal assessments: "I am haunted by a lack of definition at the center of my experience, this absence which, like a centrifuge, propels me toward the peripheral" ("Forbidden" 5). As a result, *A Reading* is peppered with observations that put the notion of an essential and unified self into question: "this is the story of my life. . . . who is this I? who asks the question already knows the answer: it is nothing, illusion, something made up out of loss, desire" (*AR 1–7* 34). Reminiscent of (Riding) Jackson's riddling "What am I? / I am what I say" in "Disclaimer of the Person," Dahlen's passage posits a subject constructed not only in language out of loss and desire, but also multiply, historically, and in memory: "there is an other, she who is in the mirror, the many faces, none of them recognizably myself, the visible history of flesh, the chains of a family, that binding which is the only limit we know" (*AR 1–7* 33).

The speaking subject in Dahlen's writing is not only constructed as a subject-in-process by the language-in-process of the writing; the subject is, in this work, herself coextensive with the writing. They are both open, interminable, and resisting closure. *A Reading* begins in the middle of a life, in *medias res*, and moving backward in time; the first sentence of the first volume reads, "before that and before that"—no capital letter, no fixed site or moment of origin (*AR 1–7* 15). In addition, there are no definite endings in the work: sections end midsentence, even midthought, and within the sections and stanzas, individual sentences end, as I mentioned above, before reaching rhetorical or syntactical completion. Though she has gone through "great stretches . . . of hiatus" Dahlen concedes that the work "was conceived as a lifelong project" (personal interview):

> I have been defensive about *A Reading*, wanting to postpone, or defer, conclusions or closure perhaps forever. It is the problem of the interminable. . . . To propose a work which is co-extensive with the literal limits of one's own life is, I think, to be in the thrall of the unconscious notion that one is immortal. For in Freud's words: "Our unconscious is . . . inaccessible to the idea of our own death." . . . The work, insofar as it is a metaphor for the life, will go on forever. ("Forbidden" 10)

The relationship between the subject and language is quite complex in writing that is coextensive with the "self." The subject is not merely constituted in language, nor is she merely a language user. Rather, she is *displaced* by language: "To become a 'speaking being' is to submit to a peculiarly human alienation from materiality. Henceforth language in my place; it speaks me" ("Something/Nothing" 172). But the subject at the same time occupies and is occupied by language, so that this displacement is ongoing yet continually deferred: "certain signs come down to us, we enter them and live there amongst them. what would you speak, living alone in silence. the center for language, once open, blooms, a long-lived flower" (*AR 11–17* 64). But "lost in it, the way we lose ourselves in our work, how can we recognize ourselves in it?" asks Dahlen (*AR 1–7* 37). Put simply, the problem becomes: How can we locate the writing subject *in* the work at all if the two are coexistent? What happens to the traditional notion of the author, in this case—the author as the one who stands outside the text and is therefore recognizable in the text as the one who writes it, crafts it into something from which readers will extract meaning?

As DuPlessis puts it, Dahlen, the "author" of this text, "is both donor and recipient, writer and text, everything and nothing, mother and child in the nest of words that defines, protects, reveals, conceals and produces it" (*Pink* 116). The author's authority, then, to set limits and determine outcomes, is undermined in the interminable text, and the reader (including the writer who is the reader), as a result, is empowered to participate in the production of meaning. And indeed, *A Reading* is an inviting text, offering a pleasurable alternative to highly crafted authorially controlled texts. And to offer such an experience is Dahlen's intent: "one of the reasons I call it *A Reading* is because I want to be another reader of this work," she explains, "I want to think of myself as a reader, and not be in a position of authority or author—that always has been a position fraught with anxiety for me" (personal interview).

But Dahlen has the feeling that what is fraught with anxiety for her is so culturally valued as normal and acceptable that its opposite—the disunified subject-in-process that Dahlen's forays into the mysteries of language and the unconscious seem to evoke—is in fact forbidden by society's regime of truth.[4] In her Freudian-Lacanian frame, Dahlen conceives of this regime of truth as the law of the father, for it is patriarchal order itself that is most threatened by what she calls, in an essay by the same title, "forbidden knowledge": "I knew . . . that it was 'forbidden knowledge,' because I don't think anybody's supposed to know that stuff; it's part of what's repressed, it's part of what makes the world tick on. You have to try to subscribe to the social goals that are set for you" (personal interview). Since the social order depends upon the illusion of a unified self, any kind of inquiry that might lead to knowledge that shatters that illusion is likewise forbidden. Dahlen feels that her interest in repressed childhood memories is also, therefore, forbidden. "amnesia, it's amazing how much is forgotten" (*AR 1–7* 34), she muses, all the while suspecting that what that amnesia is protecting us from is "a time of knowledge" that we have "bur[ied] in culture" (personal interview).

The most powerful threat to the law of the father, of course, is simply the knowledge that knowledge itself is constructed and perpetuated in the service of maintaining the authority of this law in the first place: "covering it, the alibi for the father. why the father is law, the stone. if the alibi for the father runs so deeply, if that is the lie on which. the fundamental silence" (*AR 1–7* 116). Dahlen is especially sensitive to the part the law of the father plays in the discursive and institutional practices according to which gender and sexuality are constructed. Some of the childhood memories—often fragmentary and apparently insignificant—which find their way into *A Reading* reveal Dahlen's awareness of this process. For instance, she writes: "Daddy, mom wants you to come home now, and he bending and turning, he came, came with me, back. such a man. and I a child learning the woman's part, come home now. be civilized, this is the order, we have made it, we have made these exchanges, this for that, lay it on the line" (*AR 1–7* 62). And what perpetuates "these exchanges" is the Lacanian phallus as signifier as it operates in discourse and the making of meaning: "what is real in this fantasy of the real is the phallus. everybody believes it. I believe it. you can't touch it with a tenfoot pole because it isn't there. that's how it comes to be real. it isn't there. and I'm not here" (*AR 1–7* 85). In this passage, Dahlen seems to suggest that in the insight that even the notion of the phallus is culturally constructed might lie some hope for escaping or deconstructing that semiotic cenotaph. Dahlen's humor (both in tone and the ten-foot-pole joke) reinforces the sense of hope that indeed, all is not lost.

Dahlen's (faustian?) desire to know is the motivating force behind the composition of *A Reading*. But the reading-writing subject-in-process in *A Reading* constantly asks what knowledge is, even as she seeks to know; this asking often reveals itself through contradiction. Early on in the first volume of *A Reading*, Dahlen asserts "I was not interested in preserving the mysteries, I wanted to know why" (*AR 1–7* 35). But the writing that is itself that quest— interminable, forever un-

folding its multiple meanings and unfixed propositions—insists that
the unknown cannot, in any final sense, be known. For as soon as it
seems "that you could trace the line looking into that thicket, this writing, the light and the shade, editing the rosebushes accordingly, true to
something, out there in the world," one finds that "that would be. ram-
bling, thorns" (*AR 1–7* 108). If the guiding question asked by *A Reading*
is "what could be lurking in there [the unconscious]?" (personal interview), the answer Dahlen continually seems to find is language itself:
"language language it is all made of language" (*AR 11–17* 73). And language, like the unconscious, is thick with "contradictions . . . reversals
. . . layers of meaning" so that

> the distance between
> the thing described, the event, the situation
> and the actual truth
> truth, troth
> to tell (*AR 11–17* 80)

can never be bridged and

> There will never be time to write all the sentences one may have
> been capable of writing, even about one subject. take a subject,
> anything, it is so simple, but the sentence is notched, can view
> the relationship from any one of a number (the number is infinite)
> of stances. where would you like to stand to view this one. any
> sentence is merely an example. it shows what might be done. a
> sentence is a model, in no way permanent, of thought. (*AR 11–17* 62)

This awareness of the limits of language, its inability to perfectly represent "the real," is for Dahlen on the one hand a source of grief, "betray-
ing the anxiety that the writing is a mistake, an effigy, a crude image of
life" ("A Reading: a Reading" 134). But on the other hand, even the most
extreme inarticulations of language—"loose abstractions, works on
paper. squiggles of a dying order, footmarks of deer, their droppings. the
marked and the unmarked, the book says an ethereal fluting, a prayer,
wispy, breathy. restrained. a gurgling" (*AR 11–17* 97)—may offer new
possibilities for how language might mean. For in "language. anything
there might happen. a tenuous grasp on the world" (*AR 11–17* 73).
Dahlen has no faith that purely symbolic language can lead to knowledge, so she rejects that kind of writing in favor of indeterminacy, which,
for Dahlen, carries a feminist value in its refusal of the patriarchal values

of ordered discourse: "(All this language is floating. The men make statements. They use the forms of the verb 'to be' with confidence. What I write is provisional. It depends. It is subject to constant modification. It depends)" (*AR 1–7* 76). Writing in which "it depends" may lead to knowledge, but not knowledge understood as nuggets of truth, statements of fact, or indisputable evidence.

The knowledge Dahlen so boldly seeks is of another kind, of the kind that will free her as a woman writing, as Meese's "writing : lesbian," from the law of the father: "I would not have written poetry except for that opening. otherwise madness. . . . the purely phallicized body, so burned, I meant burdened. . . . how bound to our chains. the work of a lifetime. one by one unknotting that, taking it apart at night in order not to be trapped" (*AR 1–7* 36). The gaps in symbolic language allow Dahlen to imagine a different kind of subjectivity, one not determined and fixed by the law of gender opposites and their accordingly "appropriate" sexualities. I see the shadow of Meese's lesbian smilingly slipping in through the gaps in this passage by Dahlen: "the gap, whatever is not covered, the language falls open revealing the root of bare breast, a pleasant beginning to mound in the mirror. she is taken in by it, in that relation of herself to some other, wholly imaginary whether actual or not" (*AR 11–17* 11). Dahlen at times associates this kind of knowledge with the mother, both as she remembers her own—"but mother said it was there, further back. she said you know how you go further back. she pointed to the back of her head. she said there you really did see it, as if in childhood one saw that blue and orange made brown, as if in childhood one saw the world discretely, there were the elements, one and one and one. further back, she said, we have that knowledge" (*AR 1–7* 42)—and Kristeva's imaginary chora, "unnameable, improbably, hybrid, anterior to naming, to the One, to the father, and consequently maternally connoted" (133). Dahlen uses the notion of the chora to articulate a feminine-feminist relationship between language and thought:

> forwarding the *chora* tangibly into a real day's light
> not talismanic but invested with the ordinary substantiality
> of labor accomplished apart from her
> these forms which are their meaning for me speaking
> ("Something/Nothing" 173)

But at the same time, she resists any temptation to generalize or essentialize that such notions of the so-called maternal or the so-called feminine might invite: "I doubt whether I can now say anything generally about women writers and literary form" ("Something/Nothing" 174). Still, by seeking the knowledge that is forbidden—and thereby going against the law of the father and that law's various constituent codes enforcing symbolically ordered language, such as (the perpetuation of the illusion of) unified subjectivity and compulsory heterosexuality—a writer can "send the father backwards. the two-timing father" (*AR 1–7* 36):

> shattered. what enters this house. bow down. an immense photograph of myself as a child, that unity, congruity, screen memory, living in several times at once, these were the conditions of life now. raising the flag on Iwo Jima, an image, a mythology. the uses of photography. the uses of the past. Garbo's face. her many faces. the icon. but walking in Greenwich Village, "I want to be alone," dark glasses, a woman of character, older, the eternal moment subverted. women subverting that, she is not here, she is risen as she said. (*AR 1–7* 69)

The "eternal moment" of the self and that of the feminine, which illusions the patriarchal law reinforces, are shattered and subverted—the self by layers of memory and constructed conflicting images of oneself, and the feminine by failure such as Garbo's, according to Butler's definition, "to conform to the gendered norms of cultural intelligibility" (17), her celluloid persona of feminine-heterosexual availability rendered unintelligible by her off-screen lesbian desire. It is significant that Dahlen brings the figure of Garbo, who in this way exceeds the male-female binarism assumed and imposed by the notion of unified and essential subjectivity, into the text her "lesbian : writing" is performing, a text which continues to exceed this binarism, a text which simply continues.

The male-female opposition, so deeply inscribed in Western culture and discourse, is equally deeply troubling for Dahlen. Convinced by the Freudian-Lacanian notion of the phallocentric structure of symbolic language, Dahlen writes *A Reading* partly to ask how, then, one *can* write, when one is a "woman." According to Bob Perelman, "The principal assertion that Dahlen makes—and she makes it quite strongly—throughout the book is the fact of/impossibility of her being a woman and of her writing from out of that situation" (304). If "woman" is defined as absence or lack, as she is in the Freudian-Lacanian model, then Dahlen sees her task to claim that absence as presence: "that X which was laid over it ages ago. no wonder I am a woman. now. impossible.

woman, that impossibility. that it takes place at all in any of us. . . . it is
what is lost that must be claimed. not found (impossibility) but claimed
as loss. to say it" (*AR 1–7* 78–79).

To "say" that loss involves stepping outside of the male-female
binarism as it describes opposing modes of access to language in the Lacanian frame. In one passage, Dahlen describes such a move imaginatively as a bride walking away from her wedding. At the beginning of
the description she is no more than the (absent) object of the male gaze,
while at the end she is an active agent, using language neither as a
"male" nor as a "female," but outside of that relationship altogether:

"Upon that absence he fixed his gaze."

stepping right up the breakers bashed on the beach the signal
of rising hyphens a tentative marriage. after all the vows
unsavored hinting at the go-between. why not? the list was
full of loaded words. one would come to renounce it almost
immediately. she loped off towards another vocabulary.

(*AR 11–17* 100)

That she "lopes" (rather than, say, "storms," or "slinks") implies that
she does so openly and cheerfully. Dahlen is not so much protesting
gender hierarchies as she is celebrating the possibilities for getting outside of them by using the language differently. This other vocabulary is
not just a different lexicon, but a different mode of writing altogether,
what Dahlen describes in an essay as

an interrogative style that seems to turn up frequently in the writing
of feminist women. . . . What I am calling the interrogative style of
women questions because there are no answers. They are real questions. They are questions about the ground of authority, radical ontological questions, questions about the practice of writing from a
center of experience that has been defined by others as non-existent,
an absence. ("Forbidden" 6)

I began this discussion of Beverly Dahlen's writing by describing her
work as exploration and discovery. Yet the language-oriented feminist
epistemology suggested in *A Reading* privileges invention rather than
discovery per se; knowledge must be made, and made new, not merely
uncovered in the forms in which it has already been made in Western
culture's patriarchal regime of truth. Just as the voyagers in H.D.'s *Tril-*

ogy "know no rule/of procedure" and *"have no map"* (*Collected* 543), Dahlen's writing subject must enter unexplored territory: "she said you go there and then you make the map. there aren't any maps, every journey into the wilderness" (*AR 1–7* 63). And that wilderness includes the subject herself, "the lady with the book" who is herself "an unwritten book on which this is inscribed" (*AR 8–10* 98).

A Reading continues, and as such, continues to be an unwritten book in the sense that it is perpetually unfinished, it is writing. By continuing to ask the real questions in a continual text-in-process, Dahlen keeps subjectivity, gender, and sexuality in processs, never cutting short the possibilities for knowledge, never settling into the complacency of received categories and definitions. Dahlen finds such complacency not only politically ineffective, but dangerous: "I don't think that it gets you anywhere if you stand there and say well I'm a woman and I'm a lesbian, and I'm white" (personal interview). Dahlen is skeptical of any politics or art that cuts short the process of knowing in favor of final conclusions: "I think that it's a danger for any kind of political movement if people get too complacent with their own self-namings, and it certainly is a danger to any artist to feel 'now I've arrived, I've got my goal, I found out what it is I'm writing about.' Because it's never going to be like that" (personal interview). Dahlen's goal, by contrast, is never to feel she's arrived but to keep moving, and thereby continually inhabit the moment of knowing-in-language in which "the nearest next thing is too far away to be discerned./tabula rasa the moving finger writes and having writ moves on" (*AR 11–17* 50).

Lori Lubeski

> *Just below the layer of skin will always remain a scar of this disobedient journey*
> —Lori Lubeski (*Obedient, A body* 38)

Lori Lubeski—a younger writer whose work, published in several brief small press editions and chapbooks, has not yet received as much critical attention as the other writers in this study—shares with Dahlen the propensity for incorporating personal experience, including dreams and memories, into a poetry that likewise resists coherent narrative, chronology, and closure.[5] Lubeski's unique sense of linguistic possibility finds expression in a writing style marked by syntactic and semantic oddities. For instance, sentence predication is sometimes skewed, as in "a girl playing hopscotch / falls down on her knee is scraped" (*Dissuasion*) Also, anomalous word combinations in lines such as "anyone bearing a resemblance / to the notion of safety . . . ," "coolness . . . /confiscates / your fear . . . ," and "The pain does not subside but with / an acquitted quality disengages from / impertinent situations" keep her readers pleasantly surprised by the new worlds of meaning opened by such language (*Dissuasion*). But Lubeski's investigation of subjectivity differs from Dahlen's in that it is grounded less in psychological theory, more in the poet's own lived experience as a mediated subject-in-process. Lubeski seems keenly aware that the subjectivity to which an individual has access is determined by historical social conditions. And her poetic project is directed at resisting the oppressive forces and regulatory practices at work in our society that, she feels, limit the range of subjectivities to which she has access.

Lubeski's sense of the individual subject's relation to society may be more fully understood in the context of Louis Althusser's notion of the repressive function of the state apparatus and the ideological state apparatus. According to Althusser's model (and implicit in Lubeski's poetry), the individual's access to justice, health care, financial security, and so on depends not on that individual's resources or abilities but on how he or she is interpellated as a subject by a Subject. The Subject, according to Althusser, can be any form of institutionalized authority—the church, the law, patriarchy. The Subject's authority (in relation to the subject) is enforced and maintained by state apparatuses (SAs) and ideological state apparatuses (ISAs). The function of the SA, a group that includes the army and the police, is primarily repressive. ISAs, by contrast, operate more subtly, in the form of various institutions such as churches, schools, families, legal systems, media, literature, the arts. Althusser defines interpellation as "the operation" by which ideology "'recruits' . . . or 'transforms' . . . individuals into subjects" by designating the distance between the subject and the Subject, a distance that suggests a relation of power ("from *Ideology*" 245). Lubeski seems aware of both types of state apparatus, and her writing reveals a particular concern with how the individual is interpellated as a subject by government, military, medical, and religious forces.

But Lubeski is also aware that who gets interpellated how and by whom is often determined by specific historical social particulars. Differences such as gender, race, class, and sexuality all function to signify relations of power, so that "what we are disgusted by is the amount/of labor necessary by black or dirty hands to win the money earned / quickly by white or clean hands" (*Stamina*). In addition, Lubeski is all too aware of what Butler describes as "the binary restriction on sex imposed by the system of compulsory heterosexuality" (19) according to which a woman's love for another woman is dismissed as a kind of psychological miscue by a culture that presents her with a range of subjectivities in the form of "a pie graph which does not include sexual preference," as Lubeski puts it in *You Torture Me* (*YTM*) (7). In *Dissuasion Crowds the Slow Worker*, Lubeski describes her own love as an oddity in clinical terms while at the same time representing that love as incredibly normal, marked by the same kinds of quotidian gestures of affection that characterize heterosexual love relationships:

> Displaced desire
> attracts you to women
> who make your lunch
> walk you to the train station

Alert to the fact that the options for identity authorized by her society do not include hers, Lubeski writes a poetry that investigates and expresses the effects of these repressive institutional and discursive forces on subjectivity itself.

Subjectivity is not only regulated and mediated by cultural and institutional forces, but in Lubeski's writing, it is often partial, limited, or denied. The speaker in the opening passage of *Obedient, A body* is without specific identity and in fact identifies herself accordingly: "I'm returning from the war, I'm a blank army soldier. My calves are raw, / unnerved flesh, obedient, sissy like" (27). Mediated by the military, this subject is a "blank," and even the flesh on her calves is "obedient" to the ideology that, enforced by an ISA, operates in the realm "of the *private* domain." Althusser explains that "[i]t is unimportant whether the institutions in which [ISAs] are realized are 'public' or 'private.' What matters is how they function." Unlike SAs, which function by violence, ISAs "*function 'by ideology'*" (Althusser, "Ideology and Ideological State Apparatuses [Notes towards an Investigation]" 137–38). As a result, even so-called private lives are not beyond the reach of the ideological forces deployed by ISAs that interpellate individuals as subjects.

Lubeski depicts private experience as inevitably mediated by various regulatory practices. Even one's private sense of reality is not wholly private, not constructed outside of the historical forces often thought of as being, in contrast, "public": "Fall down obediently as a dog upon command. The historical revolution / of tactless landmarks empties its film version of your interior glossy / 8×10 . . ." (*Obedient*

41). Like a dog on command, for "individuals are always-already interpellated by ideology as subjects" (Althusser, "from *Ideology*" 246),
and the individual submits to the processes by which these contending
versions of reality construct her subjectivity. Lubeski represents even
the most supposedly private of experiences—sexual desire, love,
friendships—as to some extent regulated and constructed by ISAs. For
instance, in *You Torture Me*, the speaker takes a medication (created and
prescribed by functionaries of the medical ISA) that "has side affects
[*sic*] which make it impossible for me to determine my real sex drive
from my imposed sex drive" (3). A few pages farther, the speaker
muses that "There must be another way to outwit the federal government yet the medicine has side affects [*sic*] in that I can't justify my true
intentions from my undesirable intentions. To lay awake all night by
your side dreaming of laying awake all night by your side" (5). Here,
the speaker's sense that she must "outwit" the government is continuous with her thoughts about her relationship with her lover, in which,
significantly, unconsciousness (sleep) is indistinguishable from consciousness (waking). Similarly, personal alliances are not formed independently of public economic conditions, both framed as issues in
which individual choice has been revealed to be an illusion: "in the
current deficit we are allowed only one friend and that friend has already been chosen" (*YTM* 11). Lubeski also offers poetic comment on
how the media ISA serves to perpetuate certain "private" experiences
of pain and violence: "Soap operas provide just that level of isolation,
fantasy, love, greed/and money necessary to endure the (criminal
urges) or private/sexual acts a dysfunctional family alone engages in
without/moderation" (*Stamina*).

The institutional/ideological systems that mediate individuals'
"private" lives and identities—whether one calls them ISAs and SAs
as does Althusser or "regulatory practices" as does Butler—ensure
that individuals who conform to normative values will be endowed
with a kind of public legitimacy as private subjects. In *You Torture Me*
Lubeski suggests that an individual's legitimacy depends on that person being fully integrated into the patriarchal system: "When needs
are paternal we look to the mailman, already calling us nicknames of
the ones we resemble. To be without a letter is to be undignified, a bar-
rage of inquisitions plastered, like DO NOT POST signs all over a fac-
tory wall" (9). By evoking the familiar mailman joke, Lubeski
emphasizes the extent to which legal paternity still functions in our
society as a measure of public and private legitimacy. When the question "Who are you?" is satisfactorily answered with a surname, as is
often the case, the question might just as well have been phrased

"Who is your father?"—the subtext of the question being "How authentic is your subjecthood?"

Because not only one's identity—but often also one's economic, spiritual, and emotional survival—depends on being perceived as a legitimate subject, one must be complicit in the regulation of one's own subjectivity. According to Althusser, being made into a subject by the Subject means that one has submissively responded to being interpellated. Interpellation works "in such a way that the subject [when hailed by the Subject, as in the police officer's 'hey you!'] responds: '*Yes, it really is me!*' . . . it obtains from them the *recognition* that they really do occupy the place it designates for them as theirs in the world, a fixed residence: 'It really is me, I am here, a worker, a boss or a soldier!'" ("from *Ideology*" 247). Lubeski imagines this complicity in a variety of situations described in her poetry, including the realization that one's baseline economic survival depends on the very oppressive forces that ensure one will not rise above that baseline: "when the world becomes confiscated it is your duty to the foreign investor who can, in cash, lend you the ability to continue participating in weekly activities, grocery stores" (*YTM* 2). Working as a part-time writing instructor for various colleges and universities, Lubeski is aware that employment such as hers (though without benefits or security) might itself be made possible by recent trends toward abusive administrative practices: "If the Dean weren't so infatuated with his financial stability there would be no lapse in the admission policy and thus, my position obsolete" (*YTM* 17). Even the most subjugated individuals revere those who occupy positions of power in the very system that interpellates them as subjects: "The family which (edifice) suffers together and can not rise above / (money) flutters emotional reaction upon / word of the President's assassination" (*Stamina*). The speaker in this poem feels powerless in the face of the system, yet still looks to institutionalized authority for relief:

I'm waiting for my new President to restore equality and make it possible for me to override the red tape systematic inability to provide services to those of (us majority) who live without quality control or favors from big men

who can't live without errand boys (Stamina)

Lubeski's implied protest, then, throughout her poems, is directed not only at the injustice and powerlessness she witnesses and experiences in the world, but also at the internalized oppression that takes the form of self-regulation.

Lubeski recognizes the extent to which the normalizing powers of society center on the body. Foucault's analysis of "bio-power," comprised of "numerous and diverse techniques for achieving the subjugation of bodies and the control of populations" that he discusses in *The History of Sexuality* is helpful in understanding the attention Lubeski gives in her writing to body imagery and bodily experiences (140). Foucault's explanation that "the development of the different fields of knowledge concerned with life in general" in the eighteenth and nineteenth centuries led to a new era of bio-power in which "[p]ower would no longer be dealing simply with legal subjects over whom the ultimate dominion was death, but with living beings, and the mastery it would be able to exercise over them would have to be applied at the level of life itself" (142–43) is echoed in Lubeski's observation that "the guys who read you your rights are less persuasive than the men who dig your graves" (*YTM* 1). Foucault believes that bio-power is "embodied in institutions such as the army and the schools" (262), and a broad range of what Althusser would identify as both SAs and ISAs.

But for Lubeski, some of the most troubling forms of bio-power are embodied in the medical institution. In the dream sequence that begins *Obedient, A body*, a work written out of "the gauzy nightmares of scientific doctors overriding my body" (27), the narrator describes a frightening experience at a doctor's office: "it's the strange doctor; / she holds me, strangles me, pours alcohol on my face and head, explains / Nothing; She's the science teacher at my college" (28). The speaker seems to be simultaneously attracted to and terrified by the strange doctor who, whether she is a doctor or a science teacher or both, occupies a position of power and possesses a specialized knowledge of the speaker's body. Lubeski warns the reader and her poem's speaker to be wary of the seduction, to resist being interpellated by such a Subject. She refers us to our knowledge of ourselves, though the possibility that such "private" experience is any less mediated has already been shown to be slim: "Your childhood body knows / the difference between torture and pleasure" (*Obedient* 28). Medical and dental procedures appear throughout this long work, almost always configured as painful, controlling invasions from which the subject must somehow protect herself:

when a needle penetrates the sexual organs

we could gasp or filter the emotion by looking at a photo
of a small child we love

one works for
endurance

taking off a plastic glove (35)

The ease with which Lubeski slips in a reference to Joan of Arc among descriptions such as these speaks to the similarities between the authority of the church and the medical establishment in terms of regulating the body, either in death or in life: "in a tyrant's dreams / actors incoherent / pile wood on fires to burn Joan of Arc at the stake" (36). It is noteworthy that in Lubeski's work the "tyrants" in both institutions are operating not just on bodies, but on the bodies of women. For "When even the plastic surgeon is attracted to small breasts, we know the world will end in fire" (*YTM* 10). This statement, funny and frightening at the same time, shows that Lubeski is particularly sensitive to the ways in which regulating systems seek to control women's bodies, and to the extent to which women's bodies are cultural hot spots for the local operations of bio-power. She explains the concerns that she addresses in *Obedient, A body*:

> I think much of [the piece] is geared toward the individual's lack of control, particularly in the medical field. If something literally happens to one's body, one has to be dependent on these figures, these "big" figures who we're supposed to trust to take care of us and who have an authority position in society. Partially, it's my literal bad experience with doctors and dentists, and then historically, women particularly being out of control in a man's world—plastic surgeons altering women's bodies . . . whether it be me personally or Joan of Arc, whatever the scale, women are being constantly controlled, deprived of power. (Personal interview)

As Foucault points out, the "technology of sex" that developed in the nineteenth century with "the objective of disciplining the body and . . . regulating populations" led to "the hysterization of women, which involved a thorough medicalization of their bodies and their sex" (*History* 146). Many of Lubeski's examples of medical subjugation take on a subversive power when seen as references to such medicalization of women's bodies.

In *Obedient, A body*, the speaker is not only a medical patient, but also a "blank army soldier," and a member of the Catholic church. All three institutions deploy a kind of bio-power control over the subject's body. Lubeski renders in language this multi-institutional complex of regulatory practices and the alienation that the subject experiences as a result by composing clauses and phrases which, like many of Hejinian's sentences in *My Life*, are syntactically sound but semantically bizarre, and often do not add up to complete sentences.

> A forced march into the bruised area far from the cold source of alienation the priest says we are trying so hard to conceal. Only when I embark upon this commando of habit do other worlds spin so far away from me. The texture of fog across the skin on a clouded bridge one is unable to bypass. (39)

The situation described in the first (incomplete) sentence involves a military action ("forced march") which leads directly to a medical condition ("bruised area"), and all of this is somehow under the direction of the priest. As a result of these multiple interpellations, the subject experiences distance and difficulty. The lack of verbs in two of the three sentences quoted here underscores the extent to which her agency is seriously limited.

Much as Mina Loy shattered and fragmented images in order to deconstruct and resist limiting gender categories, it is through this kind of linguistic layering, fragmentation, and juxtaposition that Lubeski puts subjectivity and sexuality into process in language, and thus resists the regulatory practices and oppressions to which she feels continually subjected in her life. Yet Lubeski is not attempting to claim for herself an "authentic" or legitimate subjectivity/identity; "I have no burning desire for license plates," she explains (*YTM* 5). Quite to the contrary, Lubeski feels that by "breaking apart the convention[s]" of writing—such as chronology, clarity and closure—that perpetuate the values associated with coherent subjectivity and intelligible genders, she might be able to "speak back to" the normalizing discourses and practices that limit agency for women and other "others" (personal interview). Lubeski proposes that "Some semblance of control can be restored by breaking apart the authority. . . . Maybe it allows the possibility of the unknown, the unanswered, in defiance of the (male) sense that there's always an answer to everything, that there's one truth, and this is what it is, and this is how to find the answer" (personal interview). Giving value to the unknown makes Lubeski's project no less investigative than one that seeks definitive answers, but like Hejinian's la faustienne, Lubeski aspires in her writing to a knowing that is as much a creation as a discovery—a kind of knowing and knowledge made possible by linguistic innovation. She explains: "the reason I'm doing 'experimental' writing is that I admire the destabilization of language. I'm interested in how we can break a story down in a way that it's re-seen or re-experienced" (personal interview).

The stories that Lubeski breaks down are not necessarily coherent narratives to begin with, but they are comprised of personal experience, which plays a primary role in all of Lubeski's writing. The dental and medical procedures described in *Obedient, A body* were actually experienced or dreamed by Lubeski herself. She describes *Stamina* as "really autobiographical"—so much so that she is not comfortable showing it to her family (personal interview). *Dissuasion Crowds the Slow Worker* incorporates several different actual events, both major and minor—a train wreck she witnessed as a child, contemporary experiences of riding public transportation to and from work, the death of her sister's infant, her love relationship with her partner. Lubeski's earliest published work, *attractions cf distractions*, is centered on one particularly painful relationship. In this sense, then, Lubeski's writing is quite truthful. But she renders the experiences in such a way that "the truth defines itself as mercury" (*Obedient* 28). That is, the reality of lived experience is ever changing and elusive in her writing, which continually thwarts narrative coherence and cause-effect relations. The reader is never sure what is "really" going on, who is doing what to whom, who the participants are, or what position the speaker occupies in Lubeski's "blurred" narratives. In a comment on her own practice requested by the editors of *Chain* to accompany her work "from *Shady Lane*" appearing in the issue whose theme is "documentary," Lubeski writes:

> When I first read the word DOCUMENTARY, I immediately assumed that my work didn't apply; it didn't literally "report facts." However, thinking more on the idea of how we "cut up our encounters to (re)see them," I felt that ALL of my work did that, and that much writing does. [My work] attempts to blur/narrate [an] . . . incident . . . through connecting other disjointed incidents of the same emotional value, thereby creating a semblance of an investigation. ("from *Shady Lane*" 144)

Lubeski blurs individual incidents by rendering them in incomplete descriptions, shifting point of view, unclear subject/verb and pronoun/

antecedent relationships, illogical semantics as in the example I gave above of the "forced march," and disruptive syntax as in this example: "a girl playing hopscotch / falls down on her knee is scraped" (*Dissuasion*). These linguistic strategies work together to connect various events that are "unrelated otherwise" by creating a layered patchwork of juxtaposed fragments "taken out of narrative order" in order to investigate the psychic or emotional experience of which these different incidents somehow all partake (personal interview).

Lubeski combines events from her distant past with more recent and current experiences, as in this stanza from *Dissuasion Crowds the Slow Worker* in which a boy photographed at the site of the train wreck some 20 years ago merges linguistically with the more recent birth and death of the baby:

> the boy will be held onto
> in time lapse photography
> describes the birth with
> a vocabulary of accident terms

Lubeski is aware that personal memories are often unreliable, at least partly imagined, seldom consistent with others' memories or so-called objective reports of the same incidents; "how many more childhoods we must reorganize," she muses (*Dissuasion*). But objective truth is not Lubeski's goal in this writing, for "sometimes what happens is not as important as the emotional content of the experience" (personal interview). Of course the emotional content of experiences with medical procedures is particularly powerful for Lubeski, leading in this passage to the connection between a childhood injury and an adult experience with medication, both instances of (bodily) interpellation:

> the grass color in nightmares
> 20 years later duplicates
> the smell of stitches
> you are given a test drug
> they see how far you stagger

> before passing out your lover catches you in her arms
> carries you to the place you will sleep (*Dissuasion*)

The lover is ambiguously both complicit in the experiment (as is the person who receives the drug) and protective of her lover against both past and present medical invasions.

Lubeski not only combines past with present events, but sometimes blurs the distinction between her own experiences and those of others. In response to a question about her pervasive use of second person point of view, she explains her process:

> sometimes it's a particular "you," sometimes many different "yous." But the "yous" are also connected in terms of their emotional equivalent to the circumstance. . . . For example, in *Sweet Land* I was thinking about different situations and little narratives involving different people, but then I bring myself into another person, who is a real other person, and then I make it my experience through that other person's experience. (Personal interview)

That other person whose experience Lubeski integrates with her own is her six-year-old niece who has been learning various patriotic songs in school:

> Songs that were sung in order of learning.
> Majestic equivalencies of patriotism.
> My country (Mediterranean Sea) gasps
> in catastrophe. You were too young then, you're
> only six, brackish water seems unthreatening,
> clouds cover the darkest sixes; murky lakes of
> the Persian Gulf personified (*Sweet Land* 13)

Lubeski processes her "self" in such a way that her own memories of being six (and learning those same songs)—reseen through the young girl's experience—is overlaid with her adult view—and her insights into how the educational ISA functions to normalize and regulate the population so that events such as the Gulf War will seem appropriate to most citizens of the "sweet land."

The accuracy of the time, place, and details of lived experiences is further disregarded in Lubeski's writing by her sense that actual events are just as real as imagined events. After all, "The body doesn't know the difference between / real and imagined fear" (*Flail*). But she turns this potentially terrifying insight to her advantage by viewing it as the opening of possibility. Since "reality" is continually constructed in discourse, it can be reconstructed in language, for "words profile/the edge of any possibility" (*Dissuasion*)—and this is her basis for hope. For Lubeski language has access to the real not by transparently representing reality, for words "never can adequately say/what is down there," but by making experience real *in* the writing, *as* the writing: "words bring out/the idea of the lost feeling" (*Dissuasion*). Actual experience, Lubeski believes, takes place in the writing itself, not prior to or outside of it: "So as the writer, whether I'm imagining it, whether or not I'm telling the 'truth' about it, I'm making the thing occur in my writing" (personal interview). In this way Lubeski's work serves as a fitting example of Nancy Gray's description of writing as experience, in which "[l]anguage and experience become interactive" as a "process of contextual experience" (Gray 5).

Lubeski's processing of experience in language necessarily involves the processing of subjectivity. Lubeski is not interested in developing a central unified persona or speaker in her writing, especially because of the painful emotional content of much of her work. She is aware of the confessional poetic convention of what she calls "that kind of tortured stance," which requires the poet to claim a unified ego whose essential being is defined by suffering. In rejecting this type of subjective position, however, Lubeski is not denying subjectivity itself. She explains:

> I can't escape my own subjectivity because the poet is always going to be speaking from the poet's point of view—that's always a given. There's always the person in there whether or not the person's intentionally absent as in that sort of writing, or whether or not the person is too present and too self–involved to see outside of the writing. (Personal interview)

In other words, Lubeski views both the "intentionally absent" and the "too present" types of subject as conventions in writing. She constructs a subject that, neither wholly absent nor coherently present, is in process in language, continually demonstrating the variety of ways in which language can construct subjectivity. The most pervasive method of processing subjectivity in Lubeski's writing is the constant shifting of pronouns and unclear pronoun references. Not only are there often more than one or many "yous" in a single piece of writing, but often the second and first person become interchangeable or imbedded in one another, as in this example from *Dissuasion Crowds the Slow Worker*:

> having come too close
> to the soft place in your heart
> suddenly jerking myself away

you huddle, make plans for involvement
in a place more fragile

as your sister
after pain has been in her life
searching for tenderness

The first three lines read relatively normally; the speaker seems to be the one who has come too close to "your heart" and then pulls herself away. But with the fourth line things get complicated, when the "you" who is the subject of the verb "huddle" is also the implied subject of the preceding verbal phrase, "jerking myself away." Therefore, the "you" who huddles is grammatically the same agent as the "myself" who is jerking away in line three. This complication is further complicated by the fact that the speaker in Lubeski's poetry frequently addresses herself in second person. For instance, the sister in the second stanza, here referred to as "your sister" is, at least in the now shadowy "real" world outside the poem, the poet's own sister whose loss of a child is one of the running themes in the work. Taking this into account, it now becomes possible to read the heart in line two of the first stanza as belonging to the speaker, addressing herself here in second person as well. But Lubeski's purpose is to explore, not to confuse. She explains: "I can keep switching off, I can be the 'I' or the 'you'—I'm going somewhere but I can get there through these different points of view and tenses. Sometimes when I start a piece I think how can I say this in a way that is exploratory of the idea rather than just putting the idea down" (personal interview).

An important implication of the fluidity of subjectivity in Lubeski's writing that results from this exploratory pronoun switching is that she proposes no essential, preexisting core-of-self lying stable beneath these varied and creative linguistic constructions of the self. In *Sweet Land* Lubeski compares the physical instability of the earth with the instability of the subject by integrating the discourse of science with disturbing dreamlike images: "On a darker street scientists begin to theory / the earth's floating atmosphere. There is no "I" / in a body found loose, unraveling mummy remains" (18). Similarly, perhaps as a component of the fluidity of subjectivity, Lubeski resists the notion of an essential "he" or "she" lying beneath the discursive constructions of gender. By "breaking into language as experience, not as representation," Lubeski is afforded "an important means of leaving old gender codes behind" (Gray 5). For instance, Lubeski's speakers are not always presented as female, even when the lived experience she is drawing on in the writing is her own. "I am the boy in the process," she writes (*attractions*). Memory plays an important role in Lubeski's writing, and the process of writing is often intertwined with the process of remembering. Interestingly, memory also puts gender into process, as in the case of the remembered train wreck that Lubeski "processes" throughout *Dissuasion Crowds the Slow Worker*. Lubeski seems to have a memory of herself, a child when the wreck occurred, climbing alone over the cars. But this and other aspects of her memory of the event are contradicted by newspaper accounts, as Lubeski discovered when she researched the accident years later, as an adult. Not only did the accident actually take place in winter, whereas she remembers running down the hot driveway in bare feet with stitches in one foot, but the lone child climbing on the cars depicted in a newspaper photograph is a boy. Perhaps she had seen this photograph in the paper as a child and remembered it as having been her own experience:

> after the train wreck entered the papers
> with a picture of the boy climbing
> on the front page you see it reproduced
> preserved image of yourself alone (*Dissuasion*)

Whether or not it really was her climbing on the cars,

> research becomes
> at length less of
> a little girl
> majority of a story
> in pieces
>
>   a slow worker arrives back
> at the train wreck, situation intact, seen climbing all over the cars,
>
>   the boy as his picture taken
>
> you are persuaded to lose
> this image leaves a gap
> in history of any young child (*Dissuasion*)

This "gap" is not only in the child's history, but in her gendered subjectivity as well, for she becomes "less of a little girl." Gender is destabilized as well in the linguistic gap in Lubeski's fragmented, layered writing technique—is this the gap through which Meese's lesbian slips in?

Lubeski is aware that gender categories carry certain culturally assigned roles, values, and relations, serving to regulate, as Judith Butler argues, sexual desire itself. The regulations enforced by the sex-gender system result in "if this, then that" propositions such as the following:

> if you substitute
> the girl for yourself
> the boy belongs somewhere
> other than longing (*Dissuasion*)

Aware of the absurdity of such logic whereby gender identities determine who may desire whom, Lubeski strives to construct in her writing a subject outside of the male-female binarism, enjoying a Steinian ungendered relation to language, whose desire is therefore also not defined in relation to the male gaze. By disrupting the text with repeated references to a male hardware store employee who has a crush on someone, perhaps one of a lesbian couple, Lubeski suggests that it is heterosexual longing that in this case functions as "displaced desire":

> the boy sleeps late
> being on vacation
> thinks of you dreaming
> seeing you tomorrow
> you point to him as we pass by (*Dissuasion*)

Whatever particular regulatory practices Lubeski addresses in a given passage, in all of her work she resists oppressive normative ideologies by putting subjectivity, gender, and sexuality into process in language. Like other practitioners of what Dahlen dubs the "interrogative style," Lubeski asks "real questions about the ground of authority" (Dahlen, "Forbidden" 6) in writing that reveals much authority to be discursively constructed and maintained. Lubeski is at least able to partially evade the ISAs by "transgressing the otherwise known as what you don't have time for" (*YTM* 2)—that is, by not recognizing herself as the subject constructed by their interpellating gestures and instead enacting a subject-in-process.

Laura Moriarty

> You can see my body
> Reread
> —Laura Moriarty (*Symmetry* 60)

Although Laura Moriarty began writing earlier than Lubeski, and has published more widely, she, too, has yet to receive much critical attention beyond book reviews.[6] However, her writing enjoys an enthusiastic audience among readers of the many small press and alternative journals in which her work regularly appears. Moriarty writes poems in both verse and prose, sometimes combining prose paragraphs with verse lines in a single work. Moriarty is also prone to writing longer, book-length works, some of which are sequences of shorter, sometimes individually titled, one-page poems (*Symmetry* and *Rondeaux* fit this description). Thus, her writing implies an openness similar to that in Lubeski and Dahlen's work, an openness due in part as well to her subtly disjointed syntax and use of repetition. As is especially apparent in her rondeaux, which I will discuss in more detail shortly, if Moriarty's poems have beginnings, middles, and ends, these mimic, repeat, and infuse each other to such a degree that closure comes only in the sense of starting anew. Another significant characteristic of Moriarty's writing is her tendency to experiment with traditional, modified, and invented forms. The external formal considerations that come into play in her writing contribute as much to her exploration of what constitutes subjectivity and gender as the sentence-, word-, and syntax-level innovations.

Lived experience does enter into Moriarty's poetry, but does not serve as the only or predominant content of the writing. In fact, autobiographical content is rarely recognizable as such in her poems because Moriarty's narrative contexts are so pared back, and details remain ambiguous. Moriarty shares with Dahlen the impulse to include in her writing readings of the cultural representations, discourses, conventions, and myths that all contribute to the constitution of whatever "personal" experience the writing comes out of. For Moriarty, a significant source of these representations is popular culture. But Moriarty's purpose is not to be all-inclusive or to construct an interminable writing that is continuous with a life. Rather, she puts her own experience into process in language by reading it through the layered lenses of the various cultural representations and conventions in which personal experience, history, identity, desire, gender, and sexuality are constructed.

Moriarty uses first-person point of view with the same frequency and matter-of-factness that a writer concerned with presenting personal history or transparent identity might. The opening series of rondeaux in *Rondeaux* is a case in point: these poems evoke the confessional mode of the diary or personal journal, and are scattered with first-person observations such as "If quiet I can hear as well as see" (9) and "With the same passion I might / have resisted or perhaps I did" (15). Moriarty comments on her use of first person: "The 'I' might have a lot of identity for me but . . . I probably won't value that much as the writer; I won't edit according to . . . whether it's true or not about me" (personal interview). Moriarty acknowledges, therefore, that "[i]t would be hard to say a whole lot about [her] life from reading [her] work" (personal interview). But this is because she is in fact intently interested in investigating the processes by which one "self" is constructed as a subject position in language.

Yet neither this linguistic process nor Moriarty's poetic analysis of it can take place completely outside of actual lived experience. Aware that she is "in life . . . having some emotion . . . having some knowledge," Moriarty thinks "hmmm, this could work in relation to language; I could use this thing that's happening to me" (personal interview). Still, she feels no impulse toward historical accuracy; Moriarty claims she does not "really care about this 'I' as the writer," and she "might quote somebody, use their 'I,' change the 'I' to 'he,' 'she,' 'it,' change it back . . ." (personal interview). Thus, the speaking subject in a Moriarty poem marks a linguistic perspective rather than an identity; it is continually created and re-created in language as the poem is written or read. And although the rondeaux series assumes the stance of a personal journal, the qualities of coherence and continuity that one expects to find in such writing are conspicuously absent. Identity is not transparently represented in this writing but put into process, constructed again and again as representation and invention merge. Writing itself becomes the most talked-about personal activity in the series, as the opening rondeau in the book makes clear:

> Each page a day
> Each rectangle outlined
> On the sky there is movement
> We are under it it is raining
> These days remembering back
> To that day actually the present
> Streets meeting already writing
> As if divided I write you and see

Each page handing it over directly
You at the same time in a speech
Make writing into life
Paper in hair and eyes
Mixed with the general storm
Inundated with each other
Each page says anything (7)

The rondeau is a French fixed form characterized by a refrain appearing first in the opening line and repeating in the middle and at the end of the poem. Moriarty adapts this form to the poetic tradition within which she sees herself working: that of the modern lyric. In her essay "The Modern Lyric" Moriarty explains, "That there is a single sensibility dominating the work is perhaps the most characteristic aspect of the lyric" (133), yet the unitary voice is not a function of the author's own sensibility, but is linguistically constructed. And though unitary on one level, the speaking subject is continually infused with multiple trajectories and plurality by the style of repetition Moriarty employs in the refrains. The elements that repeat in her rondeaux are brief fragments of speech or thought, finished out differently in each recurrence, as the forthcoming examples demonstrate. These repetitions-with-variation imply shifts in perspective on the part of the (invented) unified voice of the poem that is not therefore so unified, but in flux and multiperspectived, continually open to new meanings. This multiplicity in unity brings possibilities for "the space in writing" to open in which Moriarty can "re-invent language to write a new identity" (Meese, 13). And in Moriarty's work, that new identity is continually in process, under construction as it were, in the act of being written.

As the refrain in the second rondeaux in the series suggests, even the naked self, in her supposedly most candid and unassuming immediate reality, is a written-writing self. Tellingly, the refrain consists only of one word, "naked," and the lines in which it occurs are as follows: "Naked still on the second day," "Naked but keeping track I write," and "Naked at last again as I write this" (8). Appearing naked, then, in this case does not mean revealing the hidden inner (preexisting) truth about oneself, but rather revealing the process of construction by which the appearance of a self—naked or clothed—is made possible. This process of self-construction in writing, Moriarty suggests, is never a pure expression of unmediated desire or private experience. The self is constructed in layers of representation, of which writing takes part but never completes on its own.

The seventh rondeaux in the series highlights this layered quality of self-representation in its poetic description (representation) of a visual representation—perhaps a photo—of the "I" and an other. The poem opens with a question, "Why am I divided from him?" This division could be taking place in a number of contexts—spatially or visually in the photograph, as well as in the speaker's sense of distance from "him" in her lived experience. In addition, the division takes place in language, the question of division itself continually divided and reconfigured as it recurs in different forms as the poem's refrain. "Why am I divided thoughtlessly?" places the division within the "I" rather than between the "I" and an other, and the third and final occurrence of the refrain intensifies this focus, placing the "I" in the foreground of both the poetic and visual representations: "Why am I silent in the foreground divided?" (13). It is interesting that the speaker of the poem can within the very act of speaking also be "silent." This further internal division makes a point about agency in self-representation: the speaker is both constructing herself in writing (speaking), and is being constructed by the writing (silent).

For Moriarty, questions of self-identity are never separate from questions of relationship. For if self-identity is linguistically constructed, it is so in relation to other linguistic categories of being indicated by personal pronouns such as "we" and "you." The entire opening sequence of rondeaux in *Rondeaux* everywhere suggests that subject positions are relationally and discursively created. The writer creates not only herself but her other; "I write you" (7) as a kind of "creation of a lover on paper" (8) while "We are our own audience" (18). But in a sequence of rondeaux appearing later in the collection, Moriarty intensifies the play of pronouns to make linguistic categories of identity the main focus of the series. In one poem, the refrain consists of two words, "What" and "I," in an exploration of the question that opens the poem, "What am I," which, as becomes evident with the second line of the poem, is not a question at all but an answer: "Aloud is the answer/To what do I want," and this question, one learns at the end of the poem, is posed by a "you": "For you saying say what I want / Here name finally mine is / What I want" (69). The rondeau immediately following shifts in focus to this "you," taking as its refrain "of you." In this poem, the role of language in the mutual definition of self and other is foregrounded:

> Of you as a word
> Refers outward to the world
> Or in to pleasure

> Are you equal to
> The present includes possibility
> Only if addressed
> You have sent me a letter or not
> Or I have not the wherewithal to speak
> Of you to you
> As if you were a plan
> A construct enterable (69)

If "I" and "you" are mutually self-defined, they are always acting in complicity with one another as a "we." Moriarty puts this pronoun to the test as well, revealing it to be as slippery and impermanent as it is necessary to any notion of self:

> Undefined as we
> Only a word easily used
> To mean both
> What it means and what
> It could mean much
> More than it does
> Undefined as it is (70)

Again, this linguistic process is not merely linguistic for Moriarty—but is linguistically demonstrable precisely because it is so much a part of *lived* experience. One can neither take one's "own" identity unproblematically for granted, nor assume that one's relation with another adds up to a "we" that somehow exists independently of being so named. Moriarty gives the example of trying on clothes as an experience that foregrounds this problem, leading the shopper to ask of herself "Who is this? Do I wear this kind of thing?" She continues: "I think it's the same in relationship to people: What do I want, what does the other person want, is there a 'we' here at all?" (personal interview). In Moriarty's poetry, there often is a "we." In an untitled section in *Symmetry*, she presents the first-person plural as a subject position created in language, "Is what was said/What was written" by an individual subject who is necessarily "unsure of my position" in relation to the "you" that "we" includes. The identity "we" is therefore never wholly accessible to the "I" or "you" that supposedly comprise it:

> We wouldn't be admitted
> As an entity

We who are not visible
To either one of us
It is an argument that we are (30)

Although "we" exist only rhetorically, as this poem suggests, "we" are
no less real than "I" or "you" or any subject position, all of which take
on their qualities of reality, their recognizable forms and patterns, because they are highly conventionalized and partake of certain traditions
in which we recognize our "selves."

Moriarty shares Mina Loy's awareness that the conventions associated with love—"falling in" love, "being in" love, "unrequited" love,
and so on—are also instrumental in configuring subject positions, relations, and identities. Moriarty's interest in the rondeau form is largely a
function of her interest in exploring the convention of love of which it
partakes. As she points out, the rondeau, as a form of address to the
beloved, is "a very old tradition, and love itself is an old tradition" (personal interview). Therefore, being in love is a thoroughly mediated
"personal" experience, constructed for us in a myriad of literary, musi-
cal, artistic, and cultural traditions that dictate not only what it feels like
to be "in love," but what behaviors and emotions are appropriate to the
situation. As does Lubeski, Moriarty presents private experience as
being not free of cultural influences. In fact, Moriarty believes that our
emotions are given their form and reality by these conventions. "And so
we're in love," she explains, "and we know all the ways to be in love.
There's all these traditions about it, and so we have these vague amor-
phous emotions and we form them around these conventions, whereas
we experience it as being completely unique" (personal interview). A
rondeau in *Symmetry*, "What is said," is a meditation on the role that
language plays in constructing a love relationship. Lovers tend to speak
to one another and about themselves to others in conventionalized,
standard speeches, so that "Their words can be used against them" and
"said again/ By others pretending to be us." But if some lovers are genuine and others merely imposters, how can they be distinguished from
one another? Even if "they are men/women and we are women/men,"
the terms are easily reversed and "we" as well as the storybook lovers
are "like people who don't see themselves / Though they stand before
each other / Their words said" (37). Moriarty's focus is on the conventions of love, but not at the expense of lived experience, for the conven-
tions/constructions and actual experience are both interrelated and
mutually constitutive. "*Real life*—you're *in* a convention" she explains
(personal interview). And the speakers of her poems are often aware of

being in a convention even as they utter their (real) feelings. In "Invocation (as if to Mercury)" the speaker addresses her lover and the conventions surrounding and dictating that address at the same time:

> You are mine
> I am made to say these things
> As if we were in a play or game
> And these were moves (*Rondeaux* 81)

In "Little Egypt" Moriarty suggests that "The feeling of form without"—her term for the state of being aware that to be a lover is to be constructed in forms externally provided by convention—allows for a certain fluidity or mobility. As a result, one can act without "Sensation of volume"—perhaps without being bound to some kind of absolute authenticity or inner truth (*Rondeaux* 94).

Whereas Loy targeted the conventions in which gendered subjects are constructed in an attempt to become free of these constructions, Moriarty never presumes to stand outside of the conventions she interrogates. Her awareness of being a situated, mediated subject is central to her poetic exploration—from the inside—of the cultural conventions and traditions within which all subjects are constructed. "[I]t's kind of like Madonna doing the blonde," she explains, "there's a funny irony in that she's doing the blonde and she *is* the blonde—she becomes this blonde victim just like every other blonde victim. And that happens because she's entered the convention. . . . I think that when you enter into these conventions they take you over. . . . I'm able to write out of the culture because I'm not apart from it" (personal interview). But we are not only constructed as subjects, but as *gendered* subjects, in these conventions. Clearly, Moriarty explores the gendering of identity in heterosexual relationships in some of the poems I have already cited, but she takes a more rigorous look at gender roles and gendered identity in her poems that are meditations on a more conventional cultural form: the hollywood movie. The mainstream movie industry is certainly one of the most powerful of what Butler calls "regulatory practices of gender formation and division" in U.S. culture (16). Moriarty finds that "watching movies, one is manipulated by . . . representations . . . and aspires to them, fails to aspire to them. . . . Those kinds of representations are what we hold our lives up to to see how we're doing. We have them layered in the brain" (personal interview). These representations, then, are the stuff reality is made of.

In "The Midnight Man" (named for the 1974 movie by the same title starring Burt Lancaster)—Moriarty examines the processes that construct the figure of the movie hero, a kind of supermale who is as real as he is imagined, a complex and shifting hybrid of character, actor, and audience desire. According to the convention, we recognize him "on the trapeze, in the battlefield, shirt open to his belly, everything about him good and square like a hot meal." The convention that constructs him thus is perpetuated, or at least held in place, by viewers' expectations of the hero, so that he always acts "according to his place in your imagined matrix of events." These expectations, in turn, construct the viewer's experience as well: "The suspense that exists your first time through the movie is partly based on your need to believe in him." But because the viewer's expectations of the hero are based on composite images of the many versions in which he has appeared—other movies of the same genre, other movies starring the same actor, and so on—any particular version of the hero is revealed to be just that—a version, a representation, always falling short of "the real man" that "we imagined. However he can only be one thing at a time, though it could be anything, and we have too many possibilities to choose from." Yet the hero is not more constructed than the viewers in this scenario—both are captives to the convention that guarantees the viewers can never possess him or become him, though it is these desires that construct them as gendered subjects in his presence: "He has taken refuge in the episodic, his beloved repetitions. The means are all that is necessary. You are among them" ("Midnight" 114–15).

Moriarty focuses in some poems on how her own gendered identity is constructed in relation to cultural representations and traditions. Even Moriarty's given name, Laura, partakes of a long history of conventions and representations. Her father, a musician, named her after the song "Laura" from the 1944 movie of the same title. She relates in an interview: "So when I was . . . very little, and saw that movie, I saw it as a sort of pattern for my life." She explains how "even one's femininity" is constructed by such conventions: "You see Gene Tierney [who starred in *Laura*], and you think 'am I gonna be able to do that? I don't know—well, I'll give it my best shot!'" (personal interview). In her poem "Laura," Moriarty puts her own experience of taking the movie as a pattern for her life into process so that the result "is not my story but a story of recognition" (5). She investigates the uncertainty of identity, how we recognize ourselves in the constructions and "doubles" that surround us. In the movie, Laura is supposedly already dead, introduced as an absent presence in the form a portrait with which the hero-detective falls in love. When he discovers that she is not dead after all, Laura becomes no more "real" for him than she had been all along.

Movies of course are comprised of layers of illusion—actors playing characters who are themselves created by writers speaking words quite literally put in their mouths . . . but whose mouths? What "reality" is revealed when the layers of illusion are peeled away? Moriarty suggests that because movies are among the most powerful cultural representations of identity and gender, mirrors in which we construct and discover our "selves," the distinction between reality and illusion is not clear. "We"—the viewers, living subjects—continually participate in these constructions that are never static but in process: "The script is transparent with use. We throw it away with a certain sadness, retaining the speech of one, the cries of another. The vulnerability of the actor remains, his desperate, molested beauty." And then in the following paragraph, "Both names are used in referring to the character. She takes over the narration by force of will. She doesn't speak but it is known what she would say. We speak for her" ("Laura" 4). Moriarty invokes details of the movie's plot in her poem to suggest that the woman's feminine identity (both dead and alive, elusive, mysterious)—is at least partly constructed by male desire: "Laura doesn't narrate her own story. There is a woman. It is not a painting but a painted photograph. The painting is the real character. The man and the painting. She sleeps with the artist. But it's only sleep. He reads everything she has written. He says "You are supposed to be dead." She says "How does it feel?" (4). Laura is not a person, not an identity, but a "compositional focus," a perspective or idea. And though "He smiles at the idea of her portrait," (5) he is not as charmed by the Laura she would construct for herself: "The polar Laura he pictures at the beginning has nothing to do with the animate creature she wants to have been. By the end she is simply glad to be alive. He doesn't have to like it" (4). These contending identities or versions of Laura call to mind H.D.'s doubled Helen—also a literary tradition, but one not completely contained or safely objectified by the male gaze.

In her rondeau "Laura de Sade," Moriarty continues her exploration of the literary history of Laura, this time contemplating the Laura for whom Petrarch wrote his sonnets, whose last name calls forth another literary tradition in relation to the Marquis de Sade. Like the women in de Sade's texts, Laura is "bound"—in this case by language and literary history, to the representations that define her:

> "To wear binding like binding" she wrote
> Also "my name as the title shows
> Is Laura" a common enough situation
> To be bound as oneself . . . (*Rondeaux* 20)

Whether the object of Petrarch's love or of the libertine's sadistic desire, the woman "Entangled in leaves an animate / Becomes a sentient piercing willfully" in this poem which is itself a representation of Laura, written by a Laura.

Moriarty's interest in representations of the feminine "is partly feminist," she explains:

> Because the nude or the muse . . . it's a written thing. The sonnet was invented for Laura when she was dead. It's . . . a created written Laura, and the movie is a represented Laura. And in fact, this Laura that is in my writing that anyone reads who isn't me, is just the same kind of written thing. . . . [Women experience] coming out of that written person . . . every time we create a physical look, to become this conventionalized character. And obviously men do as well, but men, in a way, have created their own, whereas the woman character has been kind of created by men, certainly by women also, but in the woman's relation with it, it's a lot more fraught. And the fraughtness of it is interesting. (Personal interview)

Because women can and do participate in these constructions, they are not fixed or eternal, no matter how ancient or familiar they are. The cultural knowledge that defines gender and identity can be made anew, remade—precisely because, as Butler insists, "woman itself is a term in process . . . open to intervention and resignification" (33).

In "The Enthusiast" Moriarty shows that even an age-old conventionalized female role such as the king's whore can be contested and revised, put into process. Like Laura, the king's whore in this poem is an inscribed woman; in fact, her identity depends on this inscription: "I am the King's whore," the poem begins, "There is writing on a body, spread out under itself blatantly at ease" (*Rondeaux* 26). But as Meese reminds us, "the body is already in(side) language" (14) so that there is no originally clean or pure feminine body underlying the writing, lying prone or helpless to be discovered or rescued. But she can be rewritten, written over.

The king's whore is constructed as the object of male desire; in fact, she even constructs herself in the image of his image of her: "At the request of His Majesty she lay back picturing a woman like herself" (*Rondeaux* 27). But at the same time, she is a desiring subject, loving the king, "languish[ing] in the circle of his arms" (26) and actively participating in the construction of herself. She is at once the painter and the model. As the painter, she lays bare the device, renders the materials of representation a visible component of the painting: "The lady paints a picture A blood red fleur-de-lis extends itself behind her canvas into the same shape in violet There are creases in the material to show its substance" (27). But "There is a ruling pattern which sticks to her for she is also the model" (27). Yet she resists constructions of herself that limit her agency: "She thinks and speaks of herself as separate From the forms of her employment" (27) and constructs herself in such a way as to preserve her independence: "There was a black garden rendered by her with an overlaying so that the pigment was an independent skin which threatened to pull away from the picture plane" (28).

Like Moriarty's movie poems, "The Enthusiast" takes as its central concern the problem of representation itself; whereas "The Midnight Man" and "Laura" constantly refer to actors and scripts, "The Enthusiast" deals with painting and writing. Yet the poem itself is no less a representation than "the imagined context" or the curtains and statues described therein. After all, Moriarty reminds us "These verses were written" (26): The story of the king's whore is a story of representation, and the problem of identity is a problem of representation. Moriarty seeks a position of self-consciousness within the poem from which the reader-writer can participate in the making of representations and comment on that process at the same time. The most significant formal characteristic of the poem highlights this doubled perspective. Written in prose paragraphs, the poem assumes a discursive stance and its quality of being *about* representation is foregrounded. At the same time, the almost complete absence of punctuation along with frequent capitalization of the first letter of words occurring midparagraph and sometimes midsentence give the impression of verse lines that have simply been run together to look like prose. Read as verse, the poem seems not discursive but itself a poetic act *of* representation.

The poem insists, then, that although the gendered identity and sexual desire of the king's whore is multiply and variously constructed, it is not, therefore, less than "real." Moriarty joins Loy, H.D., Dahlen, and Lubeski in denying any notion of an underlying unconstructed or natural "feminine." The flesh is, after all, already inscribed, as she suggests in "The Procuress":

> A feminine form imagined
> To consist of penstrokes instead
> Of flesh we speak of her
> In the third person
> As if there were a difference

Between us the obvious one
Of being what we are
Not able to see
That this is all it is (*Symmetry* 34)

Even "we" who do the inscribing are no more "real" or less a product of imagination than the female forms we perceive and invent. Moriarty is keenly aware of gender roles *as* roles, and how these roles are constructed and perpetuated is of great interest to her as a poet. But hers is not a poetics of protest, and she is much more at ease with her own participation in the sex-gender system than was Loy and than either Dahlen or Lubeski seem to be. "[W]e're in the life that we're in, and our roles with each other are pretty conventionalized," she acknowledges (personal interview). Precisely because gender roles are conventionalized, Moriarty questions "that it makes a difference/ Which one of us is the girl" (*Rondeaux* 68). That Moriarty does not "mind doing the 'girl part'" as she calls it, may be due to the degree of agency she finds possible on the part of the "girl," even or especially in the construction of feminine conventions (personal interview). Agency on the part of the reader is important to Moriarty as well, and one of her earliest feminist interests as a writer was in "a more nurturing kind of writing . . . making an exchange that is extremely pleasing and interesting for a reader, rather than being contentious" (personal interview).

A reader can, then, with pleasure and interest participate in the making of meaning and read her own experience through the cultural representations and conventions Moriarty examines. This kind of agency, suggested also in the work of Dahlen and Lubeski, may be what comes with "recogniz[ing] 'oneself' as fully implicated in the world" which, according to Donna Haraway, "frees us of the need to root politics in identification . . . purity, and mothering" (218). Because gender and identity are discursively constructed, putting them into process in language as these three writers do reveals their constructedness, shows them to be sites of contention where writers and readers can identify and challenge socially imposed limits and participate in their construction and deconstruction.

What is remarkable is the range of poetic technique and style employed by these three different writers to achieve such similar ends. Processing subjectivity, gender, and sexuality, then, does not require or prescribe any particular poetic form. But what does link Dahlen, Moriarty, and Lubeski poetically is also what sets them apart from the "core-of-self" poetry that is more popular and commonly thought of as women's poetry in the United States. In "core-of-self" poetry, the poet claims the authority to speak with a fully present "I" from her "own" experience, of her own experience, and in her "own" voice. By not only questioning the notion of a strong core of self but interrogating the linguistic processes by which this notion is constructed and perpetuated in the first place, these language-oriented women writers leave behind ontological-epistemological certainty along with the established and predictable poetic gestures that guarantee such certainty.

Chapter 4

Feminist Phenomenologies:
Language as the Horizon of Encounter

To language-oriented women writers who conceive of writing as a process of knowing that constantly interrogates its own methods and processes, the phenomenological situation—relations among knower, knowing, knowledge—is of primary interest and implication. But their investigations of these relations, understood in the context of a larger question about the phenomenological function of language itself, depart radically from Husserlian or traditional Western phenomenology. The notion of a transcendental subject whose individual consciousness functions as a window onto the universal essences of things from which the subject is inevitably distinct, even distant, is displaced by what I referred to in my discussion of H.D. in chapter 2 as a kind of phenomenological messiness in which the knower and that which is to be known do not occupy wholly distinct realms. And, as it does for Stein, poetic language operates just at that point of overlap—is itself the zone of contact, the field of "the real."

As such, the phenomenological perspective of language-oriented women writers tends toward what Don Inde dubbs "postphenomenology"—a nonfoundational, nontranscendental phenomenology that is marked by a "sense of contingency and fallibility" (7). Inde takes the implications of variational theory—an essential component of traditional or existential phenomenology—to their logical postphenomenological ends by arguing not only that perspectives vary "within a variational frame-work," but that therefore, perspective is not "limited to one or even one dominant take upon the world . . . depth and adequacy only can come by a more radical set of multiple and even refractive perspectives" (8, 70).[1] In "Taking Subjectivity into Account," Lorraine Code examines the feminist implications of variational theory by stressing the significance of gender in experiences of knowing. She argues that the "ideals of rationality and objectivity" on which Western theories of knowledge depend "have been constructed through processes of excluding the attributes and experi-ences commonly associated with femaleness and underclass social sta-tus" (21). In other words, taking subjectivity into account means taking gender into account—not as a biological essence, but as "a primary ana-lytic category" (20), allowing a wide variety of meanings and values to be arrived at in knowing situations.

Leslie Scalapino, Mei-mei Berssenbrugge, and Carla Harryman are three writers who pay special attention in their work to the perceptual-constitutive function of language in the phenomenological situation by foregrounding the context of knowing situations—including the posi-tion of the knower and the constitutive-perceptual role that language plays. Each enacts her own version of postphenomenological variational theory that also highlights the operations of gender—Scalapino's frame-shifting, Berssenbrugge's polymorphous bodily perception, and Harry-man's playful explorations of a range of perspectival possibilities and impossibilities. For these writers, as for Hejinian, language plays more than a (merely) descriptive role in knowing, but itself functions as the horizon of encounter in knowing situations, not a fixed point but an ever-shifting continuum along which the knowing subject and "the world" meet and construct one another. Poems, in turn, do not represent some external reality but are in the McGannian sense themselves "acts of representation" (*SVPA* 246). In their writing, Scalapino, Berssenbrugge, and Harryman take the process, context, and materials of knowing into account and imply that all knowledge is socially situated and discur-sively constructed. Like Mina Loy, Scalapino, Berssenbrugge, and Har-ryman understand language to be the medium in which we come to know anything. Therefore, what we know and how we know can be not only examined but also manipulated, altered, and perpetually renewed through linguistic processes. Such perpetual renewal, during which meaning is continually in process and epistemological closure endlessly deferred, is a shared tendency among women language-oriented writers and is as evident in the writings of Scalapino, Berssenbrugge, and Har-ryman as it is in the work of the writers already examined.

In "The Field of Poetic Constitution" Lois Oppenheim suggests that poetic articulation itself is inherently experiential in this way. She argues that in poetry, language is never merely representational, but is perceptual and constitutive. In other words, poems are referential "*not* according to the realistic conception of representational thinking whereby the word 'refers back' to the thing in the world, but rather, according to the ontological dimension of perceptual and intentional referentiality" (51). In a statement that echoes both Jerome McGann and Nancy Gray, Oppenheim insists that "the poetic text . . . does not *relate* experience but *is* experience" (52). Whether or not this can be said for all poetic utterance, it is certainly the case that this experiential quality of poetry in which language plays a perceptual role is intentionally foregrounded and explored in the work of the language-oriented women writers I am considering here.

And it is this conception of poetry-as-experience that allows these writers to attend also to the ways in which gender operates discursively in the process of knowing. Some of the feminist language theories outlined in chapter 1 are again relevant here. Nancy Gray's idea that "breaking into language *as experience, not as representation*" allows women writers to leave "old gender codes behind" (4–5) points to the possibility that one's experience of being gendered need not limit or predetermine how or what one knows according to normative standards or categories. Women knowers may know differently than men, but if each knowing situation is a unique language experience, these differences will not be easily traced to biological gender alone. Johanna Drucker's observation that language structures one's relationship to the real and the imaginary (61) suggests not only that one's relationship to gender is linguistically structured, but that one's knowledge of "the world" is also partly structured by gender. Therefore, phenomenological models that claim or aspire to total neutrality, objectivity, or disinterestedness must be suspect. Language-oriented women writers offer alternatives to such models by emphasizing the real differences that come into play in knowing situations—differences in context, perspective, and language that imply that while knowing is not rigidly determined by biological gender, neither is it ever gender-neutral.

Leslie Scalapino

The image of something real is contemplated as seeing which doesn't exist there. Subject it to seeing which may not ever be its occurrence. Then the image that's real exists solely.

An event is subject to seeing not to its occurrence there.
One's seeing it is its sole occurrence.
—Leslie Scalapino (*Front Matter, Dead Souls* 49)

Like Stein, Leslie Scalapino seeks to engage her reader in a lived
exchange or confrontation with language. For the nearly twenty years
of her publishing career, Scalapino has been preoccupied in her work
with the problem of the relationship between perceiver and perceived,
knower and known.[2] In this sense Scalapino's project is—has been
from the start—phenomenological. But Scalapino's phenomenology
suggests a Marxist-feminist alternative to traditional (some would call
it "patriarchal") phenomenology. She enacts a kind of perception-in-
language that, as in Edmund Husserl's model of the subject-world encounter on which modern phenomenology is based, is both inner- and
outer-directed: in toward the consciousness of the perceiving subject
and out toward the objects of the world. But Scalapino complicates the
notion of a transcendental ego that is central to Western phenomenology in her insistence on the relevance of the social and historical context of the individual's encounter with the world. While Husserl's goal
was to attain absolute knowledge of things and human consciousness,
Scalapino's focus is on neither the perceiving subject nor the "world,"
but on the actual moment of their engagement. Scalapino's is a poetics
of perception. Where Laura (Riding) Jackson sought to approximate
the immediately existant via words that embodied human thought,
Scalapino locates an immediate consciousness of the world within the
operations of language, and foregrounds linguistic acts of perception
accordingly. Scalapino shows how perception always also includes ap-
perception—awareness of the process of perceiving. In an interview,
she describes her poetry as "trying to reach that kind of state where it's
as if you would be seeing through the lens that you're writing" ("An
Interview" 34). This lens is, of course, comprised of language itself.
Scalapino shows how language-as-perception both reflects and constitutes experience.

Attending to "the distinction between inside and outside and between perceiver and perceived," Scalapino creates in her poetry the
possibility for radical shifts in perspective (Campbell, "Neither In Nor
Out" 53). Barrett Watten suggests the source of this capacity:
"Scalapino's disciplined avoidance of totality traces a network of contingent relations in which subject and object have no fixed positions"
(51). One way this contingency manifests itself in Scalapino's poetry is
in the blurring of subject and object distinctions, even reversals of these

positions, as in this section of the poem "hmmmm" from *Considering how exaggerated music is*:

"But once", she said,   "the man whom I was with and I,
out on a walk together, outdistanced the one who followed me
by circling the block   (in order to see him from behind). We
saw him, unaware of us staring at him, simply raise his hands
(up to his chest)   and, at the spot (I thought, if he were I)
where my breasts would be,   cup the air with his hands.
Just seeing him",   the woman confessed,   "moving his hands
so slowly, up and down, the way a woman's breasts will move
as she walks (as if she were loping in slow motion),   made me
imagine, suddenly, that I was seeing myself for the last time".
[*sic* punctuation and spacing] (8)

The woman sees both the man seeing her and herself as he sees her. She and the man making the gesture are both subject and object in this encounter—not to mention the "gender trouble" this perspectival shift suggests.

In "Instead of an Animal" Scalapino complicates the perspective by shifting the point of view between first and third person and by playfully interchanging male and female gender characteristics as well as human and animal traits among the people who variously occupy the shifting positions of subject and object within the poem:

Instead of an animal, we got an old rag that was rancid-
smelling as if it were an animal.
You know how one can want to roll on it.
You know how one can want to roll on it.
You know how one can want to roll on it. (*Considering* 60)

The effect is that the reader's own position is at stake as well. By this, the midpoint of the poem, we are all animals.

Scalapino's primary means of foregrounding the process of perception is the technique of framing, and a consistent characteristic of Scalapino's poetry throughout all her published works is its serial form. A Scalapino poem—whether it is a series of verse stanzas spaced vertically down the page, or horizontal blocks of prose, or a combination of these—is a series of discrete, related frames, each situating the reader within a particular perspective toward the "reality" being perceived. In describing the work of Michael McClure, she might also be describing her own poetry: "It is valid as a serial because it is multiple, qualified articulations; mind and location are simultaneous" ("An Interview" 37).

Repetition is an important component of Scalapino's serial form. The recurrence of certain words or phrases within a poem, sometimes slightly altered, alerts the reader to the subtle shifts in context that distinguish one frame from the next. In the absence of conventional narrative and representational language, these repetitions also serve to create forward momentum and thus a sense of continuity and movement within the piece, while maintaining a Steinian being-with-knowing. Here are a few excerpts from her book *that they were at the beach*:

Stevedores—I'm immature in age—who are not made to live away from their families to work, the division is by color; they're allowed to form unions but not act—so it's evanescent.

(Because it's inactive—not just in the situation itself. Or in their later not coming to the docks—so they were striking, regardless of them being fired which occurs then).

The man having been in government—it's evanescent because it's inactive, our being immature in age—he's assassinated at an airport where we happen to come in that morning. We get on a bus which goes to the ocean—it's also beefcake but not because of the man already having died, is mature.

(We haven't seen him—as with the sailor it's contemporary in time).

A microcosm, but it's of sailors—so it's in the foreground, is beefcake—is in the past

(Therefore is contemporary in time while being seen then—so beefcake is in the past—similar to the situation of the other girls also refusing as I had to walk out onto the field, my then being immediately required to—not just in relation to them cooperating then). (28–29)

And then about twelve pages further on in the poem:

> It'd have to be some time ago—I got cake on me, handed to me by my mother, we're in a taxi. Men in another car—beside me, I'm somewhat immature in age—whistled and called to me customary stemming from seeing me eating the cake (42)

In this section, the elements that repeat include "immature in age," "beefcake," "contemporary in time," and "it's evanescent," but their occurrence is not limited to these stanzas. For example, the phrase "immature in age" occurs throughout the book-length poem. Other series and sets of repetitions swell and recede wavelike throughout the work as well, often overlapping other sets of repeating phrases. This overlapping of repetitions complicates the framing process, and in effect insists that the frame be determined perceptually and in the act of reading, rather than according to externally imposed or formal criteria.

Scalapino also uses syntactical strategies to create the frames in her poetry. She makes extensive use of hypotaxis—the embedding of modifying clauses and phrases into other clauses or sentences. Hypotaxis in itself does not skew syntax, but Scalapino embeds linguistic units in such a way that relationships between them are often ambiguous, resulting in multiple possibilities for meaning, so that, as Stephen Ellis puts it, "modifying clauses . . . placed in reference to the wrong noun . . . cause the reader to stop long enough for another 'take.' . . . yet the referential ability of the reader must lag in such a syntactical 'showdown' long enough to comprehend what seems an appreciable race toward no future but what occurs next" (65). The reader experiences these different "takes" as different frames. Ambiguous pronoun reference, also common in Scalapino's poetry, creates the same effect. Consider, for instance, one sentence from the above example: "The man having been in government—it's evanescent because it's inactive, our being immature in age—he's assassinated at an airport where we happen to come in that morning" (*that* 28). The "it" that is "evanescent" could refer to the government, or it could refer to the fact of "our being immature in age." Neither reading necessarily makes more "sense" than the other, so the reader cannot disqualify either as a misreading; one reading simply adds to another.

Part of what Scalapino's repetition and syntactical strategies serve to frame and thus foreground is the way social categories of difference operate to enforce certain normative meanings and values. Scalapino reveals how distinctions between people seen as "color" and binarisms such as girls-sailors, cake-beefcake function discursively as hierarchical distinctions of gender and race. And although the speaker in the poem seems to be recalling experiences from her past, Scalapino's use of the present tense ("we're in a taxi") and lack of narrative conventions that would order events or suggest causal relationships render these observations about gender and race "contemporary in time" so that how the categories function discursively can be continually interrogated, deconstructed.

So, while framing is conceptually modeled after a visual technique, its effects are temporal. Scalapino's intent is to present everything within a perspective of simultaneity so that "the writing is actually the event." In a statement that recalls Stein's attempt (as well as her explanation of that attempt) to construct in her writing a "continuous present," Scalapino explains: "My sense is of wanting to have the work and oneself be in present time, and not be anything else but that; the poem doesn't have any other existence except that form occurring" ("An Interview" 38). Bruce Campbell suggests that in conceiving of the frame in Scalapino's poetry as a moment rather than as a visual lens, we move from an epistemological to an ontological stance ("Neither in nor Out" 58). Time is, in Scalapino's poetry, not a field we move across, but the very structure of life itself, as if to illustrate Martin Heidegger's observation that "time fashions itself into a time only as a human, historical being-there" (84). Scalapino's use of the frame allows her to investigate the operations of language-as-experience, or what Lois Oppenheim calls "perceptual referentiality" (48).

In the late 1980s, Scalapino began to develop a particular method of framing, modeled after the comic book, which has the dual effect of presenting each "action" from a particular viewpoint and in a particular moment. Each frame is a being-in-time. In *How Phenomena Appear to Unfold* (*HPAU*), Scalapino explains: "Cartoons are a self-revealing surface as the comic strip is continuous, multiple, and within it have simultaneous future and past dimensions" (22). In "The Pearl," one of a trilogy of extended poetic works published as *The Return of Painting, The Pearl, and Orion*, the frames are defined by shifts in perspective. The reader inhabits each frame or perspective in the present tense, in the moment of each thought or event that is the action of the frame. But unlike a comic book, the frames in "The Pearl" are not necessarily visually distinguished from one another. One frame may encompass a whole stanza or paragraph, while another may be a sentence or even a phrase within a more visually defined unit, which is then not function-

ing as the frame in that case. This can best be illustrated with a short sequence from "The Pearl":

Faceless people in the heat of day pass by. Or she doesn't see them,
just them brushing by. To be utterly dependent on him.

        not able to weep—so
        desperate that is
        detached from this

That this is occurring—it occurs to her—it is not dying—so dying
seems irrelevant, it is not the matter—rather, what's the substance of
this is. The people out and the buds that precede—rather.

        buds on the trees   (*Return* 118)

In this section, each of the three sentences in the first paragraph seems
to be a different frame, and the three-line stanza that follows is one
frame. The next paragraph may be one whole frame, or may be seen as
two, the second starting with the slight shift of attention to "people" in
the second sentence of that paragraph. "[B]uds on the trees" stands out
more sharply to me as its own frame.

    Whether by way of repetition, polysemy, shift of point of view or
perspective, or any combination of these, the frames that Scalapino
creates in her poetry operate as modes of presentation—an important
concept in phenomenology that refers to *how* an object (or event or experience or thought) is seen, rather than the object itself or the perceiver.
All acts of perception take place via a particular mode of presentation. In
a Scalapino poem, each time the frame shifts, so does the mode of presentation, forcing the reader to confront the situation from another perspective. And in being made aware that this is what they are doing,
readers are also compelled to consider their own acts of perception. As a
result, and in accordance with Don Inde's postphenomenology, "perspective is not limited to one or one dominant take upon the world" (70).
As I have already indicated, repetition is one of the primary framing devices Scalapino uses. But it would not work as a framing device if the
context in which the repeated elements occur did not shift from one occurrence to the next. She explains her own intentions: "I guess the way I
use repetition is by trying to look at something precisely at the moment
you're seeing it, but then it keeps occurring again because you think of
it again or because you see it again, and the next time it comes up it

actually is not a repetition" ("An Interview" 41). The mode of presentation is different each time, so that, as in Stein's repetition-with-variation, the writing maintains an ongoing immediacy and continual renewal. As a result of these shifting modes of presentation, "The attention (of either the speaker's, or the reader's or listener's) . . . is neither in nor outside that experience" (Scalapino, *HPAU* 114).

In Husserl's phenomenology, this inner- and outer-directedness makes possible a twofold "reduction" that a person must enact in order to achieve true phenomenological insight. Husserl calls these two steps the transcendental reduction and the eidetic reduction. In Husserl's transcendental reduction the phenomenologist "bracket[s] the objective world" (Husserl, qtd. in Schmitt 59) and assumes an attitude of doubt toward the "reality" of this world. From this process arises the notion of the transcendental ego, because anything that has meaning or validity is that which has meaning or validity for the perceiving self.

Insofar as the world as presented in Scalapino's poetry is limited to what the speaking voice or subject has immediate consciousness of, she would seem to be enacting this step. But Scalapino complicates this reduction by refusing to extract the subject from the world it experiences, insisting on the reality of both the subject and the world: "I was not thinking about the woman whom I had heard about once / who could read the minds of dogs . . . once when I passed a man on the sidewalk downtown" (*Considering* 37). By thus revealing external events and the speaker's consciousness of them simultaneously, Scalapino aligns herself more with Merleau-Ponty, who rejected Husserl's transcendental reduction precisely because the individual's existence is interconnected with the world. By insisting that a writer is not "able to remove himself from the writing as a kind of objective camera-lens-like analysis of reality" (*HPAU* 112), Scalapino implies that subjectivity can neither be unified and self-contained, nor wholly rejected. The self "is the act of seeing" ("An Interview" 33).

Whereas the transcendental reduction leads to knowledge of the transcendental ego, the eidetic reduction, according to Husserl, is the means by which we attain absolute knowledge of the essences of the things we perceive. Joseph J. Kockelmans explains this process: "With the aid of memory, modifications in perception, and especially acts of phantasy, we carefully investigate what changes can be made in the sample without making it cease to be the thing it is" (31). Scalapino's framing, or modes of presentation, certainly enact the process of "modifications in perception," and in her own explanation of her use of repetition she seems to be describing Husserl's eidetic reduction: "A variation on the notion of apprehending the inherent nature of a being, object, or event as motion is suggested by the Busby Berkeley follies or a dance concentrating on one point or juncture repeated but never the same, which cannot remain identical with itself." But by focusing on the "being, object, or event *as motion*" (emphasis added), Scalapino resists the mental isolation of the object that Husserl calls for (*HPAU* 30). The phenomena that unfold in Scalapino's poetry are complex social realities in which both the subject and the so-called world are at stake, in which "social construction and private experience of reality are seen as the same, mirrored in each other. And both of these are constructions" ("An Interview" 36). Again, by focusing in her work on the process of perception, Scalapino emphasizes neither the perceiving subject nor the "world," but the actual moment of their engagement, and the constitutive function of language in this relation.

Scalapino's use of the frame and shifting modes of presentation reveal to what extent fixed concepts are products of language. As a Scalapino poem moves from frame to frame, what is fixed as the "reality" in one frame gives way to that of the next, and so on. For Scalapino, it is the movement from one frame to the next that matters: not the particular contents of any one frame. In "This eating and walking at the same time are associated all right," in which each short stanza is assigned to its own page, Scalapino traces the way language fixes and unfixes conceptual realities in a person's experience of herself-in- the-world:

Ate and I'd need to know people who were mercenaries, I'd need to
have the military
if I am going to think of nothing
ex-
cept being in a social hierarchy after I'd died. (*Considering* 88)

I've changed my mind if plants are able to be angry or can have
a
moral being
I'd be part of the social hierarchy
I'd be furiously angry. (*Considering* 89)

I've changed my mind, I don't think there's going to be a social hierarchy
after I've died
I'd have to kill someone
in order for us not to be connected. (*Considering* 90)

In addition, the open form of Scalapino's poetry precludes any possibility that an eidetic reduction could occur, because the process of variation is potentially endless. The subject's interaction with the world and others is a living process that never comes to a conclusion, and cannot be summarized or encapsulated, even when a poem "ends." Scalapino explains that "[t]he self is unraveled as an example in investigating particular historical events, which are potentially infinite" (*HPAU* 21). This resistance to closure accounts for the serial form as well as the length of Scalapino's works; her poems are all at least several pages long, and some, such as *way* and *Crowd and not evening or light*, are book-length.

As Elisabeth Frost concedes in her review of Scalapino's *Crowd and not evening or light*, this poetry does not at first seem to be "the stuff of feminist poetry" because it lacks "a clear political content, a strong personal voice, or a stance of witness" (10). Also, it is not "easy to read." Nonetheless, Scalapino's poetics of perception demonstrates a political viability that is inherently feminist. The phenomena that one encounters in Scalapino's work comprise a widely varied assortment of situations and experiences: eating, dreaming, sex and relationships, homelessness, traveling, run-ins with the KKK, racism, jobs, war. That much of Scalapino's subject matter is political in its emphasis on social injustice does not, however, in and of itself give her poetry its feminist value. Scalapino distinguishes her work from more overtly didactic treatments of political content, describing such writing as that "which eliminates social observation as a faculty because such is regarded as 'experience' which is 'subjective,'" and so becomes "purely statement of (that doctrine), i.e., statement of its own self" ("'Thinking Serially'" 48). In contrast, Scalapino's phenomenological method insists on the immediate contents of consciousness, which always include social observation. This is why poetic imagery, metaphor, and conventional narrative are conspicuously absent from Scalapino's work. She is suspicious of ordered plot because it works to reassure us by concealing, "[s]o that being assured of that is merely in fact the lie that you want to dispel, that you want to get rid of because you want to investigate what is actually there" ("An Interview" 37). What is actually there for Scalapino is our experience of the world, which is where our complicity lies. Scalapino acknowledges that her intentions in rejecting these representational values are feminist, "though not as any specific 'whole' doctrine known to me . . . we're articulated by conditions not of our choosing that are creating history—but the place where 'one' is created and exists in writing is necessarily elsewhere from this. . . . The process of the writing is an alleviation of the social rigidity" (written exchange).

Scalapino's writing does seem to alleviate the social rigidity that classifies inequality and suffering as someone else's problems, or as the fault of the victims. It is perhaps even her most minimalistic and fragmented pieces that most effectively reveal and explore the complexity of human involvement in the world:

> the bums—the men—having
> died—from
> the weather—though their
> doing that, seeing things from their view when
> they were alive
>
> . . . .
>
> so not to
> be upper class—the new
> wave baggy pants—the
> man with the dyed blonde
> hair—who's always standing in
> front of the hair salon on
> the corner (*way* 53)

Some of Scalapino's most pained and painful work comes out of the individual's experience of those aspects of reality that are simultaneously beyond one's control and part of one's inner consciousness, "so that one is constricted in it and cannot act" ("from *Waking Life*"). In *Waking Life*, a piece written at least in part in response to the 1991 Gulf War, Scalapino perceives the phenomenon of war: "There is no resemblance between the boys and the boys in the desert, that's forward in time supposedly. really, as it has reality in itself–and is separate from this. One non-reality against others in oneself, it is seen between them. as oneself is simply that."

In a sense this kind of exploration is a confirmation of the feminist credo that the personal is political, though not, obviously, in the sense of "telling" one's personal story. Because Scalapino believes that "no one is free of their narrative" ("What/Person" 52), the personal and the political are inexorably intertwined as the very fabric of perceived reality in her poems. The "personal" details that appear in Scalapino's poetry take on political implication not because they represent the heretofore untold realities of female lives and experience, but because no personal experience exists independent of social reality and context. This complicates, to say the least, one's knowledge of the world and the role that one plays in the construct of the reality one confronts, which, in turn, "challenges the reader to evaluate the culture at large" (Frost 11) as well as one's place in that culture.

Mei-mei Berssenbrugge

> The possibility of static or a gap on a starry electric night gives
> the impression of her body
> constantly engaged in transition, but she desires to enter a body
> of material by talking.
> —Mei-mei Berssenbrugge, "Recitative" (*Empathy* 34)

Like Scalapino, Mei-mei Berssenbrugge is a poet of perception. Not only is sight more consistently engaged than the other senses in her complexly sensual poetry, but also her vocabulary is concentrated with perceptual and visual terms. Her poetry offers readers a sensual experience of seeing that is almost addictive; it is difficult to look away from a poem, even as the poem itself is ceaselessly engaged in looking.[3] Throughout the poems in *Empathy* especially, objects frequently appear or disappear; perceivers are distracted, attentive; they gaze and glance. Descriptions of perspectives, angles, views, distances, and spatial relations comprise a primary gesture in Berssenbrugge's poetics, as this excerpt from "Chinese Space" illustrates: "The potential of becoming great of the space is proportional to its distance away from us, / a negative perspective, the way the far corner of the pond becomes a corner again as we approach / on the diagonal, which had been a vanishing point" (*Empathy* 29). In contrast to Stein, who avoided descriptive language in her descriptions, Berssenbrugge employs quite specifically descriptive language. But neither use description in a traditional way; Berssenbrugge describes neither the world nor its contents, but the act of perceiving itself.

Also evident in this passage is Berssenbrugge's use of frame-shifting. Frame-shifting functions here, as it does in Scalapino's work, to keep the poetry in motion, maintaining a constant newness and immediacy. But in Berssenbrugge's poetry the framing is more overtly visual, relying on descriptions of perspective itself and the way what is known or seen changes with the knower's mental and physical position.

Berssenbrugge's insistence that knowledge is thus always situated aligns her philosophically with Merleau-Ponty's thinking, so that, again like Scalapino, in her exploration of the perceptual function of language she always considers, and manipulates, the knower's position in the phenomenological situation. But for Berssenbrugge, the situatedness of the perceiver is a function of the person's material bodily existence, a point Merleau-Ponty was the first of the Western phenomenologists to make. "The perceiving mind is an incarnated body," he insists (*The Primacy of Perception* 3–4); and Berssenbrugge would certainly agree. But in her poetry she pursues this basic insight to its more radical implications than Merleau-Ponty ever did in his writing, suggesting not only that subjectivity and objectivity are not distinct or separable positions, but also that immanence and transcendence, another binarism according to which gender distinctions and relations have been reified and justified in Western thought, might be similarly integrated, even in the act of knowing.

In her incorporation of the body into the knowing situation, and her exploration of the relation between language and body in the act of perception, Berssenbrugge suggests in her poetics that there might be such a thing as what Iris Marion Young calls "feminine existence"—a nonessentialist notion that there exists "a set of structures and conditions that delimit the typical *situation* of being a woman in a particular society, as well as the typical way in which this situation is lived by the women themselves" (143–44). In a sense, Berssenbrugge's work might be seen to represent a poetic response to Elizabeth Grosz's contention in her call for a "corporeal feminism" that "[a] completely different set of perspectives—this time based on women's specificities, experiences, positions . . . is possible and needs to be explored" (xi). Berssenbrugge suggests that such perspectives are possible not by representing or describing what are conventionally thought of as feminine activities or concerns—few if any references to childbearing, domesticity, or female anatomy, for instance, occur in her writing in general. Rather, she enacts writing itself as a contact point between language, body, and "world" so that subjective bodily experience is always taken into account in how knowledge is acquired and construed.

I arrive at this view of Berssenbrugge's poetics by way of a number of interrelated tendencies in her work, all dependent on the fact that language plays a constitutive—never a passively descriptive—role in the phenomenological situation. Berssenbrugge shares Scalapino's impression that how one sees the world—even what one sees in the world—is largely influenced by how one "says it" or linguistically articulates that world. But rather than foregrounding social categories of meaning as does Scalapino, Berssenbrugge highlights the constitutive function of language in perception by linking it to desire. Writing actually enacts what she feels to be "a continuum between desires and ideas and images" (interview). In "Empathy," she writes: "An idea is a wish. / As a descriptive stream or spontaneous reaction to him, / speech serves as a starting point for uncovering a story through translation from wish into desire" (*Empathy* 57). It is in language—the "descriptive stream"—that the continuum between image and idea is realized in Berssenbrugge's work. Images and ideas are not only both comprised in and of language, but they often conflate in her work—that is, what is perceived or apprehended is often both image and idea, simultaneously visible and thinkable. For instance, in "The Swan," the subject is looking at "swans swimming at the edge of ice," perceiving them at the same time as she perceives an abstract concept: "her focus on absurdity appears / to be a spontaneous part of the desire itself" (*Empathy* 60). What she sees and thinks, in other words—what she knows at any given moment—is both constituted in language and a function of desire.

The desire that motivates Berssenbrugge's perception-in-language of image and idea is fundamentally the desire to know—to discover via direct experience of phenomena, experience in language—rather than to describe mimetically in language what is apprehended prior to the language used in the description. Berssenbrugge's poetry thus partakes of Oppenheim's "intentional referentiality," enacting a type of poetic expression in which "the verbal experience [is] not . . . the *translation* of a non-verbal phenomenon—in which the transcendental subject would be divorced from the experiential situation of language—but as the projection of the transcendental *movement* of a perceptual, intentionalizing consciousness" (49). As Berssenbrugge describes it, "being visual in writing is not being about anything. You're making something right there" (interview). Much as it was for Mina Loy in her explorations of "perceptive consciousness," perception is for Berssenbrugge quite active—never passive reception of visual stimuli. Her poem "Alakanak Break-Up" takes as its central theme or image the spring thaw of ice in Alaska, and in her poetic realization of that natural phenomena, the main action seems to take place within the perceiving subject herself rather than in the river:

Here is the event horizon. You can focus on a cone-shaped rock
in the bay. You can make it larger and closer than the ice
surrounding it, because you have the power to coax the target.
This breaks up your settlement in a stretch of infinity. (*Empathy* 16)

Because the perceiver's view is as much affected by her own intentionality as by the events occurring outside of her consciousness, her own position—her "settlement in a stretch of infinity"—is in flux rather than stable, just as the moving landscape she inhabits and beholds. Thus, perception for Berssenbrugge is not only both inner-and outer-directed, but also, as in Scalapino's work, the inner and outer realms conflate and converge, "so the innermost nature of her wishes is as much known and unknown to them as the reality of the external world" (*Empathy* 56). Thus, the perceiver-knower does not occupy a disinterested perspective on phenomena. Instead, Berssenbrugge takes subjectivity into account, much as Lorraine Code calls for in her critique of male-biased enlightenment epistemologies that posit "knowers who can be considered capable of achieving a 'view from nowhere' that allows them, through the autonomous exercise of their reason, to transcend particularity and contingency." Code explains that these "ideals presuppose a universal, homogenous, and essential 'human nature' that allows knowers to be substitutable for one another" (16). In Berssenbrugge's writing, knowers are never substitutable for one another, for perception as well as language "is a camera controlled by the participant" (*Empathy* 39). As a result, what that camera reveals is not an objective, static reality: "Your description of the amaryllis, projective, imaginary, and symbolic, still corresponds to you, / to the imaginary depth of a mirror and scene, instead of time or space having the purity of an object / that doesn't affect your sense, an ability to experience space and leave the body behind, like consciousness" (*Sphericity* 39). In addition, what is seen is continually in flux and changeable according to the changing positions and perspectives of the viewers: "Then one particle starts to move backward, suffusing her body, the way light gains character / suffusing berries or a cloud, by who sees it" (*Sphericity* 11). What matters is not only who sees it, but what his or her emotional and bodily experience of it is. By including what Code believes to have been historically excluded from enlightenment models of knowing—"the attributes and experiences commonly associated with femaleness and underclass social status: emotion, connection, practicality, sensitivity, and idiosyncrasy" (21)—Berssenbrugge suggests a poetics that might admit what she describes as "the experiences of women that are not in literature [and] are seeking a form, which has not yet been given" ("Interview with Mei-mei Berssenbrugge" 6).

Berssenbrugge helps give form to these experiences simply by taking subjectivity into account in such a way that the perceptual function of both emotions and bodily experience is also accounted for. In Berssenbrugge's poetry, "feeling is a device" (*Empathy* 35), itself active in the act of perception rather than merely a reaction to what is perceived.

Emotions can both enhance and limit a view, so that one's knowledge of a situation is always relative to one's emotional relation to it. In "Honeymoon," for instance,

She begins to acquire honeymoon as a level of representation,
    something which may call
an application of honey onto a bar of light, or the part of deep orange
    moon that is hidden or the part
that is not hidden by clouds, having a sense of, but no analysis of her
    seeing, that will explain
her feeling about an application, how the ambiguity *seems* to alter
    "how much" is seen. (*Empathy* 74)

Here, the perceiver not only sees but represents experience intentionally rather than mimetically. Frequently, emotional and bodily perception are indistinguishable from one another in Berssenbrugge's poetry, as in "Fog" where she draws on the ambiguity of the word "feeling" to evoke both emotional and physical engagement in the world as definitive of the phenomenological situation: "The fog of the way we feel our way into this focus, seeking by feeling, lies in the indefiniteness of / the concept of continuing focus, or distance and closeness, that is, or our methods of comparing / densities between human beings" (*Empathy* 48). Throughout this poem, fog functions as an impediment to clear perception while at the same time it is itself being perceived (it is impossible to see through fog without seeing the fog). Because the fog takes on a moist and cool physical presence in the poem, perception itself becomes more tangible.

In a phenomenological situation where the viewer-knower is never separable from her emotions or her body, she can never meet the basic requirements for Husserlian phenomenological insight by reducing her perception of the world to that which is outside of her own being. Berssenbrugge's knower can never attain the status of a transcendental ego, for her knowing subject has both transcendence and immanence, rather than one to the exclusion of the other. Following Simone de Beauvoir, Iris Marion Young suggests that such "a basic tension between immanence and transcendence" is typical of feminine existence in patriarchal societies (144). Because "woman" has been so thoroughly objectified in Western societies, Young insists, it is difficult for many women to act as subjects through or with their bodies without the sense at the same time of their bodies as objects. This historical social situation of women, rather than biological gender differences or a mysterious feminine "essence," accounts for frequently observed differences in how men and women use their bodies in performing such tasks as throwing, grasping, and carrying. Young concedes that "Merleau-Ponty's account of the reaction of the lived body to its world, as developed in the *Phenomenology of Perception*, applies to any human existence in a general way," but she goes on to argue that "there is a particular style of bodily comportment that is typical of feminine experience, and this style consists of particular *modalities* of the structures and conditions of the body's existence in the world" (144). Young's account of feminine bodily comportment is relevant to my analysis of Berssenbrugge's poetics not because Berssenbrugge describes herself (or any woman) in her poetry as comporting herself in any of the specific ways exemplified by Young. Rather, the way in which the body is involved in perception in Berssenbrugge's poetry demonstrates the same kind of tension between transcendence-immanence and subject-object status that Young defines as peculiarly feminine.

The poetic speakers as well as female persons described in third person in Berssenbrugge's poetry do tend to be constantly aware of "the pulls and weights of the body in motion" (*Empathy* 36) even as they undertake the most abstract and philosophical inquiries into language, perception, and how we know what we know. In "The Swan," a woman's sense of herself in the world is profoundly affected by her awareness of being the object of a male gaze:

where femininity is concerned, similar effects yield various meanings,
    as when a woman photographed
on two separate occasions on the street at random by a famous
    photographer, who's dead now,
still finds herself in a purely theoretical relationship with herself in
    relation to him,
which he refuses to merge with the indeterminacy of real light. That
    immaterial matter truly
leaves objects their own places, lighting and illuminating them.
    (*Empathy* 60)

As "immaterial matter" she is at once transcendent and immanent, embodying the "various meanings" yielded by the "effects" of "femininity." Although such unrelenting consciousness of the material body is linked in Young's analysis with physical limitations (throwing "like a girl," for instance, is marked by a lack of follow-through, failure to make full use of the body and poor aim), it never manifests itself as a handicap in Berssenbrugge's poetic perception. Perception is not less reliable or thorough for having the body involved; rather, perception is simply as bodily as it is conceptual, and therefore never divorced from the bodily experience and existence of the perceiving subject.

The subject's physical experience of knowing is as ongoing as her linguistic experience that the poem enacts, so that body and language and perception are interactive components of a single complex knowing experience. In "Fog," Berssenbrugge writes, "The body is the space of the point of a moment in your seeing him or hearing him" (*Empathy* 45). Rather than distorting or concealing knowledge (in this case, of "him"), then, the body is the *site* of knowledge. Uncertainty is necessarily a part of bodily perception for Berssenbrugge, and like Hejinian, she finds value in this uncertainty, for this is what guarantees the act of knowing is ongoing and forever beginning anew: "Therefore, we appreciate the fog, as the power to make the space continue beyond the single / perception, into raw material or youth of the body like a body of light" (*Empathy* 50). To go "beyond the single perception" means to go into the body and thus see more and see deeper, to be a being physically continuous with perception. Language is Berssenbrugge's means of realizing this physical process of perception. She even wonders if perhaps the ability to frame— "to section what you see and what you know and what you feel out of the world"—is itself a physical facility. "[W]hat if that's not something that's in your mind or your spirit but that ability to frame is something that's in the body?" she wonders (interview). And her poems explore this possibility in their focus on the connections between language and bodily experience. "My poetry is about just where the body and the word emerge from each other," she explains (interview). And where the body and language meet is the point of perception, the moment of knowing. It marks a temporal and spatial horizon toward which every long poetic line of Berssenbrugge's poetry seems to aspire.[4] In "Value" she remarks on "the way a sentence places sky along/a branch or the edge of a wing you see light through." For, "The sentence is her concrete experience of time along a scapula or the sag of his belly beside her" (*Sphericity* 40). Not only does Berssenbrugge think of her "work as a physical medium," but also the process of writing is for her very much a physical process: "I think I write for the feeling or satisfaction of actually putting one word next to another," she explains, "[i]t's a physical feeling" (interview). Perception-in-language becomes a physical experience for her readers as well; the words seem to resonate with a tactile immediacy.

That Berssenbrugge thus emphasizes the materiality of language over its transparency, and furthermore, that its materiality is linked for

her to bodily experience, guarantees that the tension between immanence and transcendence is always forefront in the phenomenological
situations her poetry enacts. She never lets her readers lose sight of the
act of perception itself or the material activity of language in perceptual
acts, even in her most abstract and discursive philosophical passages
such as this from "War Insurance":

> Instead of vanishing
> in the dark, a spoken line passes behind layers the borders of which
> cannot be perceived, of spacious intuition, as on a ricocheting surface
> of felt. Thus,
> when the mind considers the problem of him and her as a relation
> between meaning and language,
> this brings to mind the problem that language is the most formless
> means of what he or she is expressing
> and then making transparent with abstractions, such as in the
> phenomenal moment or with coincidence,
> because everything can be told from the present moment. Its sort of
> transparent experience
> begins to develop in which things are really precise without
> depending on each other.
> In this way she takes the principles of abstraction, founded on sight,
> and applies them to language. (*Empathy* 54–55)

Language, in the form of "a spoken line," takes on a physical presence
and thus acts to connect the concrete and the abstract. Language con-
nects, but not in the sense of a bridge or a conduit according to which a
concrete word symbolizes or stands in for an abstract meaning. Although Berssenbrugge is discussing the operations of language itself in
this passage, she is not reiterating this commonly evoked metaphor of
language as transparent vehicle. Rather than suggesting that the concrete represents the abstract, Berssenbrugge illustrates the ways in
which the abstract and concrete integrate, inform, and partake of one
another. This deconstruction of the concrete-abstract binarism is yet another function of the pervasive tension between immanence and transcendence in Berssenbrugge's poetry.

Perhaps the most common instances of the concrete-abstract
crossover in Berssenbrugge's work are the many cases in which emotions and ideas take on concrete dimensions and manifest themselves
physically in the landscape of a poem. *Empathy* (as the book's title
might predict) is especially rich with such examples, where, as Denise

Newman points out, "she shows in poem after poem that emotions are a tangible thing, as much as color and light are" (120). In "Naturalism," "A feeling moves like a hand across the blue and white mountain range in bright sun" (38), and the poet considers "How an emotion grew out of or failed to grow out of the landscape" (39). In "Forms of Politeness," Berssenbrugge declares that "A belief is a word-like object. You can focus your attention on it down to a point" (66). In all these instances, the knowing subject or perceiver's ability to transcend the physical immediacy of the moment and thus "bracket" the objective world in a Husserlian transcendental reduction is precluded by the infusion of the things of the mind into the tangible realm of immanent existence.

This tension between immanence and transcendence that Young finds to be typical of "feminine experience" is, according to Young, even more pronounced in pregnancy. What Young refers to as "pregnant embodiment" offers a feminist challenge to patriarchal phenomenology's "implicit assumptions of a unified subject and sharp distinction between transcendence and immanence. Pregnancy . . . reveals a paradigm of bodily experience in which the transparent unity of self dissolves and the body attends positively to itself at the same time that it enacts its projects" (161). The poems in *Sphericity*, while not "about" pregnancy per se, were written while Berssenbrugge was pregnant with her daughter Martha, and seem to be informed by the constant awareness of being pregnant. Berssenbrugge herself refers to this book as "hormonally influenced" by that pregnancy (Interview).[5] Indeed, Berssenbrugge seems to express all three of what Young identifies as the primary characteristics of pregnant embodiment in this book.

Young suggests that "[t]he pregnant subject . . . is decentered, split, or doubled in several ways. She experiences her body as herself and not herself" (160). In Berssenbrugge's poem "Experience," this split manifests itself in the sensation that the self might exist in separate worlds and at different stages simultaneously: "The idea of illusion suggests that existences in different worlds, herself at different / stages, or moving from one metaphor to another, can compare" (*Sphericity* 31). In "Ideal," what starts out as a possible reference to conception in which there are "two particles" of which a one, or a "third event," are comprised, becomes an image of a woman herself comprised of several or many "sheaths":

Two particles that make a continuum or ideal, in how the space
    between them relates to a third event,
as how clouds against a windowpane admit space that continues to a
    cloud on the mountain,

a sheath of a space of feeling in material sheaths of her body for a
    perceived order, depend
on your having felt the relation. (*Sphericity* 10)

This woman is a many-layered subject to say the least, and what she
(and we readers) see of the world is similarly layered and riddled with
discontinuity, gaps, spaces.

Another important quality of pregnant embodiment according to
Young is the sense that "the boundaries of [the] body are themselves in
flux." Or, from the point of view of the subject herself, "[i]n pregnancy
I literally don't have a firm sense of where my body ends and the
world begins" (163). In "Sphericity" Berssenbrugge describes just such
a sensation:

> I can correlate
> my sensation of reddening with changes in the sky. I can't graph
>   my sense of this position of my body,
> which has no degree, but is more like time on either side of you.
>   Each point of the space
> marks the center of a sphere, as if your eyes were a point.
> (*Sphericity* 26)

Not only has the speaker a sense that her body is changing, in flux
("reddening"), but she also has difficulty locating the position of her
own body in space (and so calls in the dimension of time, such a crucial
gauge for measuring pregnancy, a condition itself marked by change
and time). Berssenbrugge's image of the center of a sphere and eyes as
a point recall Loy's poem "Parturition," in which the subject's position
is defined not as a physical presence in space, but as "a circle of pain /
Exceeding its boundaries" (*LLB* 67).

Finally, as is the case in feminine bodily comportment in general,
Young claims that "[p]regnant consciousness is animated by a double
intentionality: my subjectivity splits between awareness of myself as
body and awareness of my aims and projects" (165). Again in "Sphericity," Berssenbrugge suggests that a woman in motion, performing a
bodily task, is as aware of her own materiality in that act as she is of the
aim of her action: "Emphasizing not only the ground upon which her
movement builds, but matter it forms, the idea / of movement is a material, also, like the transparency of light about a blue ridge *being* apri-
cot" (*Sphericity* 25). To be in motion, these lines suggest, is to experience
the materiality of being itself. This double intentionality as it appears in

Berssenbrugge's work does not seem to indicate an impediment to sub-jectivity or a barrier to knowledge. And Young also argues the point that it does not. "Existential phenomenologists of the body usually as-sume a distinction between transcendence and immanence as two modes of bodily being." She continues: "These thinkers tend to assume that awareness of my body in its weight, massiveness, and balance is al-ways an alienated objectification of my body, in which I am not my body and my body imprisons me." But this distinction and its contin-gent alienation simply does not adequately describe or account for much feminine experience of being in the world, whether pregnant or not. Therefore, Young insists that "[i]t is inappropriate . . . to tie such a negative meaning to all experience of being brought to awareness of the body in its weight and materiality" (164).

Berssenbrugge certainly implies no such negative meaning to this kind of bodily awareness, for the tension between immanence and tran-scendence is precisely what allows her poetry to evoke the kind of pro-ductive epistemological uncertainty such as that which Lyn Hejinian associates with "la faustienne" or feminine knowing. And this is what makes Berssenbrugge's works so satisfying to read. She poetically en-acts Merleau-Ponty's insight that in perceiving anything, the knowing subject "can never exhaust its possibilities or empty it of meaning. It al-ways offers . . . more; there is always more to be known" (Riley 480). Berssenbrugge's seemingly ever-lengthening poetic line is in fact di-rectly tied to her intention to offer in her poetry an ongoing word-world encounter for the reader. She explains: "I've really been trying to create an experience in the reader in which they are changed but they can't re-iterate what happened or how it happened. So a long line helps me in doing that because you can't grasp the whole line in your mind." The poetic experience of knowing cannot be totalized or fully grasped if readers "have to keep letting go and surrender themselves to the lan-guage or the dynamics of the poem" ("Interview with Mei-mei Berssen-brugge" 6). Berssenbrugge hopes that this suspension of closure and certainty will create what she calls "a subliminal experience"—a kind of knowing that is "beyond or below words or more basic than words," in-volving the body and emotions even at the same time that it is enacted in words. Language thus functions as a perceptual horizon in Berssen-brugge's poetics of bodily epistemology, and therefore suggests a more radical poetics than even Cixous's "writing the body." In her work, writing itself is "the dialogue between [the reader and/or writer] and the source of language" (interview).

Carla Harryman

> Screens, frames, windows randomize the story of youth I'd fol-
> low like a sheepdog, who like a false language adheres to a pre-
> determined selection of sheep or slips or flies to show that I
> must lie. Or else.
>
> —Carla Harryman (*Vice* 33)

As do Scalapino's and Berssenbrugge's, Carla Harryman's poetic
project depends on the insight that language and literary-artistic modes
of representation do play a definitional role in one's encounter with "reality."[6] Harryman's response is to try to change that reality by manipulating the terms of the encounter. Rather than articulating linguistic
perspectives with painterly precision as does Berssenbrugge, or exploring the social nuances of person-world encounter via repetition-with-
variation as does Scalapino, Harryman is engaged in what she calls "an
aggressive kind of play" or Wittgensteinian "language game" in which
she (sub)merges genres, subverts writing conventions, and interrogates
the norms of narrative and genre (personal interview). Harryman's
project is motivated by her sense of play—of writing *as* play—in at least
four senses of the word: drama, manipulation, variation, and fun. By
subverting literary and linguistic norms and thus thwarting readers' expectations, Harryman breaks the frames through which people observe
events and that determine how these events will be interpreted or understood.[7] As a result, Harryman's writing imaginatively posits nonnormative ways of seeing. The results are often absurd and quite funny,
as in this excerpt from "Typical Domains":

> On the beach slaves pass by solving problems.
> "This is mere bliss. There must be a better procedure."
> "Oh, stop it D, you're tickling me." Beautiful limbs flap in the
> wind like tortoises out of their shells. Boats run to the beach and
> slaves pour into them.
> The beautiful limbs flapping in the wind said, "D, I don't be-
> lieve in you."
> At this point the creatures projected their identities into cli-
> max. (*There* 55)

But at the same time, such absurdity offers a powerful transformative
critique, for Harryman's writing demonstrates Inde's claim that "per-

spective is not limited to one or one dominant take upon the world" (70). Harryman is especially concerned with finding ways in language to admit the various forms of knowledge and experiences that have been and continue to be denied, suppressed, or marginalized by dominant and normative discourse in Western culture.

Of particular interest to my feminist reading of her work is its sensitivity to the ways in which women's, children's, and "feminine" experiences and forms of knowledge have been privatized and excluded from public discourse. Among the literary influences she claims—an eclectic list that includes a broad range of writers and artistic movements—Harryman places the "phantasmatic images of women to replace women's historical invisibility" and "the travesty of the representation of the feminine" ("An Interview" 519). Harryman believes that there are "forms of knowledge that might not have received the attention they deserve" (e.g., women's personal experience) and that it is important that such knowledge be given form in language because "[l]ack of articulation about significant daily experience undermines consciousness, creates a condition for repression, doubt, insecurity. Then social norms that may not serve the best interest of 'the mother' or 'the child' [for instance] can take hold" ("An Interview" 523–24). For Harryman, this lack of articulation is a problem of language and discourse; dominant forms of language use and literary form often fail to acknowledge the full range of human experience. Harryman considers her own gendered experience of normative discourse and concludes that there exists a "gap between my experience and the discourse that's available to me—whether it's theoretical, philosophical, or just sort of quotidian media" ("An Interview" 532).

It is these gaps between discourse and experience that Harryman intends to both foreground and fill in her writing. She attempts to construct "an imaginary eros that can violate forms of knowledge and turn them into something else" ("An Interview" 527). Just as Gertrude Stein worked to thwart reader's learned habits of reading and perceiving, Harryman demonstrates how normative discourse functions to structure reader expectations and frames by, as Bob Perelman describes it, "working to bend, if not break, whatever framing devices the reader may discover" (307), thereby suggesting that other nonnormative and potentially more inclusive or liberating meanings and modes of knowing are possible. Harryman simultaneously employs a range of linguistic strategies that serve to bend or break these frames, including genre bending and blending, the "distribution" of narrative, radical personification, the subversion of conventions of identity and gender and the deconstruction of culturally reified oppositions, binarisms, and categories. The most conspicuous challenge Harryman poses to genre distinctions is the consistency with which her own writings successfully elude easy genre classification. She often combines verse and prose in the same piece, and the language she uses in both forms partakes of a range of discourses: narrative, philosophy, fantasy, theater, nonsense. Her writing demonstrates that the division between the critical and the creative upheld by conventions of genre and form is not only constraining and arbitrary, but illusory. Yet the cultural demands to uphold genre distinctions are intense, if unspoken. Harryman thumbs her nose at the prohibition she most consistently disregards in these lines (taken directly from Derrida, but not cited) which open the book-length work *Vice*:

> Genres are not to be mixed. I will
> not mix genres.
> I repeat: genres are not to be mixed.
> I will not mix them. (4)

In the 90 pages that follow, the mixing of genres is perhaps Harryman's primary gesture. Her objection to being designated as a poet by publishers and critics is related to this interest in transgressing genre boundaries: "I'm exploring genre. . . . I like to put families of language in conversation with each other, such as theoretical discourse, fiction, and nonsense—I use the page to perform the dialogue, first, although I think of the page also as a staging device. . . . The performance/conversation occurs between the kinds of language put into play" ("An Interview" 514–15). In fact, many of Harryman's writings are designated as "plays," but they function as plays primarily in the sense of combining into performance various traditionally nontheatrical discourses in this playful way.

For instance, "La Quotidienne: An Atmospheric Play" is itself a performance on the page—already staged on the page, that is, rather than being merely a written plan for a live performance.[8] The play begins with a series of indented spoken lines, apparently delivered by different characters, though how many and who they may be is nowhere specified. As a result, the different types of discourse presented function as characters of a sort, and a dialogue develops among them. The following is an excerpt from the first page of Scene One:

—On the street the casually dressed person barks at his family. The doctor strolls by appraising them. "Extraordinary," says the doctor, whose balance is being restored by what everyone knows about horrible things. "The animal is slavish and fierce but a potentially agreeable pet." Then he says, "Heirloom."
—Stop scrutinizing that fading image.
—Am I that girl in the pasture wearing heirlooms?
—I'm trying to be philosophical about my things.
—Only for the most balanced minds does it seem possible to guard reality against distortions to which it is otherwise subjected in its transit through the psychic individuality of the one there.
—Let us rhapsodize. I am clinging to a rock. (*Animal Instincts* 81)

In this case, the "speakers" move from nonsense to an almost sincere-sounding narrative ("Am I that girl?") to psychological discourse and back to nonsense. In Scene Six there are no speakers or lines delivered, only two narratives visually overlaying and thus interrupting each other on alternate lines, beginning thus:

An actor tells the story rather than shall we say tells the world or tells
    the book.
                The actor tells the world
The strangest stories lack a person's voice: statues set the stage on
    edge when
                        What to do
                                    (*Animal Instincts* 86)

And she continues in the same vein. By putting these different kinds of language use in dialogue with one another, Harryman not only creates a form that is inherently unable to conform to any particular recognized literary genre, but also she emphasizes the extent to which what is acceptable and what is unacceptable in writing has to do with the proper or proprietary alignment of language use and genre. Harryman explains why she feels it is important to transgress these boundaries:

There are what I consider faux divisions of genre, or great simplifi-cations of aesthetic knowledge, in our contemporary culture. The reification of genre is disadvantageous to contemporary women artists, because generic terrain "appears" to be limited to forms that may not be conducive to mapping out consciousness that invents it-self or its forms of cultural expression, which is part of the cultural work of women right now—the creation of cultural forms. ("An Interview" 515–16)

Just as Mina Loy felt half a century before her that new forms of consciousness would be made possible by new forms of language use, Harryman suspects that by shattering the prescribed boundaries of literary form, new or as yet unacknowledged modes of consciousness might find form in language.

Related to Harryman's subversion of genre is her interrogation of the operations of narrative and narrative conventions. "I prefer to distribute narrative rather than deny it," she writes in "Toy Boats," a piece first published in *Poetics Journal's* 1985 symposium on narrative (*There* 2). Her response to the symposium's inquiry is direct: "The question of the status of narrative presupposes a hierarchy of literary values I don't entertain in my work. Narrative is neither an oppressor to be obliterated nor the validating force of all literary impulse" (5). Harryman "distributes" narrative throughout her various writings by toying with narrative conventions, allowing narratives to begin but then dissolve or disintegrate, interrupt and be interrupted by other types of discourse.

"Sublimation," the first piece in *Animal Instincts*, opens with a parenthetical statement about narrative beginnings, in first-person narrative form: "I had wanted to begin slowly" begins the narrative. But then "I would never come to the point" because the various narrative gestures that are distributed throughout the long opening paragraph—gestures such as references to the passage of time ("The filthy language we spoke yesterday has been replaced") and causal relationships between events ("That is what was bound to happen")—never evolve into a coherent or continuous narrative. The sentences, narrative in form independently, do not build on one another in the way we expect the sentences in a story to do: "Sadly, one might step into a boat that is docked near a cement walkway where people lounge, watching the replacement of baseball by another, inferior, sport. And float. There is no need to be moved by distant snickering. Explanation has been used up" (9). But then a page later, a coherent if brief narrative is permitted to develop over the course of several sentences: "Because you don't touch me I am completely exposed and your being is centered on the exposure. We are drawn to each other by resistance and the excitement of touching is replaced by not being touched. This goes on a very long time, you standing in the doorway and I lying on the bed" (10). But this narrative and its characters almost immediately dissolve into references to a small boat in Mallorca, the Potomac, and a cabbage patch. Then, the speaker (or *a* speaker) suddenly (re)appears and suggests that some other narrative has been at some point interrupted and might now be continued: "Where were you in your story? (A woman was about to give you advice" (10). However, this story has not appeared or even been referred to previously in "Sublimation."

In "Fish Speech" Harryman interrogates the narrative conventions of "before" and "after." "In the beginning," this piece begins, "there was nothing. No cattails, no wigs, no paws. There was no doom" (*There* 41). By playfully evoking both the language of Genesis and the "natural" history of evolution, Harryman contests the opposition nature-construct implied by these narrative forms. Both man-made objects (wigs) and natural things (cattails) are socially constructed, Harryman suggests, because this distinction itself could not even be conceived of outside of discourse or prior to narrative itself. "In the beginning, there was nothing to hold and nothing to hold in mind, since there was no beginning, no nothing, and no mind" (*There* 42). In her investigation of narrative and its various forms and conventions, Harryman is teaching her readers to be on guard, skeptical, and therefore active makers of meaning, unconstrained by normative frames and preestablished habits of perceiving.

Another device with which Harryman breaks the frames that determine readers' expectations is the relentless personification of the non-human, even of the nonconcrete. Harryman personifies rhetorical devices in order to suggest that they, too, are active "characters" in the performance of her writing: "metaphor is over-used" and "description flees to the hinterlands" (*There* 31). Objects, too, quite matter-of-factly take on human characteristics: in *Vice* a house is "aggressive" (33) and, in a later more whimsical section, a rock "turns on its hindlegs and pleads innocence. It filches a panoply of events. It lurches into mother's room and comes out shocked. That is the condition of the rock" (43). When asked about this rock in an interview, Harryman comments: "It's like a cartoon. This can be read in another way; whereas the rock is usually situated in the symbolic, it is here transformed into a vehicle for narrative. It has to act. Symbolic conventions are thus transgressed" ("An Interview" 525). This kind of transgression emphasizes the degree to which our knowledge depends on and is limited by certain discursive conventions and norms. In this case, Harryman wonders, "What if we didn't see rocks as profundities, or barriers . . . what if we saw them as thieves, or something else?" ("An Interview" 526). It is possible, she suggests, that the knowledge one comes to in such an experiment might be that which is kept invisible or inaccessible by the conventions one breaks in these experiments?

Harryman also subverts the related conventions of identity and gender in her writing. In fact, she puts both into process in language, as do Dahlen, Lubeski, and Moriarty, but Harryman does so in order to investigate and demonstrate how the assumptions of "authentic" identity and essential gender function discursively to frame and limit what and how we know. In "In the Mode Of," the narrator contemplates both an expressionist painting of a nude and the gendered relationships constructed by the various subject-object positions available in such an encounter: "So here I am . . . trying to decide how I would view this nude if I were a man and how I would view this nude if I were a woman. If. One is a woman then it is likely she has studied how men look at nudes. If. One is a man has one studied the way a woman looks at nudes?" (*There* 9). The question of gender partakes, for Harryman, of the question of identity, and both have a hand in how one apprehends phenomena. She explains her intent with this piece:

The work was written to see if I could get away with not identifying the gender of the "I." Or course, it is highly likely that every woman who reads this work will identify the "I" as being female. I wanted that. But the joke (inside joke) about it is that many men identify with the speaker as being male. My position, as writer, is that there is a freedom in messing with concepts of identity and gender, and that there is a realm of playful objectification that is related to having the experience and history (that is, female) of being objectified, individually and as a class. ("An Interview" 531)

That Harryman's project is undertaken in good humor, motivated by a sense of play rather than a taste of sour grapes, as it were, makes her radical critique both inviting and fun. And in her "radical questioning of the representation of subjectivity in writing" ("An Interview" 527), Harryman foregrounds the ways in which identity and gender are always assumed in writing, assumed, that is, in two senses. First, the reader assumes that characters, narrators, and so on, are literary representations of real or originary beings, whether fictional or "historical." But, to evoke the second sense of the word, these imagined beings are themselves assumed identities—constructed in and by the writing itself so that "a person is an episode but the wilting subject strips the maneuver of its tight name, a lineup of masks" (*Animal Instincts* 25).

Male-female and self-other are not the only culturally reified binarisms that Harryman seeks to challenge and deconstruct. She perceives
that many such binarisms are value laden and function as moralizing or
controlling elements in normative constructions of "reality." In "Fairy
Tale," whose title refers to the Kuwait-as-princess, United States-as-
knight-in shining-armor metaphors the White House and much of the
media used to construct and justify the Gulf War, Harryman tells her
own revisionist and highly self-aware tale of a little Iraqi girl who is "as
thrilled by this world as any well loved and well fed child would be in
any other story" (*There* 90). The girl is able to save her family from the
bombs that drop on her city by refusing to buy into the hierarchical opposition "good" versus "bad" on which all wars depend for their logic
and validity. She is forewarned by a visiting storm cloud that "the men-
dacious ones will come to your city and they will try to destroy it" and
they "will tell you they are dividing good from bad" (*There* 90–91). And
these destroyers do come, and the girl is afraid,

But she resists saying that anything is either good or bad.
    She calls the water water and the sky sky and people people.
She calls agriculture and nature agriculture and nature, music music
and silence silence, the Kurds, the Palestinians, the Turks, the Jewish, the Muslims, the Christians, the Kurds, the Palestinians, the
Turks, the Jewish, the Muslims, the Christians, she calls a cloud a
cloud. (*There* 93)

As a result, the little girl and her family survive. The moral of the story
(this being a fairy tale, after all)—besides a sort of postmodern version
of the pen being mightier than the sword—is that one does have control
over one's reality—linguistic-perceptual control.
    "Margin" is one of Harryman's "game" writings, writings modeled
after written rules for board and card games. The game described in
"Margin" is called "Who Do You Think You Are?" (to return to the theme
of identity) and its players seem to enjoy acting out their own self-con-
ceived identities. But Harryman's description of the game makes clear
her own critique of the categories of identity and difference on which the
game depends. One of the favorite versions of the game, popular among
immigration bureaucrats, employs the "Citizenship Game Board." Although the job of the immigration bureaucrat is to "investigate the legitimacy of aliens" (*There* 104), the game's premise "is that most people
perceive themselves as marginalized" . . . in fact, "all civilization is built
on the expectation of, or desire for, marginality" (*There* 102–03). Therefore,

who is the alien? "It is a good question who she is" because "*[t]he inner voice of the bureaucrat screams silently, 'Everybody but me!' . . . Let me in!*" (*There* 104–05). By playfully putting the rules of the game into play, and so complicating the opposition center-margin (of which alien-citizen is of course a subset), Harryman suggests that these binarisms are merely perceptual tools, without which we might devise less limiting tools, allowing us access to a greater range of knowledge and experience.

In *Vice*, Harryman writes "I do not write with inner truth" (54). When asked in an interview if she could write with inner truth if she wanted to, she responds: "No. I just experience writing as thinking. The writer, the reader, or the writer who is the reader tends to have certain world views that have something to do with her self-construction(s). A detachment from authenticity is native to my self-construction" ("An Interview" 520). Harryman's detachment from authenticity manifests itself in her writing as the incessant desire to call attention to discourse as discourse—its limits, surface, and intentions. Writing does not transparently reveal or describe inner truth or meaning; writing is meaningful in that it constructs meaning—it is an active operative in the phenomenological situation. Harryman wants the operations of language to be apparent even as those operations are carried out, so she invites endearingly familiar characters into her texts, such as Aunt Mildred, who in "Property" "inserted a powerful fingernail under the corner of the veneer"[9] to show that much of perceived "reality" is a veneer, is the surface of discourse, and also to show that what's beneath the veneer is not as consequential as the veneer itself, is merely "Some 'deep image' like a three-way collision which occurs beneath the exterior form and as a consequence has no effect on daily habits" (*There* 68).

In fact, Harryman is critical of writing that attempts to conceal its own intentions and materiality—its role in constructing the reality it presents. In an essaylike section in *Vice* she brings in the example of art museum catalog copy whose author is guilty of just such an attempt. As a result,

The catalog experience is identical to newscoverage experience in that the images that are exploited are framed as distant events. . . . This framing creates an illusion of social cohesion while the images themselves directly contradict the hallucination. The reader or audience experiences both the effect of the hallucination and a more primary response to the image, which, if it has any power at all, suggests contexts excluded by any particular rendition of it. The problem is this primary response is unacknowledged, and thus inarticulate. (55)

In an interview, Harryman continues this critique:

> What I mean is that even "informative" writing like wall material
> can call attention to its own limits without invalidating its discur-
> sive objectives. It can demonstrate, like Steven Benson might when
> igniting a series of mishearings with additional self-conscious mis-
> hearings, that what "it" says may not be as important as what a
> viewer sees when she looks at a work of art. It can announce itself
> as having a slant, its own aesthetic bias, etc., but not if the "author"
> of the explication believes that the person looking at the work of art
> is entirely dependent on her explication of the work of art. This
> is an issue for anybody in any writing medium who wishes to
> communicate something to someone else. Simply imagining the au-
> dience's presumed ignorance is not an adequate basis for commu-
> nication. ("An Interview" 517)

Clearly, Harryman finds an epistemological and political value in being
aware of discourse as discourse even as it shapes what one perceives.

Several of Harryman's most characteristic gestures in her writing
serve to foreground the constitutive role of language in the phenomenological situation. As do Scalapino and Berssenbrugge in their own
ways, Harryman also attends to the position and situation of the knowing subject. But taking subjectivity into account for Harryman means
taking into account that subject positions are themselves discursively
constructed. In expressing her skepticism toward absolutes at the end
of "Toy Boats," Harryman comes to the conclusion that "[t]he ground is
the constructed ideology" (*There* 6); there is no neutral or interest-free
"ground" on which one can stand to get a clear or objective view of the
world. This is why the narrator in "In the Mode Of" can assume different (gendered and therefore discursively constructed) perspectives
when looking at the nude, each perspective resulting in a different perception. Similarly, because "[i]nside the box of words is where the
woman appears," the characters in "Portraits" can, with the help of language, slip in and out of various gendered or gender-ambiguous subject positions and thus affect the outcome of the subject-world
encounter (*There* 150). As a "female male," DeQuincy's "androgynous
complexity draws rings of discourse around the Victorian female's
fainting Cartesian viewpoint" (*There* 149). The knowing subject's viewpoint is inherently comprised of such rings of discourse.

And, as many of the language-oriented women writers I have discussed so far in this study suggest in their work, writing itself is com-

prised of rings of discourse—no expression, statement, phrase, or description is wholly original or independent of prior expressions and statements. What we see and comprehend of the world, including how we articulate these views, is largely constructed in and by preexisting discourses. To emphasize this point, Harryman incorporates into her writing a great deal of appropriated material. Some of her many textual sources include H.D. (herself a skilled palimpsestist), Freud, St. Augustine, the Marquis de Sade, Rousseau, and nonliterary texts such as promotional brochures, art gallery reception invitations and art catalogs. These appropriations are seldom clearly identified or cited in the text, though sometimes footnotes inform a reader of the range of sources from which the material in a particular piece was culled. In a few cases the appropriated material is obvious, as in the dialogue between Sade and Rousseau in "There Never Was a Rose without a Thorn," in which the speakers are Writing of Rousseau and Writing of Marquis de Sade and a footnote identifies both textual sources.

Whether appropriated material is identified or not, Harryman is not trying to trick anybody; on the contrary, her intention is to disabuse the reader of faith in such misleading and inhibitive concepts as authenticity and originality. "What is interesting is influence and usage not authenticity," she explains. "I think of Freud as a kind of concoction, a neo-classical aesthetician, a Victorian scientist and a modernist theoretician" (interview 62). The influence and usage of Freudian discourse in Western culture has been to validate and reify the very masculinist modes of self-world encounter that Harryman's language-oriented feminist epistemology seeks to question and undermine. She continues: "An outsider like me i.e. a female, one who provides the 'background' or subcentrality to the male—the central figure in Freud—might feel free to create an outsiders [sic] vocabulary" (Interview 62). This outsider's vocabulary, in turn, does not serve to construct a female-centered view, but rather, to playfully illustrate that the very notion of a center (male or female) depends on a notion of origins and inner truth that is imaginary. Beneath the layers of discourse is more discourse. In "Animal Instincts," the first-person narrator contemplates this very issue. "Out of my window the view blocks what's behind it," the piece begins. And then a few paragraphs further: "Perhaps this is the reason, or excuse, for my biography. Privacy may be caught out on a limb, but one can backtrack through endless plagiarisms to a fictional era, pure discourse that can be imitated, that can take advantage of modern life" (There 75). The only pure thing that lies beneath the surface of discourse is discourse itself. Harryman takes this insight as an invitation to

invention. She explains: "Sometimes charging into the unknown involves writing something down that one imagines has been said but
never written, creating a shift in meaning and context by adding to its
communicative medium. In fact, there is not so much difference between re-using, pillaging, and pioneering when it comes to cultural
construction. The terrain is there to be opened up" ("An Interview"
516).

So, far from stripping language of its power and influence, recognizing the significance of the surface of discourse is the key to language's ability to deconstruct normative (i.e., limited) models of
knowing and suggest or permit alternative modes of perception. Harryman uses language not to represent an already-given reality, but to
discover and invent. "[T]he way I use sentences is involved with discovery," she explains, "I have rejected certain ideas about centrality.
There is not one meaning or finding . . . nor is there necessarily a primary story or theme fed by a bunch of sub plots. Nor is there only a ca-
cophony of sounds and jumbled thought. There are other orders by
which people think and live . . . which I want to call up, find out about"
(Interview 65). These other orders, of course, include certain kinds of
women's experience.

Harryman's collaboration with Lyn Hejinian, *The Wide Road*, uses
language in such an exploratory way, to find out about a realm of
knowledge that has been especially marginalized, stylized, and discursively regulated in our culture: female sexual imagination. *The Wide
Road*, as I mentioned in chapter 1, is written in the first-person plural, so
the speaker is a multiple, potentially incoherent feminine subject. This
in itself is transgressive, but even more so because the content of the
writing includes women's heterosexual fantasies. Harryman describes
the writing as a kind of girl talk that is "literarily transformative" because "it's not real girl talk." She goes on to explain:

> It's just not exactly or only about girl talk topics. We infuse other
> topics with the desire inherent in girl talk. That is not permitted;
> you can't just do that. So the freedom is in doing something that's
> not permitted. But the great thing about it is that it's *so* not permit-
> ted that it's not even talked about, so it doesn't feel like it's not per-
> mitted. Sharing heterosexual fantasies in writing is an uncharted
> territory. It's not as if people say, "you can't do that." It's unstated.
>
> Interestingly, we have absolutely no problem with it. It doesn't
> even feel like we're violating anything; I don't feel like I'm being
> bad. It's like play. So I think that this has to do with what is knowl-

edge, what is social knowledge, and what is private knowledge and all that. ("An Interview" 524–25)

These questions about social and private knowledge are highlighted in *The Wide Road* by the blending and juxtaposing of various recognizable forms of erotic discourse, from sensual description typical of romance fiction ("They sleep among a scent of onions and cumin mingled with the sweet fragrance of speckled lilies") to the objectifying stance and peculiar vocabulary of popular pornography: "A jerk of the covers on the bed reveals a fleshy and muscular, freckled mound of a male's ass, as large also as the width of our abundant bed. With confident grandeur, blunt plinthlike legs support this marvelous work of art" ("from *The Wide Road* 26). One point of this description seems to be that none of these established discursive forms are adequate, nor are they wholly inaccurate. Female desire is constructed in and by such discourses, even as it exceeds them:

We have romantic and real desires. These are logical eroticisms. We can merge more than we already have.

a saturating thought
of shadows

We like to have sex outdoors in the sun where the sun can see into our pants. We pull ourselves a little open. This feels a little daring, a little unabashed, a little fertile, and it's all of these. The sunlight begins to focus on us, the colors swirl and converge, the heat on us increases, even burns slightly between our legs, as the sun looks in.
The sun can't measure. (Harryman and Hejinian, "A Comment" 91)

In exceeding normative discourse on female sexuality, *The Wide Road* suggests that there is not one experience of feminine desire, but many; it represents an unexplored realm of knowledge to the writer-explorer. And in such writing language itself is the shifting, tenuous meeting ground where the individual encounters the world.

But the individual, in the phenomenological imagination of Harryman's writing in which identity and gender are always in question and the epistemological ground from which one views the world is likewise discursively constructed and changeable, is, not surprisingly, an actor or mask-wearer—always an assumed identity. Her narrators are posers who tend to draw attention to their own lack of authenticity. No one ever seems to be one thing, and no one is what one seems in Harryman's dramas. The initial speaker in "Typical Domains" proclaims "I enjoy all the roles I play" (*There* 49). And much to the reader's enjoyment, she plays many, including roles within roles. For instance, a few pages into the piece, a character identified only as It speaks the following: "I hold back the desire to be named. Each night, wearing a different disguise, *she* finks on a guest, then slips back to bed and into her lover's arms. In her lovemaking, I surface with masks that reproduce the tattletale actress. This lousy part promotes me to ace" (*There* 57). Harryman's speakers are not debilitated or alienated by their lack of essential identity; on the contrary, they are thereby empowered to explore and test assumptions about identity and reality—about what knowing is. Harryman shifts the phenomenological mode of presentation in her writing not by shifting visual frames per se, as does Scalapino, but by shifting the identity of the knowing subject. This passage from *Vice* illustrates the way in which the phenomenological situation itself is altered with each new identity the characters assume:

If I decide to go after the historian next to the window looking out the window I will pretend to be a clothes designer pretending he's a manufacturer of clothes and he won't be able to tell if I'm serious or not if I really think he's someone who only looks like someone else until he either shrugs me off and stays an historian or gives in and becomes nothing too, and the trick then will be not to tell him not to be honest and sentimental but continue to change colors names motifs just to see what happens when the car gets to where it is we're going. (79–80)

Not only is Harryman intent on discovering "what happens" as she dons and discards various masks and identities, but she is also making an important point about the phenomenological situation itself. Just as Scalapino and Berssenbrugge preclude Husserl's transcendental reduction from taking place in their writing, so does Harryman, by insisting that the phenomenological moment is not comprised of an autonomous self objectively confronting a separate world. Rather, like language itself, person-world encounters are culturally inscribed, social events—in which there is always room for play. Harryman uses language to demonstrate the social relationships that create the illusion of autonomy, the sense that one can create meaning in language independent of another's interpretation of that language. In an interview she explains: "I'm interested in a measure of dialogue in which, on the one hand, somebody asks a question and somebody answers the question: on the other, the person answering the question is only talking to herself and the question itself is only heard as a question she would ask herself, something that would be a product of her own mind" ("An Interview" 517–18). Such dialogues abound in Harryman's writing, such as this short excerpt from "Property":

MAY: So, breaking up ground.

HELEN: When one says lily pad but means grasshopper what trick is that? The lily pad sits placidly on stagnant water. We don't get off our asses because there are too many life forms but because the harshness of reality can be eliminated by comparing one thing to another.

PAM: Working for a living and living are the same thing.

MAY: Murder! (*There* 69–70)

What's important in dialogue, Harryman suggests, is not that people understand one another, but that people find a sense of community and connection in the exchange. "In fact, it's fascinating," she comments, "to some extent civilization rests on the belief that we know what each other is talking about. Or sometimes talking is like sex; you just want to be with somebody and it's not important whether or not you're able to understand the other person" ("An Interview" 518). Human conversation, then, is never an interchange between autonomous individuals; rather, it is a social event that constructs both the sense of autonomy and the sense that real information has really been exchanged that we associate with dialogue.

Perhaps "Autonomy Speech" is the piece in which Harryman most thoroughly explores these questions of autonomy. The very notion of autonomy is undermined on the most basic level of the writing, for this, like many of Harryman's writings, is comprised of text appropriated from other sources, including *The Wide Road*, Donna Haraway's "Cyborg Manifesto," and the psychological writings of L. S. Vygotsky. Moving from one type of language use or "game" to another, in and out of dialogue, from internal monologue to third-person narrative, the text continually thwarts any gestures toward wholeness or autonomous identity for the speaker that any one of these modes might initiate on its own. Declarative statements butt up against noun phrase fragments flanked by isolated words overrunning the right margin in boldface. These language units are the performers in Harryman's dramatic insistence that

> There is no autonomy save
> the daily
> the banal emptied out, the forms of human practice that have no
> formal language. If there were a formal language for pouring pep-
> per onto the clay no one would ask what happens when you have
> to pee. (*There* 38)

In other words, since there is no formal language for pouring pepper onto clay (an act apparently actually performed by Harryman's son Asa, who is mentioned by name in the piece), it can be seen as an autonomous act. It describes an experience in the realm of child's play, for many of which experiences there is no formal language, no acknowledged knowledge. Significantly, the child's encounter with the world is only autonomous in the sense that it is social. Harryman believes that many aspects of parent-child relations are in the realm of unacknowledged knowledge, and that such relations offer special insights into autonomy. In an interview she discusses

> the experience of having a child and the sense—the very ongoing
> sense—that whatever individuation actually is, whatever that real
> dynamic is (which is not adequately accounted for in the psychoan-
> alytic tradition), it has to do with the basic fact that when the child
> has autonomy from the parent, it's because the child understands
> that the parent can grant the child autonomy. Which is like society.
> So that familial relationships are very like the construction of soci-
> ety. There is never a time that a human being is not in society.[10] ("An
> Interview" 520)

The gist of this insight is of course not altogether new to Western phenomenological thought. Merleau-Ponty certainly points in this general direction in his emphasis on lived experience and on the individual as a "network of relationships" among interrelated experiences ("What Is Phenomenology?" 373). But by exploring these relationships on the level of language, Harryman is able to demonstrate the extent to which "individual" and "world" are not two separate realms that meet in the phenomenological situation, but rather, are always already integrated, on the level of language. By thus jettisoning the Cartesian notion of autonomy, Harryman is able to enact a kind of "language as experience" à la Nancy Gray that does indeed leave old gender codes behind—the gender codes that say certain experiences do not exist because there is no language for them. In "Gender and Epistemic Negotiation," Elizabeth Potter points to the "communal nature of knowledge production and the ways in which the politics of gender, class, and other axes of oppression are negotiated in the production of knowledge" (165), suggesting that the denial of this aspect of knowledge might account for the kinds of gender biases in discourse that Harryman is so concerned about. Harryman seems to share Potter's view that "the isolated individual cannot produce language—much less the knowledge it embodies; language must be public" (164), and she accounts for this insight in her writing by disrupting the linguistic conventions that perpetuate the Cartesian epistemological ideals that effectively erase whole realms of human experience from linguistic articulation and acknowledgment. In the chapter that follows, I show how Susan Howe disrupts conventions in order to recover certain human experiences that she feels have been systematically erased from historical records.

Chapter 5

"Cries open to the words inside them":
Textual Truth and Historical Materialism
in the Poetry of Susan Howe[1]

> To articulate the past historically does not mean to recognize
> it "the way it really was" (Ranke). It means to seize hold of a
> memory as it flashes up at a moment of danger. . . . In every
> era the attempt must be made anew to wrest tradition away
> from a conformism that is about to overpower it. Only that
> historian will have the gift of fanning the spark of hope in the
> past who is firmly convinced that even the dead will not be
> safe from the enemy if he wins. And this enemy has not
> ceased to be victorious.
> —Walter Benjamin, "Theses on the Philosophy of History"
> (*Illuminations* 255)

> If History is a record of survivors, Poetry shelters other voices.
> . . . Poets try to keep love safe from the enemy.
> —Susan Howe, "*The Difficulties* Interview" (25–26)

Susan Howe shares Carla Harryman's concern that established literary forms and discourses might suppress or disallow certain modes
of knowing. In particular, Howe focuses on historical discourse,

putting knowledge of the past, as well as the processes by which history is socially and discursively constructed, into process in language.[2]
Howe writes a poetry that is at once a critique of conventional historiography and a mode of historical inquiry. She hopes to "tenderly lift
from the dark side of history, voices that are anonymous, slighted—
inarticulate" ("Poetics" 15). These are the "antinomian," lawless and
"feminized" voices that she feels have been nearly silenced in the ordering forms of conventional historiography and historical texts. Perhaps surprisingly for a project so politically motivated, Howe's is a
poetry of unusual beauty, "a play of force and play / of forces / falling
out sentences" (*ET* 99). Her work's seductive logic often depends on a
coherence derived from complex sound patterns, yet word choice never
seems forced or artificial. On the contrary, assonance and alliteration
seem a natural consequence of already necessary word combinations.
But this is poetry for the eye as well as the ear: Howe makes use of the
page as a painter does a canvas. As a result, language takes on a spacial
as well as aural existence:

> small boy-bird of the air
>
>   moving or capable of moving
> with great speed
> rapidly running   flying   following
>   flight of an arrow
> known for the swiftness of her soul. (*ET* 163)

And fittingly, language is both her subject and her tool in this project:
"[W]ords are like swords," she explains. "'S' makes word a sword.
When you slice into past and future, what abrupt violence may open
under you?" (SSH 34). With each slice of her double-edged (s)word,
Howe simultaneously seeks and subverts, discovers and disrupts; quoting textual fragments, thwarting narrative, disrupting syntax, and fragmenting words, she foregrounds language, emphasizing its materiality.

    But at the heart of Howe's feminist project of historical recovery lies
an apparent contradiction, similar to the paradox in H.D.'s work. Her
poetics implies a positivist belief that historical "voices" are somehow
really there to be recovered—that there is "real" content hidden beneath
or within the literary representations of history. Indeed, Howe rejects
the antifoundationalist view that past events are wholly the products of
discourse, that "history is only a series of justifications or that tragedy
and savagery can be theorized away." After all, [t]here is *real* suffering

on this little planet" (*Birth-mark* 164). Yet neither does Howe suppose that historical documents can be read unproblematically as transparent representations of a "real" past. Howe's entire project also depends on her view that history is discursively constituted. Howe's poetic-historical method is consistent with those poststructuralist and feminist theories of history which hold that historical truth is socially-discursively constructed.[3] But at the same time, Howe *believes* in truth. Aware of the paradoxical nature of her own project, she explains to Lynn Keller in an interview:

> I think there is a truth, even it's not fashionable to say so anymore. . . . I believe with Walter Benjamin that the story is in danger of being lost the minute someone opens one's mouth to speak; but you've got to open your mouth to speak, and there *is* a story, and it's probably going to be lost anyway, but whatever that story is, whether you call it fact or fiction, or an original version, it's something real. ("An Interview" 30–31)

It seems that Susan Howe rides the rift between empiricism and textuality, sharing the empiricist's interest in material details, but remaining suspicious of empirical methods of obtaining these details, which, she believes, can best or only be recovered textually. Like H.D., Howe seeks knowledge through writing while insisting that all meaning is ultimately textual. This paradox, rather than weakening or discrediting Howe's project, as might be expected, is in fact what drives that project, validates it, and gives her poetry such force.

Howe has devised a poetic strategy for writing history that seems a perfect example of what Jerome McGann conceives of as "a hermeneutics of a repressed or invisibilized content" ("Introduction" 4). Her poetic innovations with language and form create a kind of writing that both avoids the totalizing gestures she objects to in conventional history such as cause-effect explanations, coherence, and closure, and pays close attention to the particular, local, apparently minor details that resist these gestures. In this way, she performs the recovery of the past by letting it into her work (textually) instead of claiming to master it by means of "objective" representation of an extra-textual "reality."

Since the truth that Howe seeks is that which has been excluded from or occluded by historical records, and so can often be found only in the "gaps and silences" (*Birth-mark* 158) of those documents, it is not the kind of truth that can be attained by means of any "Distant coherent rational system" (*Singularities* 17), such as scientific reason, according to which these voices were excluded in the first place. Historians who try to uncover the "truth" by means of rational explanation, "Sharpshooters in history's apple-dark," will inevitably miss their mark (*Singularities* 22). Howe believes that it is possible to recover the marginalized voices of the past, but only when we give up any claims of objectivity. For Howe historical truth is not "Knowledge narrowly fixed knowledge / Whose bounds in theories slay" (*Singularities* 12), but an "Untraceable wandering / the meaning of knowing" (*Singularities* 25)—the kind of knowledge enacted in the processes of language, and therefore, indicative of a reality inextricable from the text in which such knowing is performed.

Howe's language-oriented feminist epistemology undermines the assumption that the "textual" and the "real" are distinct, opposing categories. This opposition is commonly taken by historians and literary critics alike to be natural and inevitable. But as poststructuralist historian Michel de Certeau convincingly argues, this distinction is maintained and reinforced in both disciplines by a network of related oppositions that were "legalized in the eighteenth century as a result of the split between the 'humanities' and the 'sciences'" (*Heterologies* 17): subject and object, the objective and the imaginary, theory and practice, the past and the present.[4] In her negotiation between the "textual" and the "real," Howe explores the constitutive role that language plays in the production of historical truth as well as how gender, also discursively constructed, functions to maintain the power relations that determine what counts, at any given historical-cultural moment, as "truth."

The language-oriented feminist strategies she devises in her poetry to do this transform the character of historical knowledge itself; no longer the goal of historical investigation, knowledge *is* that investigation, constructed as an interactive engagement with both the reader and the past. Howe offers ways of knowing historical truth that are not positivistic or empirical, but performative. In her poetry, language does represent historical truth, but only in the sense of McGann's "recovered" theory of representation, according to which, "art imitates not merely the 'fact' and the 'ideal' but also the dynamic relation which operates between the two" ("Introduction" 14). McGann argues that the poetic represents the real by *performing* this relation: poems are not "representations; they are acts of representation" (*SVPA* 245). I find in Howe's poetry what McGann later describes as "truth-functions which are not encompassed by the coherence and correspondence theories of truth" (*Towards* 6).[5]

Both the coherence and the correspondence theories of truth assume that the production and consumption of texts are separate processes. But Howe does not see it this way, and central to her poetics is a challenge to such distinctions between writing and reading. In a deconstructive gesture which, as I have shown throughout this study, is a shared tendency among language-oriented women writers, Howe posits writing as a mode of reading. Like H.D., Laura Moriarty, and Beverly Dahlen, she reads history, myth, culture, and the literary, religious and historical documents in which such cultural knowledge is preserved and disseminated—is *constituted*. Although Howe did not, of course, directly experience the past events that she writes about, she does sense that her own life and experiences are located within a particular history. What feminist historian Catherine Hall calls "the feminist injunction that you should always start with yourself and what you know and experience" is for Howe not so much an injunction as a compulsion (16). "I feel compelled in my work to go back," she explains to Edward Foster in an interview, "not to the Hittites, but to the invasion or settling or whatever current practice calls it, of *this* place" (*Birth-mark* 164). Howe focuses in many of her poems on the history of early North America and its inhabitants, the history of which she, a white middle class intellectual woman raised in New England, is a part. In "Secret History of the Dividing Line," collected in *Frame Structures: Early Poems 1974–1979* (*FS*), Howe writes a reading of the private journals of William Byrd, an early American surveyor of Virginia and North Carolina. In this poem, Howe examines the settling of the North American wilderness, the wars and migrations and "netting of fences" (96) that served to partition and divide the New World along property, gender, race, and class lines. "Articulation of Sound Forms in Time" continues this theme, focusing in particular on the experience of Hope Atherton, a minister of Hatfield, Massachusetts who accompanied Colonial troops in an attack on Indian settlements in the Connecticut River Valley in 1676. Howe wrote "Thorow" throughout the winter and spring of 1987 during which time she immersed herself in Henry David Thoreau's journals. In this work Howe is especially interested in Thoreau's representations of Native Americans and the wilderness.

But not all of Howe's works are readings of North American history; she understands that the European "invasion or settling or whatever" of this continent is part of the larger history of Western imperialism, and her investigations occasionally attend to moments in European and British history as well as Western myth and religion. Howe's collection of most recent poems, *The Nonconformist's Memorial*

(*NM*), includes two such works. "A Bibliography of the King's Book or, Eikon Basilike" is Howe's reading of a book—or more accurately, of the textual history of a book—that was first published and distributed in England following the execution of King Charles I. And in the volume's title poem, "The Nonconformist's Memorial," Howe conducts a reading of the very same text that H.D. "revises" in her poem *Trilogy*: the Gospel According to St. John. Whatever texts or discourses Howe takes as her subject in a given work, her intention is the same. She reads in order to recover certain elements that have been obscured or excluded from accepted historical accounts.

Interventions in History: Recovering the Feminine

Before examining in greater detail some of the methods of recovery Howe employs in her poetic readings of these various texts and discourses, I would like to look at Howe's theories regarding why—and how—certain voices get silenced in historical discourse in the first place. Howe's poetry is difficult, to say the least, but I believe that in the context of her theoretical concerns and intentions, even her most eccentric poetic gestures may be understood as meaningful acts. Howe's most comprehensive statements of her poetic-historical theories may be found in *The Birth-mark: unsettling the wilderness in American literary history*, her collection of essays on various topics in American literary history. In one of these essays, entitled "Incloser," Howe explores the problem of literary and historical exclusion. She writes: "Every statement is a product of collective desires and divisibilities. Knowledge, no matter how I get it, involves exclusion and repression. National histories hold ruptures and hierarchies. On the scales of global power, what gets crossed over?" (45). Howe suspects that knowledge or "truth" is inseparable from relations of power, and that discourse functions to police this relation. Recalling Foucault's claim that "[e]ach society has a regime of truth, its 'general politics' of truth . . . the types of discourse which it accepts and makes function as true" ("Truth and Power" 1144), Howe maintains that "when we move through the positivism of literary canons and master narratives, we consign ourselves to the legitimation of power, chains of inertia, an apparatus of capture" (*Birth-mark* 46). But Howe's efforts directed against such an apparatus of capture is informed by her sense that just as important as the question of how "the silenced factions waiting to be part of any expression" (DI 24) become silenced is the question of *who* those silenced factions are: Whose voices, perspectives, and experiences are deemed unrepresentable or irrelevant or incommensurable by a society's "regime of truth"?

Howe's sense that "in paternal colonial systems a positivist efficiency appropriates primal indeterminacy" suggests that she is alert to the role that gender plays in such processes of exclusion (*Singularities* 41). I do not mean to imply that Howe believes only or all women have been unfairly represented in historical documents. Rather, Howe seems to be joining feminist critics from Simone de Beavoir to Postcolonial and Third World theorists who have analyzed how certain cultural, social, and linguistic processes have relegated the category "woman" and all things conceived of as "female" or "feminine" to a position of object or "other" in Western thought and discourse, in which the speaking subject is inevitably constructed as male.[6] In *The Writing of History* (*WH*), Certeau attributes the impulse to exclude to modern Western history's "differentiation between the present and the past," subject and object, same and other. Certeau explains that "*[I]ntelligibility is established through a relation with the other*; it moves . . . by changing what it makes of its 'other'—the Indian, the past, the people, the mad, the child, the Third World" (3). Although Certeau does not include "woman" or "the feminine" in his litany of types that usually play the role of the "other" in historical discourse, I find that his analysis elucidates Howe's feminist poetics.

Resisting the tendency in dominant discourse toward marginalizing all that is other to the patriarchal, Susan Howe often does center her attention in her writing on the actual women who really lived and whose "voices," though "incoherent inaccessible muddled inaudible," are nevertheless still discernible, she believes, in historical texts and discourses (*Singularities* 21). Sometimes their presence is most clearly indicated by their absence. In the introductory material to her poem "Articulation of Sound Forms in Time," for instance, Howe observes that "what the historian [of the battle between white settlers and Indians known as the Falls Fight] doesn't say is that most of the dead were women and children" (*Singularities* 3). Accordingly, Howe makes sure that the "Little figure of mother" finds a place in her poem, both as "She is and the way She was," as a "Lost fact dim outline" as she appears to Howe in the historical records. In Howe's poem a woman's "Outline was a point chosen," in order to ensure that her "Face seen in a landscape once" will remain visible (*Singularities* 37). In "The Nonconformist's Memorial," Howe concerns herself in her reading of The Gospel According to St. John with "the obscure negative way" that a particular female figure, Mary Magdalene, is therein represented, "Dense in parameter space"

(*NM* 33). And in an earlier work, "The Liberties," collected in *The Europe of Trusts* (*ET*), Howe "rescues" Stella Johnson, Jonathan Swift's unacknowledged lifelong companion, whose letters to him were lost (perhaps destroyed by Swift himself for his own protection) and whose presence in literary history is thus limited to what is contained in his journals and letters to her. Howe has also written extensively in her poetic scholarly work about North American women, including Emily Dickinson and two Puritan women: Mary Rowlandson, author of the first Captivity Narrative written and broadly distributed in New England, and Anne Hutchinson, who, in 1637, was banished from the Massachusetts Bay Colony for her "heretical" preachings.

But not only women's voices are muffled in history's discourse. Howe's is an antiessentialist view of gender: whoever is outside the bounds of the law, order, and codes of behavior is equally subject to historical invisibility. In early American history, these "feminized" others include American Indians (who were never within the bounds of Puritan order to begin with) as well as whites of both genders who strayed beyond the bounds of Puritan law. Howe's interest in recovering not only the female but also the feminized might place her with those poststructuralist theorists who, according to Janet Todd, "have put . . . the idea of woman before the experiences of women" (14). But I would warn against any such simplistic categorizing of Howe or her methods. Howe's understanding of how certain voices get silenced in history depends on her notion of gender as, in Joan Scott's definition, an "analytical category." Scott argues that historians must attend not only to the experiences of women, but also to the processes of "how gender operates historically" and how "meanings are constructed through exclusions" (22, 9).[7] It seems to me that these are the very processes Howe refers to when she writes that "[l]awlessness seen as negligence is at first feminized and then restricted or banished" (*Birth-mark* 1). Howe has her ear tuned to the "muffled discourse from distance" of the banished, whom she seeks to rescue from their "Destiny of calamitous silence" (*Singularities* 25, 32).

Among the banished in North American history, Howe counts the land itself. One of the most symbolic and effective means by which white settlers contained and tamed (feminized) the "wilderness" (as such, already feminized) was to survey, parcel, and fence off the land. "I am trying to understand what went wrong when the first Europeans stepped on shore here . . . ," explains Howe. "Isn't it bitterly ironic that many of them were fleeing the devastation caused by enclosure laws in Britain, and the first thing they did here was to put up fences?" (*Birth-*

mark 164). She explores this impulse in "Secret History of the Dividing Line," which, as I already mentioned, is based on the journals of surveyor William Byrd.[8] On the second page of the poem Howe introduces the central tension of the work, a tension between "the permanence/of endless distance" and the imposed boundaries that render "Frame of our Universe / Our intellectual wilderness / no longer boundless" (*FS* 90).

In these early pages, Howe is responding to the poet Charles Olson, who has also been an important influence on her work. He too was interested in the history of New England, dubbing its European immigrant citizens "THE LAST FIRST PEOPLE," the irony of which Howe explores in her poem by beginning this section with this line. Howe is responding to Olson's oft-quoted statement, significantly *not* quoted in Howe's poem: "I take SPACE to be the central fact to man born in America" (11). Howe explains in an interview: "I am a woman born in America. I can't take central facts for granted" (DI 21). The connection between the containment-destruction of the wilderness and the exclusion of women (and other "others") from historical records is immediately apparent to Howe, for both gestures reveal the role that gender plays in the operation of power. Just as the American wilderness was divided by land surveyors and property owners, "discourse in the Massachusetts Bay Colony . . . was charged with particular risks for women, who were hedged in by a network of old-world values (*Birthmark* 3). Thus the position of any woman in America is similarly defined and delimited, marked.

In "The Nonconformist's Memorial," Howe shows how the same old-world values led to the partial erasure of Mary in the Gospel of John. Like Anne Hutchinson, Mary is a female figure whose

> Preaching constantly
> in woods and obscure
>
> dissenting storms
> A variety of trials (*NM* 4)

was deemed threatening by the regime(s) of truth that police Christian religious discourse.[9] "The act of Uniformity / ejected her" so that her presence in scripture is obscured in various ways: "Citations remain abbreviated" and "in Peter she is nameless" (*NM* 5–6). As Howe explains, "Mary, the disciple, the first one who witnesses the resurrection, the one whose story we go by, gets dropped away almost at once" ("An Interview"11). The female is, again, the most readily feminized in discourses

that resist "headstrong anarchy thoughts" such as Mary's in their striv-
ings for coherence and unity (*NM* 6). Howe's choice of the word "headstrong" here emphasizes that the anarchy that Mary threatens is
gendered, for very rarely does "headstrong" describe male behavior;
the term is usually reserved to indicate willfulness in females. But
Howe writes her poem to illustrate that it is through "this very process
of her interruption and erasure" that Mary remains present in the
Gospel, and we see "that she's continuing through these narratives"
("An Interview" 11).

Howe's sense of the interplay between what is represented and
what is unrepresentable by the discourse of the Gospel is consistent with
Certeau's claim that "any autonomous order is founded upon what it
eliminates; it produces a 'residue' condemned to be forgotten, but what
was excluded re-infiltrates the place of its origin . . . it inscribes there the
law of the other" (*Heterologies* 3–4). Howe's poetry of recovery depends
on such a Freudian notion of the inevitable "return of the repressed"
(*WH* 4), which in turn allows for agency on the part of the poet. Instead
of "aim[ing] at calming the dead who still haunt the present, and at offering them scriptural tombs" as Certeau accuses traditional historians
of doing (*WH* 2), Howe devises modes of investigation and representation that make the lawless factions and voices of alterity more easily apparent. She presents Mary in her poem as one of history's repressed
"others" who, like Certeau's ghosts, still haunts the text. "In the synop-
tic tradition Mary/enters the tomb," writes Howe (*NM* 12). On perhaps
the most literal level of all, the tomb she enters is the "scriptural tomb"
of the text itself, to which the discourse of the Gospels of the New Testament would relegate Mary. But Howe ensures that this tomb will
nonetheless become "No abiding habitation" for her by revealing that
"The Gospel did not grasp" her "least coherent utterance" (*NM* 7, 23,
26). Such utterances make Mary's presence known, and the incoheren-
cies in Howe's poem emphasize the irony of a discourse of testimony
that attempts to muffle the voice of its most important witness.

Again, Howe traces this irony to the operations of gender in history: "If you are a woman, archives hold perpetual ironies," she explains, "[b]ecause the gaps and silences are where you find yourself"
(*Birth-mark* 158). The New Testament's regime of truth cannot "grasp"
Mary's utterance—cannot fully contain, subsume, or expel from the
Gospel the experiences and expressions that are incompatible with the
ideological purposes of its various authors. Howe's belief that historical
truth may be found in such traces and utterances finds support in

Jerome McGann's idea that "these particulars always appear as *incommensurates*: details, persons, events which the work's own (reflected) conceptual formulas and ideologies must admit, but which they cannot wholly account for" ("Introduction" 14). McGann argues that the incommensurate is the source of positive poetic knowledge, and that the chief social value of poetic works lies in poetry's ability to represent the incommensurate.

Because Howe likewise finds poetic truth and value in these incommensurates, she is wary of historiography that represents history as unified, "As if all history were a progress," or "A single thread of narrative" (*NM* 7). Such an image of what Foucault calls "total history" and identifies as illusory, a function of Western society's regimes of truth,[10] is purchased at too high a cost for Howe, because in order for the past to appear unified and continuous, not only must antinomian voices be suppressed, but also the operations of gender, power, and language in the production of historical representation must be obscured, ignored, or even denied. Howe wants, rather, to reveal and foreground these elements and operations. Therefore, she works more in the tradition of Foucault's genealogist who concentrates on the minute and close-at-hand than in that of the traditional historian who chases the "corruptible first figure" (*Singularities* 17) of original causes. Howe believes that "every source has another center so is every creator" (*Birth-mark* 39). In renouncing her search for origins, the genealogist does not abandon her inquiry into historical *beginnings*, but rather than looking for sameness in these beginnings, she is sensitive to *difference*. Howe's poetic image of a "pitchfork origin" (*Singularities* 25) implies that she conceives of historical beginnings as instances of Foucauldian emergence. Foucault describes points of emergence as marked "not by inviolable identity" but by difference and disparity ("Nietzsche" 79). The several prongs of Howe's pitchfork would preclude the discovery of any single point of origin when probing the past with such an implement.

Although Howe's project cannot be characterized as entirely antinarrative, relying as it does on a kind of philosophical-political-poetic quest narrative in the tradition of the twentieth-century long poem, she resists the kind of conventional, closed narrative that has been the preferred form of historical representations of "total history" since the Enlightenment. Such resistance is consistent with her poetics of recovery, for she suspects that "the true story . . . comes to/nothing" (*ET* 88) in historical representations that impose narrative form and closure.[11] Much as H.D. does with the Trojan War legend in *Helen in Egypt*, Howe dismantles the narratives of the texts she reads and refuses to recast, even into revised coherent narrative, the elements she recovers, the "forgotten forgiven escaping conclusion" (*Singularities* 31). The exclusion of these elements is especially significant for Howe because she views this exclusion as inherently gendered: "Yes, she, the Strange, excluded from formalism" (*Singularities* 41). Howe attempts to include the strange, the incommensurate, in her poetry by thwarting narrative closure and coherence. "Exiles wander / and return from fiction or falsehood" (*FS* 105) in Howe's poems that deconstruct the texts they are readings of.

Howe's title, "Articulation of Sound Forms *in Time*" (not *of* time), announces her nonnarrative intentions with this work. Hope Atherton is the wandering exile who returns from falsehood in this text, and a feminized wanderer, at that. Howe's treatment of Hope in this poem illustrates her theory of the gendered operations of historical erasure as well as the specific strategies of recovery she employs to counteract that erasure. Because his experience, as well as his account of it, did not fit the master narratives of the Massachusetts Bay Colony, at that time struggling to maintain order and to distinguish its "civilized" communities from the "savagery" of the Indians[12]—that is, because his narrative did not cohere into a moralizing closure in accordance with the discourse which his society "accepts and makes function as true" (Foucault "Truth and Power" 1144), Hope was rejected. Ironically, he was repudiated by both the Indians to whom he tried to surrender and, on his eventual return to Hatfield, his own townspeople who were unwilling or unable to accept his story. Howe recasts his address in an increasingly fragmented speech:

> Loving Friends and Kindred:—
> When I look back
> So short in charity and good works
> We are a small remnant
> of signal escapes wonderful in themselves
> We march from our camp a little
> and come home
> Lost the beaten track and so
> River section dark all this time
> We must not worry
> how few we are and fall from each other
> More than language can express
> Hope for the artist in America & etc

This is my birthday
These are the old home trees (*Singularities* 16)

The discontinuity from one line to the next seems to indicate the contesting discourses of which the history of the Falls Fight is comprised.
Accounts given by Hope, the Indians, and white soldiers conflict; the
historical record is incomplete; and Hope ended up on the opposite side
of the swollen Connecticut River that was supposedly impossible to
cross at that time. He died shortly after his ordeal in the wilderness. But
in this stanza Howe overlays Hope's contested plea to his congregation
with her own plea directed at her own contemporaries to resist and oppose the apparati of capture that continue to domesticate and suppress
insurgent expression in both literature and history. She forges a linguistic link between the past and present by playfully recasting key words
from the Falls Fight accounts such as "Hope" and "fall."

Hope's name is especially charged with meaning for Howe, so that
her representation of him as one of history's "feminized" others implies
a more extensive critique of antifeminist historiography. "In our culture
Hope is a name we give women," she explains. "Signifying desire, trust,
promise, does her name prophetically engender pacification of the feminine?" (*Singularities* 4). Howe is intrigued by the ways in which Hope's
historical presence seems to frustrate the subject-object opposition on
which Certeau believes Western history insists and depends—the same
subject-object distinction essential to Western phenomenology that
Leslie Scalapino, Mei-mei Berssenbrugge, and Carla Harryman frustrate in their poetic projects. Describing her first impression of Hope,
Howe writes: "He had this borderline, half-wilderness, half-Indian, in-
sanity-sanity experience" (DI 25). He came out of the wilderness "same
and not the same," not classifiable as insider or outsider, civilized or
savage (*Singularities* 17). By welcoming him into her poem in this un-
classifiable, incoherent state, in an accordingly halting and thwarted
narrative that "*does not* reduce" his experience "to conceptual finished-
ness" (McGann, "Introduction" 12), Howe "represents the incommensurable" (McGann, *SVPA* 72).

Although she does preface her poem with some narrative background in the form of a brief historical account of the events surrounding the Falls Fight, including an extract from a letter by Stephen
Williams (also in narrative form), Howe does not "tell" Hope's story in
her poem. Even in the section of the poem entitled "Hope Atherton's
Story," rather than narrating, she explodes and explores both the events
and the language used in various historical documents in which the

events were recorded. Thus, she *performs* the paradox of her own approach to historical "truth" in her treatment of Hope's story:

> Two blew bird eggs plat
> Habitants before dark
> Little way went mistook awake
> abt again Clay Gully
> espied bounds to leop over
> Selah cithera Opynne be
> 5 rails high houselot Cow
> Kinsmen I pray you hasten
> Furious Nipnet Ninep Ninap
> little Pansett fence with ditch
> Clear stumps grubbing ploughing
> Clearing the land (*Singularities* 8)

Certainly some narrative elements are still apparent through the fragmented syntax and peculiar diction and spelling in these lines. Temporal markers such as "before" and "again" suggest that events are ordered chronologically, however vaguely, and the combination of past and present tenses serves a similar function. But the presence of these various narrative elements in Howe's poetry does not necessarily result in the kind of totalizing closure typical of narrative historiography. Jerome McGann's theory of "dialogic discourse" is helpful in explaining why not. McGann acknowledges that in light of recent critiques of narrative such as Hayden White's and Certeau's, narrative may seem devoid of subversive power. But he insists that this is not necessarily or always the case. Discourse in which "the story . . . is continually subjected to a critique from other materials, including other narratives," may be able to "invade the strongholds of . . . ideological narratives and force them to face their meanings and their limits" (*SVPA* 145, 151). Howe's use of narrative in "Articulation of Sound Forms in Time" seems to fit this model. The variety of verb tenses in the above stanza, for instance, while indicating narrative, at the same time thwarts the coherent development of any single narrative or chronology because the different tenses occur randomly, shift without warning, and do not seem to represent specific or distinct points in time or points of view. This example illustrates just one of a range of "invasion" tactics Howe employs in her poetry.

Other examples may be found in "The Liberties," where Howe disregards certain conventions of historiography by combining and intertwining narratives of different types in a way that calls to mind Carla Harryman's transgressions of generic boundaries. For instance, she blurs the sanctified distinction between history and fiction by devoting nearly as much of the poem to reading-"recovering" the character Cordelia of Shakespeare's *King Lear* as she does to recovering Stella Johnson, and in one section of the poem, "God's Spies," she brings Stella, Cordelia, and the ghost of Jonathan Swift together into a single scripted play. In the earliest scenes, Stella and Cordelia are in dialogue, responding to one another's questions and statements: "STELLA: Don't Leave me. / CORDELIA: I won't" (*ET* 184). But by the fourth scene the two are beginning to merge, to the point that they are finishing each other's speech: "STELLA: It is— / CORDELIA: —Not true" (*ET* 187). And by the end of this scene they are fully integrated into the same fragmented speech:

> TOGETHER (*Urgently*): Space—room—gate—lid—
> noise—ruin—heart—breast—years—family
> souvenir—wedding ring—whatsoever—
> clear as day—(*Pause*)
> Hurdles. And stems of trees. (*Pause*)
> Hearing at night when silence is deep—Unity—
> something there—really nowhere—(*Pause*)
> A path
> into the light.
>
> *They return to the rock and sit down.* CORDELIA *pulls the coats out of her knapsack.*
>
> CORDELIA: (*Urgently*): put on one coat, two coats, three coats!
>
> *They bundle themselves up and sit closely huddled together for warmth. Complete darkness. Silence.* (*ET* 187–88)

By bringing characters from two different types of narrative together in this way, she is also, of course, subjecting both narratives—including the "fictionality" of one and the "historical actuality" of the other—to a mutual critique. The passage also implies that these female characters are able to help each other out of the darkened silence of their respective scriptural tombs by crossing the boundaries of subjectivity—boundaries rendered fluid in Howe's poetic language. Such mutual interrogation and integration function here as feminist survival tactics, guaranteeing that Stella and Cordelia will be equally fictional, equally real, huddled together in the dark into which the (illusory) binarism reality-textuality casts them.

Howe also invades the stronghold of ideological narrative through the entrance to that stronghold guarded by objectivity. She often reads narratives against and through her own life and history, thus drawing attention to her role in the production of her poem and the "history" it is a reading of. This is Howe's method of taking subjectivity into account. Although personal experience never seems to be the primary focus or motivation for her poetry—as it might be for Dahlen or Lubeski or even Berssenbrugge—Howe sometimes puts her "self" into process in language in ways that call to mind the projects of some of her language-oriented contemporaries. Howe's treatment of Hope Atherton's address to his congregation, which I have already discussed, is one such example. Another may be found in section III of "The Liberties," where Howe acknowledges her interest in the Irish history the poem treats—an interest based on the very personal circumstance of her own Irish heritage:[13]

> Across the Atlantic, I
> inherit myself
> semblance
> of irish susans (*ET* 213)

Such self-consciousness is another means of presenting a more "authentic" history:

> I can re
> trac
> my steps
> Iwho
> crawl
> between thwarts
> Do not come down the ladder
> ifor I
> haveaten
> it a
> way (*ET* 177)

Howe assumes that the most truthful narrative is the one found "between thwarts," the one that can only be traced or followed once the coherence that we normally require in order to trace or follow the logical progression of events—the coherence that is after all imposed on events by discourse—has been "eaten away" by gestures such as self-reflexivity. Another such gesture may be found in "Thorow." In the prose introduction to that poem, which Howe has tellingly titled "Narrative in Non-Narrative," she offers the historical circumstances of the writing of that poem—her winter at Lake George, her experiences of reading Thoreau's journals. Howe suggests that this (personal) history is as much—inevitably so—the subject of the poem as any other "history" there explored. "I thought I stood on the shores of a history of the world where forms of wildness brought up by memory become desire and multiply," she writes (*Singularities* 41).

None of Howe's poetic texts is reducible to any one version or vision of history-reality because she keeps them active, allowing elements from a variety of different narratives to play off one another. Howe opens "The Liberties," for instance, with a factual history of Stella Johnson's life presented in an objective, "scholarly" voice. The section that immediately follows, "Stella's Portrait" subverts the objective authority of this opening narrative by (dis)continuing the history in a fragmented "portrait" of Stella. The "portrait" is a collage of details, facts, speculations, and excerpts from poems and letters, many written by Swift. Howe arranges the information in such a way that frustrates the reader's expectations that historical narrative will be meaningfully ordered according to causality, continuity, chronology: "Sometimes her eyes pained her. When she was twenty-four she shot and killed a prowler after her servants had fled the house in terror. William Tidsall proposed marriage. With Swift's encouragement she turned him down. Three poems she transcribed into a manuscript volume have been attributed to her." Part of Howe's purpose in presenting material in this way is to demonstrate that "No authentic portrait exists"; the very notion of authenticity is problematic to begin with (*ET* 152). And this is a key component of Howe's performative poetics. It may seem contradictory for Howe to dedicate herself to recovering marginalized voices while claiming that objective access to a real past is impossible, but this contradiction is only apparent. Because all historical "facts" are never wholly separable from the modes of representation that give them form, the "real" *is*, to a great extent, also (already) "textual." By parenthetically citing a variety of sources in a single sentence of "Stella's Portrait," Howe suggests that a mode of portraiture that gathers and combines information from a variety of perspectives, even or especially when that information is contradictory, might be more historically accurate than a mode that obscures these processes of the production of historical "truth." Much as Gertrude Stein created poetic portraits by means of repetition-with-variation that foreground the processes and medium in which they are constructed, Howe suggests in her portrait that these same interrelations among language, perception, and knowledge operate in representations of history: "She had raven-black hair (Swift), a pale and pensive expression (Mrs. Delaney), was plump (Some), extremely thin(Others)" (*ET* 152).

Intertextuality and the Material Word

Many of the elements that Howe brings together in her work are directly quoted from different narratives and versions; like Dahlen and Harryman, she culls text from written sources and lifts the fragments—words, phrases, passages, expressions—into her poems. "My writing has been haunted and inspired by a series of texts," she acknowledges (*Birth-mark* 45). Howe's poems become rich fields of intertextuality, for she does not limit her reading to any one kind of text, or any one point of view, drawing equally from histories, orations, letters, encyclopedias, psalms, captivity narratives, sermons, literary manuscripts. Bits of Thoreau's journals are scattered throughout Howe's poem "Thorow" (the unique spelling of which is taken from one of Hawthorne's letters) and I have already mentioned that "Articulation of Sound Forms in Time" opens with excerpts from a letter. "Secret History of the Dividing Line" contains fragments from a variety of texts—not only Byrd's journals—including soldiers' letters:

> Dear Parents
>
> I am writing by candlelight
> All right so far
>
> after a long series of collisions
> had a good night's rest.
>
> Belief in the right of our cause.
> Tomorrow we move (*FS* 91)

Howe also excerpts written accounts, perhaps from captivity narratives, of Indian ceremonies as glimpsed by white settlers:

A series of movements
half grotesque, half magical
whoops, yells, uncouth forms
RAIN FELL INCESSANTLY
IT BECAME QUITE DARK (*FS* 117)

Howe brings these quotations into her poems not in order to reconstruct a total image of the past, nor to offer evidence in support of a particular interpretation of the past. On the contrary, quotations function in Howe's poetry to frustrate the development of any such complete image of the past, allowing for the conflicts and messiness that the posture of completeness always rejects. Howe's citational method results in a layered text, much like H.D.'s palimpsests, and functions, similarly, to deconstruct normative versions or visions of "reality" by allowing elements from different and contradictory discourses to exist simultaneously, in active, often contentious, relation to one another. "You open your mind and textual space to many voices," Howe explains, "to an interplay and contradiction and polyphony that forms lines and often abolishes lines" (DI 24). The result is a poem-history (or "portrait") constructed out of difference rather than sameness, to return again to Foucault's distinction between points of emergence and origin. But just as important, this collage is not static—and Howe does not intend it to be, as is clear from her use of the word "interplay," and the value she places on the process of "forming" and "abolishing" lines. McGann's notion of incommensurability as a mark of poetic truth is again helpful here.[14] Howe's poems are fields of action comprised of "details and prospects which are at odds or in tension with other details and prospects. What is central and what is peripheral, even what is present and what is absent, all make their appearance and shift their positions in relation to each other" (McGann, *SVPA* 7). Rather than smoothing over or blending the differences among the various historical and textual elements she brings together, Howe emphasizes the incommensurate. As a result, her detailed palimpsests never settle into stillness, and the tension among details never abates.

A crucial component of this poetic method is Howe's sensitivity to the material dimension of language. Howe finds precedent for the poetic-historical methods she champions in the historical materialism of Walter Benjamin. She feels a deep kinship with Benjamin, whose commitment to recovering the silenced voices of history she shares. In his "Theses on the Philosophy of History" Benjamin writes: "For every image of the past that is not recognized by the present as one of its own concerns threatens to disappear irretrievably" (*Illuminations* 255). And, like Howe, his primary method of recognizing the past is to collect quotations from a range of sources and construct texts out of them. In a recent talk she gave on her own creative process and influences as a poet, Howe spoke of Benjamin's historical-materialist method almost interchangeably with her own, particularly when describing how quotations function in poetic texts constructed by historical materialists such as herself and Benjamin: "Fragments, details, sparks of spirit, letters in times, quotations can interrupt the transcendent flow of a poem or an essay . . . with a real force . . . you do not take a quotation because it's wonderful and you worship it but [because] it's like a piece of dynamite, it's like a shock interrupting some kind of transcendent flow" ("The Poet"). Howe also shares with Benjamin the belief that introducing such interruptions is valuable because it is the means by which the historical materialist "blast[s] open the continuum of history" (Benjamin, 262). Readers of Howe's poetry are thus unable to rely on continuity as an ordering principle. "[L]iberating divergence and marginal elements" (Foucault, "Nietzsche" 87), "slipping from known to utmost bound" (Howe, *Singularities* 19), Howe *defamiliarizes*. Readers are liberated from their associational habits, freed to experience an original encounter with language, and with understanding. But even if "Inarticulate true meaning/lives beyond thought" (*Singularities* 30) for Howe, it does not live beyond language.

Howe finds language to be meaningful to the extent that it is *material*. Notice the metaphors in which both Howe and Benjamin discuss the process of collecting quotations and historical fragments from the context and continuum of history. For Howe, quotations are "dynamite" and they "shock" the reader. Benjamin wants to "blast" history open. Howe has even described herself as one who must "quarry" in her reading of historical texts, as if she digs or cuts through the sediment of the past in search of precious rock (Metcalf 52). It seems fitting that both Howe and Benjamin conceive of their projects as mining operations, for mining is a process that yields a material product, but also has significant material effects on the land from which it is mined. The historical continuum, like the earth where a mine has operated, is left blasted open. Interestingly, mining is not the only process of extracting natural resources to which Howe's and Benjamin's historical materialism has been compared. Hannah Arendt takes the metaphor under water in her introduction to Benjamin's *Illuminations* in which she compares Benjamin to "a pearl diver who descends to the bottom of the sea, not to excavate the bottom and bring it to light but to pry loose the rich and the strange, the pearls and the coral in the depths" (51). This description fits Howe as well in that she reverses the method of the traditional historian who, in his desire to make sense of history, privileges a coherent narrative at the expense of the insignificant (rich and strange) details that do not fit. Howe herself chooses an agricultural metaphor in order to suggest that truth is physical, not metaphysical: "Stripped of metaphysical proof / Stoop to gather chaff," she advises, for the chaff, what is usually discarded, is more valuable than the grain (*Singularities* 27). Such a harvest seems to be precisely what Foucault's genealogist hopes to reap by "cultivat[ing] the details and accidents that accompany every beginning" ("Nietzsche" 80). But even when the metaphors are not so consistent or clearly developed, the terms in which Howe discusses her writing process are strikingly physical. She may be describing her own method as well as Emily Dickinson's when she writes: "Forcing, abbreviating, pushing, padding, subtracting, riddling, interrogating, re-writing, she pulled text from text" (*My Emily Dickinson* 29).

Not only does Howe conceive of the reading/collecting process as physical, but just as significantly, she treats the products of the process, history's once-repressed and now-recovered "scraps, instants, rejectamenta . . . quotations, thought fragments, anagrams . . . the material details" (Howe, "The Poet")—whether imagined as rock, pearl, coral or chaff—as materially manifest. Benjamin's notion of the monad is useful here: Because a text so constructed by the collector-historical materialist is, as Benjamin puts it, "based on a constructive principle" that releases each quotation, fragment, or thought from the causal connections on which the constructive principle of history-as-continuum depends, each fragment so released "crystalizes into a monad [the basic constituent element of physical reality]. A historical materialist approaches a historical subject only where he encounters it as a monad. In this structure he recognizes . . . a revolutionary chance in the fight for the oppressed past" (262–63). Of significance here, is not only the materiality of the monad, but its scale in relation to other material forms, being *the basic constituent element* of any form. Arendt explains that "Benjamin had a passion for small, even minute things. . . . The smaller the object, the more likely it seemed that it could contain in the most concentrated form everything else" (11–12). Howe has a passion for minute elements of language and text—single words, sounds, phonemes, and fragments—and I understand her attention to these in the histories she reads as her attempt to encounter historical subjects as monads. In the context of her project of recovery, Howe's interest in linguistic monads suggests that she perceives history's operation of capture and silencing to take place most often, or most effectively—perhaps even alerting the least amount of suspicion or resistance—on this level of minute detail.

Just such an awareness, that the local and particular is where power manifests itself, might help account for Howe's attraction to Benjamin's notion of the monad; part of the "everything else" that a small textual or linguistic detail might contain is the very microphysics of power that Howe hopes both to reveal and to disrupt in her poetic readings of historical discourse.[15] Along one branch of these microphysics of power, of course, lie "the silent and hidden operations of gender" (J. Scott 27). Joan Scott's Foucauldian analysis accounts for the way Benjamin's monadic method, in Howe's hands, becomes a feminist strategy, operating on two levels. First, the monadic elements Howe collects and presents carry traces of the voices that have been silenced, whether female, feminine, or feminized. By foregrounding them in her texts, Howe not only *encounters* them but also *releases* them from their tombs of silence. And in the process, she calls attention to the operations of gender according to which these elements were, at various historical moments, feminized in the discourses she is reading.

The social value of Howe's monadic method implied by identifying it as a feminist strategy becomes more plausible when that method is seen as an instance of McGann's "reconstituted" referentiality. The material minutiae that Howe gathers from the language and texts of history can never be purely linguistic, according to McGann's theory, because the literary system of which they are part "operates . . . in concrete social space and conditions which can be specified" (*SVPA* 4). Therefore, the particulars that comprise the palimpsest he so values and which Howe delivers, "are not mere data, objects, or monads; they are heuristic isolates which bring into focus some more or less complex network of human events and relations" ("Introduction" 12). Howe presents the material details that she gathers from the textual debris of history in such a way that permits them to function this way.

Furthermore, like Benjamin's historical materialist, a collector "who recites events without distinguishing between major and minor ones" (Benjamin 254), Howe does not classify elements or discriminate among them for the reader. Howe's poetry "preserves [heuristic isolates] in a state of (as it were) freedom. The particulars are grains of sand in which the world may be seen—may be seen again and again, in new sets of relations and differentials" (McGann, "Introduction" 12). "This is not to deny that quotations are staged by the quoter," assures Howe (DI 24). Surely a poem constructed of difference is not necessarily less constructed than one that favors sameness. But, Howe explains, "data has generally been gathered by men from men telling their visions" (DI 24). Howe "stages" quotations according to very different criteria than those followed by the authors of the texts she gathers them from. In her poetry, quotations become monads or heuristic isolates, to be directly encountered in language, as language.

For example, Howe often arranges phrases, words and lines of poetry paratactically, placing them side by side rather than in the causal hypotactic relationships typical of analytical or chronologically ordered discourse. In many of her poems, she includes a few sections like the following in which words and word fragments are arranged equidistant from one another, in the form of a text block with justified left and right margins:

> green chaste gaiety purity sh inca
> deity snare swift leaf defile dispel
> poppy sh snow flee falcon fathom sh
> flame orison sh children lost fleece
> sh jagged woof subdued foliage sh
> spinet stain clair sh chara sh mirac
> (*FS* 116)

This visual parataxis helps to disconnect the words and fragments from syntactical, grammatical, and logical relationships, so her readers may encounter them as monads. One result is that in these sections the sound of each word comes alive, becomes primary. Language is material. And words such as "anthen" and "uplispth" and "enend," rather than referring to realities beyond themselves, assume immediate physical presences (*Singularities* 59). The sound of a word—its most physical characteristic—is the test of its truth value for Howe: "to an almost alarming extent . . . sound creates meaning," she claims (SSH 31). Butterick notes that because of Howe's attention to sound in her work, "words survive at their primordial limits. The result is a report as from under hypnosis, where thresholds have been eased and language and its components, including mumbles, halts and even hisses, arise" (321). This survival is precisely what she is after. When giving a public reading of her work, Howe even whispers some words. "[T]hat way they sound like another voice—the hissing return of the repressed," she explains ("An Interview" 11). By emphasizing the sound, shape, physical presence of language, Howe hopes to allow even the most uncontainable elements of history to persist and survive.

Howe spotlights word roots and cognates, fragmenting not only syntax but words themselves as if to see what they might contain. Unconventional—often archaic—spelling and the intermingling of Latin, Anglo Saxon, French, Indian, and Greek word forms are common in her poetry:

> rest chondriacal lunacy
> velc cello viable toil
> quench conch uncannunc
> drumm amonoosuck ythian
>
> ———
>
> scow aback din
> flicker skaeg ne
> barge quagg peat
> ~~sieve catacomb~~
> stint chisel sect
>
> ———   (*Singularities* 10)

This kind of fragmentation is what Andrew Schelling refers to as Howe's "ceremonial" etymology, a term that calls to mind H.D.'s "linguistic alchemy," and that poet's very similar exploration of word roots and derivatives. Howe's poetry, by "breaking the impasse of philology," Schelling explains, "locks literal tongues with the dead, activating the language they used, projecting their speech onto the page" (116). Howe believes that by encountering history on the level of the linguistic monad, she—and her readers—can encounter the past more directly. She even describes writing as "a physical event of immediate revelation" (*Birth-mark* 1) whose purpose is to render audible and visible the "sounds and spirits (ghosts if you like) [that] leave traces in a geography" (*Birth-mark* 156). Howe's sense that language can contact the "spirits" of history depends on a philosophy of language according to which "the spirit and its material manifestation are so intimately connected that it seems permissible to discover everywhere chance correspondences" (Howe, "The Poet").[16]

If this notion seems Messianic, it is; in his Judaic studies Benjamin found himself drawn to the "theological type of interpretation for which the text itself is sacred" (Arendt 4) and in her studies in early American literature and thought, Howe is taken by the Puritans' belief that divine truth could be embodied in the written word—not only in the Bible, but in poetry as well, which often took scripture as its model.[17] But, whatever the spiritual dimensions of such a position, neither Benjamin nor Howe arrived at this shared view of language through ascribing to the religious doctrines in which the theory has been articulated. Oddly, it seems more likely that both arrived at the idea by way of their political interests. Benjamin recognized in Marx's theory of the superstructure what Howe recognizes in the processes by which historical voices are feminized, exiled, and therefore recoverable: that language's relation to "reality" is not merely or simply one of representation; language is also constitutive of reality.

The sense that language is therefore an important site of the connection between spirit and matter expresses itself for both poet-historians as a view of language as numinous: plenitudinously meaningful, never reducible to any single or fixed meaning. In fact, language functions in Howe's historical materialism much as it does in H.D.'s spiritual realism. For both poets, words do function as containers or vehicles for meaningful content, but only to the extent that they themselves *are* the content; they cannot be exchanged for or replaced by their meanings. In "Articulation of Sound Forms in Time," words are so full of themselves that verbal expressions take on a three-dimensionality, moving across the page in the form of "Cries hurled through the Woods." And Howe suggests that when we open up a verbal expression to look inside, what we find there is language: the cries are "open to the words inside them" (*Singularities* 23). This is the same discovery, remember, made by H.D.'s protagonist Julia while translating from the Greek, that "the words themselves held inner words" (*Bid Me to Live* 162). Howe's linguistic monads—whether words or fragments—function like H.D.'s hieroglyphs: they are meaningful for her to the extent that they are finally untranslatable, numinously indeterminate.

The "Visible surface of Discourse"

Howe's notion of a nonrational, nontotalizing truth is consistent with her methods of poetic representation, which, as I claimed at the beginning of this chapter, may be seen as truthful to the extent that her poems are not themselves representations, but rather, *enact* representation. Because of what he calls the "'performative' aspect of the poetic" (*SVPA* 75), McGann insists in *The Beauty of Inflections* that "'meaning' in the literary experience will also be reconceived as the process by which literary works are produced and reproduced" (10). This process of production includes the "various institutional forms which are not themselves 'literary' at all" but in which literary works are encountered and constituted ("Introduction" 4). Of particular interest to both McGann and Howe are the publishing and printing institutions: McGann insists that textual criticism and bibliographical work must "be conceived of as central to hermeneutics" (*BI* 6); and Howe writes a poetry that activates the most *performative* material dimension of language, the typographical, bibliographical details that comprise both the texts she reads and those she writes.

Howe makes tangible the "Visible surface of Discourse" (*Singularities* 36) in a number of ways. First, she offers frequent reminders that historical events are inseparable from their textual embodiments, and these textual embodiments are never static or fixed, but are themselves *events*. Howe has a tendency, for instance, to narrate meteorological events in statements that simultaneously indicate textual conditions: in "Secret History of the Dividing Line," "Flakes of thick snow / fell on the open pages" (*FS* 104); in "The Liberties" "sleet whips the page" (*ET* 100). Both images emphasize that textual production is a significant site of historical loss and recovery; antinomian voices are subject to bibliographical erasure. They can be washed away by the sleet of printing conventions, whited-out by the snow of copyright laws. Note, too, that the distinction between "natural" events and "cultural" acts is compromised in these images that insert texts into the natural landscape and bring rain and sleet into the pages of a book. Howe tries to counteract the weathering effects of textual history by reading bibliographically, as it were—attending to the bibliographical events according to which nontextual events are physically organized and produced as texts. She even integrates bibliographical descriptions into her poems. In "Eikon Basilike," for instance, following ten pages of verse stanzas exploring the "Bibliography of the Authorship Controversy" surrounding the King's Book, is a prose block that includes information such as "the text is mostly black letter" and "This edition is Steele 3239. with coat of arms, no. 67, measuring 1 15/16 × 1 11/16 in." (73). In several instances Howe presents textual variants in standard bibliographical form, such as in this stanza:

K CHARL | WORKS | VOL I
K CHARLE | WORKS | VOL II
Numbers of Prayers, 3.
pp. 1 - 102 ending "FINIS"
It has remains of light blue silk
strings (*NM* 80)

Such bibliographical array is one example McGann offers of a form of discourse that "can maintain its own integrity within a narrativized field" as I mentioned earlier in the context of Howe's nonnarrative tendencies (*SVPA* 145). McGann explains that bibliographical description does not require narrative explanation or context in order to be meaningful. Since readers can refer to standardized guidelines for reading bibliographical discourse, "the entry, in its arrayed form, offers these (and other) materials in a discourse that is already full of significance" (*SVPA* 138). Furthermore, bibliographical discourse is especially full of significance because it offers a historical representation that includes a dimension of history's mode of production.

Additionally, in nearly all of her poems Howe disrupts printing conventions. She overlays lines of text, crosses horizontally printed lines with lines placed vertically and at various angles across the page. In some cases the whole page becomes a visual collage, comprised of words that function more like brushstrokes in a painting than linguistic signifiers (see Fig. 1). In passages such as these Howe's talent as a visual artist (in 1961 she graduated from the Boston Museum School of Fine Arts, where she majored in painting) clearly informs her poetic technique.[18] In this example, Howe has also drawn attention to the textual construction of some individual words by allowing the letters within the words to fall out of line, as happens when the type is incorrectly or carelessly composed in letterpress printing. How does one "read" such a page of text? In places in "Eikon Basilike" the physical layering of text on text renders some of the words themselves completely illegible (see Fig. 2). In these cases Howe has emphasized the material nature of language to such a degree that its referential function is totally disabled. These words cannot mean in the normative sense; they simply *are*—they are physical presences on the page. The reader confronts language "[n]ot to look off from it / but to look at it" (*Singularities* 50). But in none of these examples are the words static or fixed presences: Howe's visual collages are fields of action, drawing the viewer's eye this way and that, highlighting points of intersection, the multiple direction of language at cross-purposes. These passages represent the most radically *physical* instances of palimpsest in Howe's poetry.

In "The Nonconformist's Memorial," Howe creates a different visual effect by flipping a three-line stanza upside down and laying it over another three-line stanza that is printed right side up. Each upside-down line is placed directly under a right side up line, so that the two lines of text lie against one another, base line to base line, but without

Cannot be
every
where I   Parted with the Otterware

entreat
snapt   at the three Rivers, & are
s o l u t i o n   Re solve
picked up arrowhead
hieroglyph   Gone to have a Treaty

                                           with the French at Oswego
battleau
At this end of the carry
islet
& singing their war song

                                           neck
sheen   The French Hatchet

                                           dusk
Their Plenipo   squall   Messages

                                           splint
disc   coin   cedar
                          chip   grease
                                           cusk
lily root
                   a very deep Rabbit
                                           wavelet
swamp
of which will not perm[mit] of
                                           shrub
fitted to the paper,   the Margins
                                           mud
Encampt   Fires by night   Frames should be exactly
                                           waterbug
wood
canoes   c o v er y   Cove
                                           places to walk out to
Tranquillity of a garrison
Escalade
Traverse canon night siege Constant firing
Traverse canon night siege Constant firing

Gabion
Parapet

Fig. 1.   from Susan Howe's "Thorow" (*Singularities* 56)

England's Black Tribunal : Containing The Complete
Tryal of King CHARLES the First by the pretended
High Court of Justice in *Westminster-Hall*, begun *Jan.*
20, 1648. Together with His Majesty's Speech on the
Scaffold, erected at *Whitehall-Gate*, on Tuesday *Jan.* 30,
1648.   It passed with the Negative.

they kept prisoner

Fig. 2.   from Susan Howe's "A Bibliography of the King's Book or,
Eikon Basilike" (*NM* 59)

physically touching. The mirrored lines take on a three-dimensional
quality, as if each is extending from a shared axis into a different plane
(see Fig. 3). This mirrored quality is reinforced by a more precise mir-
roring that occurs between this verso page and its facing recto page: the
lines are mirrored exactly so that the first line of text on the facing page
reads "As if all history . . ." Howe explains that

> The mirroring impulse in my work goes way back . . . At first when
> I used mirroring in my writing I was very sedate about it, and it in-
> volved repetition in a more structured way. But with "Thorow" I
> had done one scattered page and made a xerox copy and suddenly
> there were two lying on my desk beside each other, and it seemed
> to me the scattering effect was stronger if I repeated them so the
> image would travel across facing pages. The facing pages reflected
> and strengthened each other. ("An Interview" 9)

The purpose of this visual presentation is not just to emphasize the materiality of language, but to draw attention to the textual history of the
Gospel of John and Mary Magdalene's contested presence there. Howe
continues:

> The reversed line in between—"Actual world nothing ideal"—
> would be an interruption to the narrative that you're trying to
> start. Then the third line that's right-side up—"She was coming to
> anoint him"—that was what was happening, but the reversed text
> on either side was a kind of break-in, some other thought going in

In Peter she is nameless
Actual world nothing ideal

headstrong anarchy thoughts
A single thread of narrative

She was coming to anoint him
As if all history were a progress

Fig. 3.   from Susan Howe's "The Nonconformist's Memorial" (*NM* 6)

some other direction. It also conveys her erasure. I'm trying to illustrate what I'm saying by putting this part upside down. ("An Interview" 9)

Howe is not just illustrating what she is saying; her poem is *performing* Mary's erasure, and performing it in such a way that the mode of production of the text that erases her is center stage in the performance—thus wandering her way through knowledge.

Howe intends such bibliographical performances to serve a hermeneutical function in her poetry. She believes that even the "tiniest tiniest essences, such as commas, blank pages, blots, erasures, all count" ("The Poet"); they count not only because they function, like all of Howe's textual minutiae, as heuristic isolates, but also "[b]ecause so many of the documents that come down to us have been homogenized or sanitized in favor of some eternal image of the past . . . even the subtlest changes in the original copies affect the truth" (Howe, "The Poet"). In *The Birth-mark* Howe writes, "I know records are compiled by winners, and scholarship is in collusion with Civil Government. I know this and go on searching for some trace of love's unfolding through all the paper in all the libraries I come to" (4). But in her introduction to "Eikon Basilike," "Making the Ghost Walk about Again and Again," Howe emphasizes that her hermeneutical bibliography is not based on the belief that truth can finally be located in authorial intention or "original" manuscripts. "Can we ever really discover the original text?" she asks. "Was there ever an original poem? What is a pure text invented by an author? Is such a conception possible? Only by going back to the prescriptive level of thought process can 'authorial intention' finally be located, and then the material object has become immaterial" (*NM* 50).

Certeau describes this loss of materiality as a defining feature of normative historiography, and one of its most grievous shortcomings: "the real as represented by historiography does not correspond to the real that determines its production" (*Heterologies* 203). Howe avoids this fallacy in her own poetic historiography by never allowing the material to become immaterial. Howe's bibliographical hermeneutics, as well as her other poetic strategies that foreground the materiality of language, are aimed at recovering a historical truth that is material, located in the material of language. Howe displays the representational operations at work in her own poems even as she employs such a display to lay bare the modes of production of the histories she reads.

A Poetics of Encounter

Howe's performative poetics demonstrate that she conceives of the texts she reads and those she writes much as McGann urges historical critics to appreciate any literary work, not "as an autonomous system of verbal signs, on the one hand, or on the other as the (free or determined) creation of reader and/or critic . . . [but] as a complex event in socio-historical space, the always particularized interchange of a present with a past" (*BI* 5). By (re)presenting historical details and particulars of the past as heuristic isolates—"lived realities" rather than static images of the dead past—Howe performs such particularized interchanges in her poetry. This allows her to encounter history's "others" in such a way that they are "not—to borrow Coleridge's phraseology—'objects as objects'; rather, they are objects-as-subjects" (McGann, "Introduction" 11). Since her project depends on *interchange with* rather than *distinction from* the past, Howe's meeting ground with the past can never be the supposed neutral-zone of objective historical accounting, which, according to Certeau, is never really neutral, for "[i]n pretending to recount the real, [historiography] manufactures it"; the "'past' is the object from which a mode of production distinguishes itself in order to transform it" (*Heterologies* 207, 216). Rather, Howe meets her other in language, in the telling of the poem itself. "[T]he past is present when I write" she explains (DI 20), locating the encounter in a *process*—the process of language experienced in the act of writing or reading—rather than in any one fixed interpretation or moment, or in the text itself. In fact, the text "itself" does not really exist as such—the "texts" of Howe's poems are actualized only in the human (social) process of historical knowing, of interchange *with*. When I read her poetry, I feel at

Home in a human knowing

Stretched out at the thresh
of beginning

Sphere of sound (*Singularities* 26)

In other words, historical knowing seems more "real" to me, in the sense of being immediately actual, than does any final product, such as "knowledge of the past" that is contained in (and by) historiographical texts that differentiate themselves from the "real" that they supposedly represent. Howe describes her own intent as being "not to explain . . . not to translate . . . but to meet the [other] with writing . . . to meet in time, not just from place to place but from writer to writer, mind to mind, friend to friend, from words to words" (*Birth-mark* 158).

In order to meet the other with writing, Howe is willing to venture from the safety of objectivity into the realm of the unknown, meeting her historical others on the terms and textual turf where she finds them: "Voices I am following lead me to the margins," writes Howe, "[i]n order to hear them I have returned by strange paths to a particular place at a particular time, a threshold at the austere reach of the book" (*Birth-mark* 2, 4). For Howe the margin is quite literally a textual margin as well as a conceptual space on the edges of the dominant culture, for it is in the marginalia, what is written in the blank spaces of a text, that she finds traces of the voices that have been exiled from the privileged, centralized content. According to Peter Quartermain, Howe "treads borders, boundaries, dividing lines, edges, invisible meeting points. Her language returns to such cusps again and again, for they mark extremities, turning points, limits, shifts, the nameless edge of mystery where transformations occur and where edge becomes center" (186). This kind of transformation seems to occur within Howe herself as well as in language. She allows herself to become infused with the other, so that she writes in "Thorow," as if addressing Thoreau, whose journals her poem is a reading of, "You are of me & I of you, I cannot tell / Where you leave off and I begin" (*Singularities* 58).

Not only does the historical other assume a subject rather than object position in Howe's writing, but so does her reader, who is invited to actively participate in the production of meaning. And this is what many of her readers find so pleasurable about her work. For instance, Bruce Andrews has commended Howe for not addressing her readers from the position of a "sovereign absent-one" in order to "guarantee a smoothed, anti-social address," by turning the reader into a consumer. Instead, Andrews finds "a multiplicity of social intersections" in Howe's writing (69). Howe is in dialogue with both the present reader and the past, so that, in Certeau's terms, "[a] hierarchy of knowledges is replaced by a mutual differentiation of subjects" (*Heterologies* 217). Howe's writing restores ambiguity between all the oppositions that serve to enforce the perceived opposition between the "textual" and "the real": subject and object, the actual and the imaginary, theory and practice, the past and the present. By taking this dialogic approach, Howe avoids the equally limited and limiting traps of both positivism and relativism. For neither does she claim to tell the whole story or history and to do it without bias, and nor does she allow that the "truth" of history is wholly arbitrary or detached from the social scenes of its (ongoing) construction.

My argument, as I have said, is that Susan Howe's poetic-historical project involves a deconstruction of the opposition textuality-reality on which most conventional historiography depends, and that, in turn, this deconstruction is a defining feature of the language-oriented feminist epistemology on which her project rests. Jerome McGann's insistence that "we must reconceive of the literary 'text' as the literary 'work,' i.e. as a related series of concretely determinable semiotic events that embody and represent processes of social and historical experience" offers a model of literary representation according to which such a deconstruction is not only possible, but inevitable (*BI* 10). McGann claims that while all literary texts are in this way performative rather than referential, it is in *poetic* texts that the incommensurability of the heuristic isolates, lived realities, differences, and changing truths that comprise social reality is most apparent. "The poetic work is a nexus of reciprocating expectations and intersections between the various persons engaged over and within the poetic event. Criticism, therefore, has to explain the way those communicative resources operate" (*SVPA* 85–86).[19] Howe's poetry itself reciprocates and intersects with McGann's ideas, and gives them a peculiar feminist twist in her poetic-critical writing: her poetry attempts the critical function of "reading" history and historical texts by performing the incommensurability of historical reality, a reality comprised of "competing human interests by which meaning is constituted" (McGann, *SVPA* 72).

What makes Howe's language-oriented epistemology, already so accurately theorized by McGann, also a *feminist* epistemology is that she highlights in much of her work the operations of gender in the constitution of meaning, and in the competing human interests that go into the making of the past. So, Howe's focus on the material, textual dimensions of history allows her to explore "how history operates as a site of the production of gender knowledge" (J. Scott 10). Such an analysis depends on a deconstruction of the textual-real binary opposition in all its guises, for it rests on the assumption that "experience only exists through its conceptual organization" (56). Susan Howe's poetic project is the best example I know of what Joan Scott, herself a historian, describes as "not simply a literary technique for reading but an epistemological theory that offers a method for analyzing the processes by which meanings are made, by which we make meanings. This theory is, moreover, profoundly political in its implications for it puts conflict at the center of its analysis, assuming that hierarchy and power are inherent in the linguistic processes being analyzed" (8–9). Instead of resolving conflicts by excluding the voices that disrupt the narratives of history, Howe puts conflict at the center of her analysis, letting it take place in poems that do not pretend to master the past. But at the same time, it is Howe's McGannian conception of the literary "work" as not merely a text but a constellation of social acts that enables her to perform this kind of language-oriented analysis while avoiding the danger Scott warns against, of conflating "language," "even when carefully defined, with 'words,' 'vocabulary,' and literal usage" (67). To Howe, the world of language and the world of the human are one, "For we are language Lost / in language" (*ET* 99). And language is the "Mortal particulars / whose shatter we are" (*Singularities* 50).

I like Andrew Schelling's choice of the term "ceremony" to describe Howe's language acts. A ceremony is an action that is performed, usually serving a social function. Similarly, in Howe's poems it is the gesture that language performs, not what it refers to, that makes language most meaningful. Howe puts language into action, drawing on the numinousness of language, its materiality, its social reality, to perform "Immediate Acts" of feminist recovery. And these are acts of love, "Love for the work's sake" (*NM* 23).

Notes

Preface

1. Although the writers who are the subject of this study are not necessarily "language poets" per se—though some are—they are all working out of this tradition, within the political and philosophical frame articulated by "language poetry." The particular writers I treat in this study fit less problematically into a broader category of language-oriented writers, a category that might include "language poets" as well as writers who do not consider themselves to be "language poets" and/or were not present for or involved in the early discussions, theorizing, and publishing activity of that group. I also categorize as language-oriented some writers who reject or critique some of the assumptions of "language poetry." The designation language-oriented writing simply strikes me as being more fluid, less definitive, less group-identified. I use it to refer to works that, as Charles Bernstein puts it in his afterword to "43 Poets (1984)," "in quite different ways, keep open the question of how meaning is constituted and take this question to have political, tonal, aesthetic, syntactic, grammatical, prosodic, sociological, physical, and biological consequences" (112).

The designation "writing" is also more inclusive than "poetry," and it indicates the extent to which language-oriented writers are challenging and crossing generic boundaries. While most of the writers I will discuss sometimes or often write in verse with line breaks, many also blur genres or write in other recognizable genres such as plays, dialogues, prose narratives. As a result, it is obviously problematic to refer unilaterally to these writers as poets and to their work as poetry. Indeed, Carla Harryman insists that she has never thought of herself as a poet because of her deep interest in narrative and prose forms, though she acknowledges that many of her readers are poets, and many of her concerns intersect with those of writers who do consider themselves to be poets ("An Interview" 514–15).

2. I do not mean to imply that language-oriented women writers have actively sought publication in these venues. On the contrary, many of these writers have chosen to publish only with small, alternative presses, intentionally disassociating themselves and their work from the mainstream literary trends and academic values of which language-oriented writing offers a critique.

3. In order to focus the scope of this project, I have had to omit many more language-oriented women writers than I am including. Writers whose work I particularly value but who are not highlighted in this study include Kathleen Fraser, Harryette Mullen, Rae Armantrout, Norma Cole, Tina Darragh, Jean Day, Diane Ward, Lynne Dreyer, Fanny Howe, Erica Hunt, Abigail Child, Susan Clark, Myung Mi Kim, Jena Osman, Johanna Drucker, Susan Gevirtz, Elaine Equi, Joan Retallack, and Colleen Lookingbill. I hope this study will generate interest in these, and the many other language-oriented women writers I have not named, as well.

Chapter 1

1. Dahlen, personal interview.

2. In addition, Rae Armantrout was a "founding" language writer, and Hejinian attributes her own entrance into the "language writing" scene in 1976 to an invitation from Armantrout to read in the Grand Piano series in San Francisco's Haight district.

3. While the ratio of women to men remained consistently at about one to three throughout the first four collections of "language poetry"—Charles Bernstein's "Language Sampler" collected for *The Paris Review* in 1982, his "43 Poets (1984)" in *Boundary 2*; Ron Silliman's *In the American Tree* (1986); and Douglas Messerli's 1987 anthology *"Language" Poetries*—this trend is finally broken in Dennis Barone and Peter Ganick's anthology *The Art of Practice* (1994). Fully half of the writers whose work is here collected are women. That only one-quarter of the 81 writers anthologized in Douglas Messerli's 1994 *From the Other Side of the Century: A New American Poetry 1960–1990* and only one-seventh of those in Eliot Weinberger's 1993 *American Poetry Since 1950: Innovators and Outsiders* are women should not be taken as an indication of a decline in numbers of women doing linguistically innovative writing. On the contrary, a majority of language-oriented women writers began to publish widely after 1985. Therefore, and to give the editors of these two volumes the benefit of the doubt, the emphasis in both collections on work published prior to 1985 could account for the fewer number of women in each. Yet enough innovative work by women was available by 1982 to induce at least one magazine, *How(ever)*, to devote its pages exclusively to innovative writing by women. Published in newsletter format, and running from 1982 to 1988, *How(ever)* enjoyed the editorship of a number of women writers, including Kathleen Fraser, Beverly Dahlen, and Susan Gevirtz.

4. By "workshop poetry" I mean the kind of verse Charles Altieri refers to as the "scenic style" and identifies as the dominant poetic mode of the late seventies. This poetry is marked by "unobtrusive" craft, "a sense of urgency and immediacy," and of "spontaneous personal sincerity" (10). The poetic values implied by this kind of verse tend to be promoted and privileged in American college and university creative writing courses. In their early theoretical writings, many "language poets" refer to the kind of writing they do not do, by way of contrast, as "workshop poetry."

5. Although I draw heavily on Joan Scott in distinguishing language-oriented feminist epistemology from feminist standpoint epistemology, she is but one of many feminist theorists who view language as constitutive of gender and power relations. Judith Butler's notion of the "performativity" of gender; Jane Flax's writings on gender, psychoanalysis, and knowledge; Donna Haraway's critique of Harding's "standpoints," to name a few, all partake of a postmodern engagement with language and knowledge that is flourishing among many feminist theorists.

6. Lyn Hejinian's books, in addition to those cited in this study, include *A Thought Is the Bride of What Thinking* (Tuumba, 1976), *A Mask of Motion* (Burning Deck, 1977), *Gesualdo* (Tuumba, 1978), *Writing Is an Aid to Memory* (The Figures, 1978), *The Guard* (Tuumba, 1984), *Redo* (Salt-Works, 1984), *Individuals* (with Kit Robinson/Chax, 1988), *Leningrad* (with Michael Davidson, Ron Silliman, and Barrett Watten/Mercury House, 1991), *The Hunt* (Zasterle, 1991), *Oxota: A Short Russian Novel* (The Figures, 1991), *Wicker* (with Jack Collom/Rodent, 1996), *The Little Book of a Thousand Eyes* (Smokeproof, 1996), and *Sight* (with Leslie Scalapino/Edge, 1999).

7. Hejinian's sense of the differences between metonymy and metaphor seem to partake of the "bolder" conception of metonymy described by Rene Wellek and Austin Warren in their *Theory of Literature*: "Recently some bolder conceptions of metonymy . . . have been suggested, even the notion that metonymy and metaphor may be the characterizing structures of two poetic types—poetry of association by contiguity, and poetry of association by comparison" (184–85). Paul de Man makes a similar distinction in "Semiology and Rhetoric," where he defines metaphor as "a paradigmatic structure based on substitution" and metonymy as "a syntagmatic structure based on contingent association" (229).

8. *Sleeps* is an earlier working title for the series of poems Hejinian refers to in "La Faustienne" as *The Book of a Thousand Eyes*.

Chapter 2

1. (Riding) Jackson, *PLR* 134.

2. Benstock's focus in this article on expatriate American women writers makes her comments especially relevant here, for three of the four American writers whose work I am considering in this chapter were born and spent their

childhoods in the eastern United States, but spent much of their adult lives abroad—Stein in Paris, H.D. in London, (Riding) Jackson for fourteen years in England and Mallorca, although she returned permanently to the United States in 1939. Mina Loy traced an opposite trajectory: born and raised in London, she spent some years in Florence during and after her first marriage, and first came to New York in 1916, where she lived off-and-on for the next three decades. Loy became a naturalized U.S. citizen in 1946, and spent the last years of her life with her daughters in Aspen, Colorado.

3. (Riding) Jackson's view is in some ways consistent with those of contemporary feminist "standpoint" epistemologists who similarly argue that women are able to perceive social inequality more accurately than men. But for standpoint epistemologists, this difference in perspective is traceable to the marginalized positions that women have been socially forced to occupy—including those in the domestic realm. For (Riding) Jackson, women's domesticity is a function not of patriarchal oppression so much as their natural inclinations and abilities. For a comprehensive overview of feminist standpoint epistemology, see the articles by Sandra Harding and Nancy Hartsock in Harding and Hintekka, eds., *Discovering Reality: Feminist Perspectives on Epistemology, Metaphysics, Methodology, and Philosophy of Science.*

4. For an extended analysis of this very question, see Susan Schultz's essay "Laura Riding's Essentialism and the Absent Muse."

5. Michael J. Hoffman's *The Development of Abstractionism in the Writings of Gertrude Stein* (1965) offers a careful and still-useful assessment of Stein's use of language as matter in the context of various major intellectual and aesthetic trends of her time.

6. For two different interpretations of sexual content in Stein's writing, see Lisa Ruddick's essay "A Rosy Charm: Gertrude Stein and the Repressed Feminine" and Catherine Stimpson's articles "Gertrude/Altrude: Stein, Toklas, and the Paradox of the Happy Marriage" and "Gertrude Stein and the Transposition of Gender," in both of which Stimpson takes normative cultural constructions of gender and sexuality into account as she traces connections between Stein's representations of gender and sexuality in her writing and biographical details of her relationship with Toklas.

7. Paula Bennett convincingly substantiates her claim by offering a myriad of examples from poetry written by nineteenth-century American women in her article "Critical Clitoridectomy: Female Sexual Imagery and Feminist Psychoanalytic Theory."

8. The most influential and thorough theoretical consideration of the sentence from a language writer's point of view is Ron Silliman's *The New Sentence*.

9. Loy 150.

10. Loy studied art in London, Munich, and Paris and throughout her early twenties, from 1903–1907, she showed her paintings in Paris at the Salon d'Automne (Burke, Introduction 230). After coming to the United States in

1916, she continued to paint, as well as sculpt, design clothing, and make lamp shades.

11. Loy's perception of the role that binary thinking plays in gender hierarchy not only predates Jacques Derrida's critique of Western metaphysics by some 30 years, but also anticipates contemporary feminist deconstruction such as that theorized by Barbara Johnson in her book *A World of Difference*.

12. An important distinction between Kristeva's and Loy's theories of female subjectivity (besides the 60 years that separate the articulations of their ideas) may lie in their attitudes toward the fragmentation of subjectivity they describe. While Loy's hope that new linguistic forms will lead to new (supposedly less constricted) forms of consciousness is consistent with Kristeva's belief in the political viability of avant-garde writing that celebrates poetic language and subjectivity in process, Loy seems more conflicted over the issue than Kristeva. Even Carolyn Burke acknowledges this when she writes, "Now it seems to me that Loy's poetry was written at least as much from her trouble over the issue of subjectivity as from a quest for identity or a stable position of female selfhood" ("Supposed" 132).

13. With the publication in 1996 of a new biography by Carolyn Burke and Roger L. Conover's new edition of her selected poems (which serves as my source in this study), Loy seems to be enjoying a bit of a renaissance. Burke offers a possible explanation for this delayed recognition: "She has been neglected because she paid no heed to the requirement for consistent self-presentation in an age that, increasingly, valued professionalism and its external sign, the career. [Loy was an actor, painter, poet, lampshade designer . . .]. It may be that in her multiplicity, Mina speaks to us now, in the era of the postmodern, *because* she followed no one path and did not present a unified body of work" (*Becoming Modern* viii).

14. H.D. was bisexual, and had several significant relationships with lovers of both genders throughout her life. With Winifred Bryher, who called herself simply Bryher, H.D. enjoyed a particularly deep and lasting alliance. The two women traveled and lived together for many years. For a history of this relationship, see Gillian Hanscombe and Virginia L. Smyers, *Writing for their Lives: The Modernist Women 1910–1940*.

15. These are the terms in which H.D. praised John Gould Fletcher's *Goblins and Pagodas* in her review of that work.

16. This interest is perhaps traceable to H.D.'s own upbringing in a family that practiced Moravianism, a Christian doctrine that emphasizes the mystical or supernatural quality of faith and salvation. For critical assessments that focus on mysticism in H.D.'s writing, see Adalaide Morris, "The Concept of Projection: H.D.'s Visionary Powers"; Robert Duncan's *H.D. Book*; and Joseph Riddel, "H.D. and the Poetics of Spiritual Mysticism."

17. This is a term Duncan uses throughout his *H.D. Book*.

18. As recent sources cited throughout this chapter indicate, this does seem to be changing finally.

Chapter 3

1. Beverly Dahlen's books, in addition to those cited in this study, include *Out of the Third* (Momo's, 1974), *A Letter at Easter: To George Stanley* (Effie's, 1976), and *The Egyptian Poems* (Hipparchia, 1983).

2. Though I do not know what Freud himself thought about how or when the process of free association in psychoanalysis might end, Dahlen takes as her epigraph for *A Reading 1–7* George Steiner's observation that, as Wittgenstein had earlier proposed, Freud's method must necessarily be without end. Therefore, Steiner suggests, "An exercise in 'total reading' is also potentially unending" (*AR 1–7* 11).

3. Dahlen is quoting Freud, in a line she repeats more than once in *A Reading*.

4. Here I rely on Foucault's claim that "[e]ach society has a regime of truth, its 'general politics' of truth . . . the types of discourse which it accepts and makes function as true" ("Truth and Power" 1144).

5. Lori Lubeski's books, in addition to those cited in this study, include *Trickle* (Boron, 1997).

6. Laura Moriarty's books, in addition to those cited in this study, include *Two Cross Seizings* (Sombre Reptiles, 1980), *Persia* (Chance Additions, 1983), *Duse* (Coincidence, 1986), *like roads* (Kelsey St., 1990), *The Case* (O Books, 1999), and two books still forthcoming at the time of this writing: *Spicer's City* (Poetry New York), and *Cunning* (Spuyten Duyvil).

Chapter 4

1. The kind of tolerant pluralism Inde is here describing is characteristic not only of various Western postmodern and feminist worldviews, but also of older, Eastern perspectives such as Buddhism, by which both Scalapino and Berssenbrugge have been influenced as well.

2. Leslie Scalapino's books, in addition to those cited in this study, include *This Eating and Walking at the Same Time Is Associated All Right* (Tombouctou, 1979), *Objects in the Terrifying Tense/Longing from Taking Place* (Roof, 1993), *Defoe* (Sun & Moon, 1994), *Goya's L.A.* (Potes & Poets, 1994), *The Line* (Meow, 1994), *The Weatherman Turns Himself In* (Zasterle, 1995), *The Front Matter, Dead Souls* (Wesleyan/New England, 1996), *Green and Black: Selected Writings* (Talisman, 1996), and, with Lyn Hejinian, *Sight* (Edge, 1999).

3. Mei-mei Berssenbrugge's books, in addition to those cited in this study, include *The Heat Bird* (Burning Deck, 1983), *Summits Move with the Tide* (Greenfield, 1982), *Endocrinology* (Kelsey St., 1997), and *Four Year Old Girl* (Kelsey St., 1998).

4. With each of her books, Berssenbrugge's poetic lines seem to get longer and longer, often pushing at the physical boundaries of the printed page and

book. The two books I discuss in this chapter, *Empathy* and *Sphericity*, are 8 1/2 inches square, allowing more space on each page from left-to-right than conventional book sizes or shapes.

5. *Sphericity* is dedicated to Berssenbrugge's daughter as well as to her mother—also named Martha—who had recently died. The "sphere" to which the title refers, then, is the birth-death continuum. The pregnant body might be conceived of as a sphere emblematic of this greater sphere.

6. Carla Harryman's books, in addition to those cited in this study, include *Percentage* (Tuumba, 1982), *Under the Bridge* (This, 1980), *Property* (Tuumba, 1982), *The Middle* (Gaz, 1983), *In the Mode Of* (Zasterle, 1991), and *Memory Play* (O Books, 1994).

7. Here I am relying on Erving Goffman's definition of "primary frameworks" in terms of which individuals perceive and understand events. In *Frame Analysis*, Goffman explains that these frameworks are culturally defined: "Taken all together, the primary frameworks of a particular social group constitute a central element of its culture, especially insofar as understandings emerge concerning principal classes of schemata, the relations of these classes to one another, and the sum total of forces and agents that these interpretive designs acknowledge to be loose in the world" (27). Significant to my discussion of Harryman's poetics are the related facts that these frames are therefore discursively constructed and serve a normative function: "In sum, observers actively project their frames of reference into the world immediately around them, and one fails to see their so doing only because events ordinarily confirm these projections, causing the assumptions to disappear into the smooth flow of activity" (39).

8. Although many of Harryman's plays have been produced in live performances, these are not necessarily more complete or actualized than the written form—they might, in fact, be seen to emphasize the extent to which the writing *is* the performance.

9. The Aunt Mildred passage is taken verbatim from Nigel Demis's novel *Cards of Identity*.

10. This idea grows out of Harryman's own experience as a parent as well as discussions she had with her husband about Jessica Benjamin's book, *The Bonds of Love*, much of which, Harryman explains, "has to do with the relationship of the mother to the child and acknowledging it" ("An Interview" 520).

Chapter 5

1. Howe, *Singularities* 23.

2. Susan Howe's books, in addition to those cited in this study, include *Hinge Picture* (Telephone, 1974), *Chanting at the Crystal Sea* (Fire Exit, 1975), *The Western Borders* (Tuumba, 1976), *Secret History of the Dividing Line* (Telephone, 1978), *Cabbage Gardens* (Fathom, 1979), *Pythagorean Silence* (Montemora, 1982), *De-*

fenestration of Prague (Kulchur, 1983), *Articulation of Sound Forms in Time* (Awede, 1989), and *A Bibliography of the King's Book or, Eikon Basilike* (Paradigm, 1989).

3. By presenting Howe's sense of the past in the context of poststructuralist and feminist theory, I do not mean to imply that she is familiar with all of the theorists I cite in this chapter or that she has developed her poetics of history according to their ideas. As the notes to many of Howe's scholarly writings attest, she has read Foucault as well as other French theorists such as Hélène Cixous and Julia Kristeva. Walter Benjamin is of great interest to Howe, as I discuss later in this chapter. But Susan Howe began writing poetry before she began reading theory, and the theorists she has since discovered to be most useful to her are those who, as Lynn Keller phrases it in her recent interview with Howe, "have provided a kind of space for" the work Howe herself was already undertaking ("An Interview" by Keller 29).

4. In *The Critical Difference: Essays in the Contemporary Rhetoric of Reading,* deconstructionist Barbara Johnson argues that all such binary oppositions, including the opposition man-woman, are inherently hierarchical. Relevant to my reading of Howe's poetry is Johnson's view that one term in a binary opposition is always privileged, but that this apparent primacy of one term depends on "a binary difference that is . . . an illusion. . . . The differences between entities . . . are shown to be based on a representation of differences within entities, ways in which an entity differs from itself" (xi).

5. McGann claims that "from the point of view of science and philosophy, truth may be measured in one of two ways." He goes on to quote Hilary Putnam in defining these ways as the correspondence theory of truth, according to which "truth involves some sort of correspondence relation between words or thought-signs and external things"; and the coherence theory of truth, according to which truth "is some sort of ideal coherence of our beliefs with each other and with our experiences . . . and not correspondence with mind-independent or discourse-independent 'states of affairs.'" McGann finds that both theories "equally posit an ideal of part-to-whole orderliness" (*Towards* 5–6).

6. For a variety of such theories, see Simone de Beauvoir's *The Second Sex,* Margaret Homans' *Women Writers and Poetic Identity,* Trinh T. Minh-ha's *When the Moon Waxes Red,* and Gayatri Chakrovorty Spivak's *In Other Worlds: Essays in Cultural Politics.*

7. Joan Scott takes as her starting point Foucault's idea that gender is produced in discourse and that discourses on sexuality, in turn, sustain power relations according to which gender hierarchies are created and legitimized. In *The History of Sexuality,* Foucault claims that "[w]hat is at issue," in determining the relationship between power and sexuality, ". . . is the overall 'discursive fact,' the way in which sex is 'put into discourse'" (11). Scott agrees, arguing that "gender is a primary field within which or by means of which power is articulated" and not an essential, biological category (95). Therefore she believes that "we cannot write women into history . . . unless we are willing to entertain the notion that history as a unified story was a fiction about a

universal subject whose universality was achieved through implicit processes of differentiation, marginalization, and exclusion" (197). It seems to me that Susan Howe is more than willing to entertain this notion in her poetry that seeks to undo these exclusions.

8. Byrd's public account of this same expedition bears the title *The History of the Dividing Line betwixt Virginia and North Carolina. The Heath Anthology of American Literature* describes the differences between Byrd's public and private accounts: "instead of depicting public events, *The Secret History* narrates the private exploits of the surveyors. While the public history offers 'an account of the good' the team did, this history offers what one 'smart lass' they meet suggests be told as well, 'an account of the evil'" (Lauter 541).

9. As Howe is very aware, The Gospel According to St. John is both of unknown authorship and not the work of any one author. An untraceable history of revisions, additions, deletions, and variants comprise the text. Each modification took place in a particular circumstance of power relations, so, in keeping with Foucault's idea that regimes of truth do not exist a priori or independently of the social discourses in which they operate, no single or fixed regime of truth can be identified as having more or less control than any other such regime over Mary's presence (or lack thereof) in the Gospel.

10. Foucault rejects the idea that "at the root of what we know and what we are" lies some deep, essential meaning such as "truth or being," believing this to be a normalizing notion that supports oppressive thought systems (such as the notion that gender differences are essential, natural, fixed) and allows "regimes of truth" to enforce their laws in discourse ("Nietzsche" 81). In contrast, Foucault claims that "What is found at the historical beginning of things is not the inviolable identity of their origin; it is the dissension of other things. It is disparity" ("Nietzsche" 79). Foucault therefore encourages historians to forego the search for origins and instead practice "genealogy."

11. Hayden White's analysis of the operations and effects of narrative in historical representation is helpful here. White claims that narrative serves a legitimizing, moralizing function by imposing an order and coherence on events that we associate with "truth." Narrative closure, in particular, serves this moralizing impulse: "The value attached to narrativity in the representation of real events arises out of a desire to have real events display the coherence, integrity, fullness, and closure of an image of life that is and can only be imaginary" (*The Content of the Form* 24). In *Metahistory: The Historical Imagination in Nineteenth-Century Europe*, White explains that "Providing the 'meaning' of a story by identifying the *kind of story* that has been told is called explanation by emplotment. . . . Emplotment is the way by which a sequence of events fashioned into a story is gradually revealed to be a story of a particular kind" (7). White relies on Northrop Frye's *Anatomy of Criticism* in his identification of four major modes of emplotment: Romance, Tragedy, Comedy, and Satire. For White, the most significant problem with emplotting historical events into familiar narrative forms is not that history is thereby somehow falsified—for he believes that historical

reality is always already figurative—but rather, that in the process of making historical events understandable, narrative dispels the "very strangeness of the original" events it recounts, what he calls "the dynamic and disruptive forces in contemporary life" (*Tropics of Discourse* 50, 88).

12. In his introduction to *American Poetry of the Seventeenth Century*, Harrison T. Meserole explains that "Whatever their genealogy (there was some conjecture that the Indians might have been descendants of one of the biblical Lost Tribes), the Indians assumed diabolical dimensions during the brutal King Philip's War of 1675–76. Their image in verse was then 'Scare-crows clad with oaken leaves . . . Like *Vulcans* anvilling *New Englands brains*'" [sic] (xx). According to Cecelia Tichi, the Indians were often "regarded as a going indication of God's disposition toward the tribe whose mettle was being tested" in Puritan historiography (63).

13. Stella Johnson lived most of her life in Ireland near Swift, and Susan Howe's mother was born in Ireland. Howe herself has spent a great deal of time there and considers her Irish heritage to be an important component of her identity.

14. McGann takes as the starting point for his "recovered" concept of referentiality the method of an historian, Milman Parry. Parry chose to represent the past as "a picture of great detail." But McGann faults Parry's representations with falling short of accurately representing the truth of the past because "when he actually made the picture for his audience, the layers and intervenient distances tended to disappear." Susan Howe is not guilty of "this blurring of the palimpsest" ("Introduction" 11).

15. Here I rely on Foucault's theory that the operations of power are most apparent on the level of the local, minute, particular—especially the body. For an excellent explication of Foucault's analysis of the "microphysics" of power, see Lois McNay's *Foucault: A Critical Introduction*.

16. Here Howe is quoting loosely from Arendt's introduction to Benjamin's *Illuminations* (11).

17. In "The Honeyed Knot of Puritan Aesthetics," Michael Clark explains how the scripturalism of the Reformation " led the Puritans to value language—especially but not only that of the Bible—as a significant domain in itself independent of the supplementary, interpretive connection to the world that Calvin described" (71).

18. For Howe's comments on the visual dimension of her poetry, see Lynn Keller's "An Interview with Susan Howe" and Janet Falon's interview, "Speaking with Susan Howe."

19. How McGann distinguishes, then, between poetic texts and texts in general is not entirely clear. As elucidating of Howe's poetics as I find McGann's theory, I do share Michael Fischer's uneasiness with what he calls in his review of *Social Values and Poetic Acts* "McGann's essentialist talk of 'the poetic' . . ." in which "'poetry' or 'poetic discourse' seems static, defined (by McGann) once and for all" (36–37).

Works Cited

Alcoff, Linda, and Elizabeth Potter, eds. *Feminist Epistemologies*. New York: Routledge, 1993.

Allen, Jeffner. "Poetic Politics: How the Amazons Took the Acropolis." *Sexual Practice/ Textual Theory: Lesbian Cultural Criticism*. Ed. Susan J. Wolfe and Julia Penelope. Cambridge, UK: Blackwell, 1993. 307–21.

Altieri, Charles. *Self and Sensibility in Contemporary American Poetry*. New York: Cambridge UP, 1984.

Althusser, Louis. "from *Ideology and Ideological State Apparatuses*." *Critical Theory Since 1965*. Ed. Hazard Adams and Leroy Searle. Tallahassee: Florida State UP, 1986. 239–50.

———. "Ideology and Ideological State Apparatuses (Notes Towards an Investigation)." *"Lenin and Philosophy" and Other Essays*. Trans. Ben Brewster. London: NLB, 1971. 121–73.

Andrews, Bruce. "Suture—& Absence of the Social." *The Difficulties* 3.2 (1989): 67–70.

Arendt, Hannah. Introduction. *Illuminations*. By Walter Benjamin. Harcourt, 1968. 1–55.

Armantrout, Rae. "Feminist Poetics and the Meaning of Clarity." *Sagetrieb* 11.3 (Winter 1992): 7–16.

Barone, Dennis, and Peter Ganick, eds. *The Art of Practice: Forty-Five Contemporary Poets*. Elmwood, CT: Potes & Poets, 1994.

de Beauvoir, Simone. *The Second Sex*. Ed. and Trans. H. M. Parshley. New York: Knopf, 1952.

Benjamin, Jessica. *The Bonds of Love: Psychoanalysis, Feminism, and the Problem of Domination*. NY: Pantheon, 1988.

Benjamin, Walter. *Illuminations*. Ed. Hannah Arendt. Trans. Harry Zohn. Harcourt, 1968.

Bennett, Paula. "Critical Clitoridectomy: Female Sexual Imagery and Feminist Psychoanalytic Theory." *Signs* 18.2 (Winter 1993): 235–59.

Benstock, Shari. "Beyond the Reaches of Feminist Criticism: A Letter from Paris." Benstock, *Feminist Issues* 7–29.

———, ed. *Feminist Issues in Literary Scholarship*. Bloomington: Indiana UP, 1987.

———. *Women of the Left Bank: Paris, 1900–1940*. Austin: U of Texas Press, 1986.

Bernstein, Charles. Afterword. "43 Poets (1984)." *Boundary 2* (1986): 12.

———. "Language Sampler." *The Paris Review* 86 (Winter 1982): N. pag.

Berssenbrugge, Mei-mei. *Empathy*. New York: Station Hill, 1989.

———. Interview. By Judi Lynn Judy. 26 March and 15 May 1992.

———. "Interview with Mei-mei Berssenbrugge." By Laura Moriarty. *The American Poetry Archive News*. 5.1 (Spring 1988): 1–2, 6–7.

———. *Sphericity*. Berkeley: Kelsey St., 1993.

Bowers, Jane Palatini. *Gertrude Stein*. New York: St. Martin's, 1993.

Burke, Carolyn. *Becoming Modern: The Life of Mina Loy*. NY: Farrar, 1996.

———. Introduction to Mina Loy in Scott, B., *Gender* 230–238.

———. "Mina Loy's 'Love Songs' and the Limits of Imagism." *San Jose Studies* 13.3 (Fall 1987): 37–46.

———. "The New Poetry and the New Woman: Mina Loy." *Coming to Light: American Women Poets in the Twentieth Century*. Ed. Diane Wood Middlebrook and Marilyn Yalom. Ann Arbor: U of Michigan P, 1985. 37–57.

———. "Supposed Persons: Modernist Poetry and the Female Subject." *Feminist Studies* 11.1 (Spring 1985): 131–48.

———. "Without Commas: Gertrude Stein and Mina Loy." *Poetics Journal* 4 (May 1984): 43–52.

Butler, Judith. *Gender Trouble: Feminism and the Subversion of Identity*. New York: Routledge, 1990.

Butterick, George F. "The Mysterious Vision of Susan Howe." *North Dakota Quarterly* 55.4 (Fall 1987): 312–21.

Camboni, Marina. "H.D.'s *Trilogy*, or the Secret Language of Change." *Letteratura d'America* 6.27 (Spring 1985): 87–106.

Campbell, Bruce. "H.D.'s 'Hermetic Definitions' and the Order of Writing." *American Poetry* 5.3 (Spring 1988): 24–31.

———. "Neither In Nor Out: The Poetry of Leslie Scalapino." *Talisman* 8 (Spring 1992): 53–60.

de Certeau, Michel. *Heterologies: Discourse on the Other*. Trans. Brian Massumi. Theory and Hist. of Lit., Vol. 17. Minneapolis: U of Minnesota P, 1986.

———. *The Writing of History*. Trans. Tom Conley. New York: Columbia UP, 1988.

Chessman, Harriet Scott. *The Public Is Invited to Dance: Representation, the Body, and Dialogue in Gertrude Stein*. Stanford: Stanford UP, 1989.

Clark, Michael. "The Honeyed Knot of Puritan Aesthetics." *Puritan Poets and Poetics: Seventeenth-Century American Poetry in Theory and Practice*. Ed. Peter White. University Park, PA: Pennsylvania State UP, 1985. 67–83.

Code, Lorraine. "Taking Subjectivity into Account." Alcoff and Potter 15–48.

Dahlen, Beverly. *A Reading 1–7*. San Francisco: Momo's, 1985.

———. *A Reading 8–10*. Tucson: Chax, 1992.

———. *A Reading: 11–17*. Elmwood, CT: Potes & Poets, 1989.

———. "A Reading: A Reading." *Poetry/Talks*. Ed. Bob Perelman. Carbondale: Southern Illinois UP, 1985. 113–34.

———. "Forbidden Knowledge." *Poetics Journal* 4 (May 1984): 3–19.

———. "Homonymous: A Meditation on H.D.'s *Trilogy*." *Sagetrieb* 6.2 (Fall 1987): 9–13.

———. Personal interview. 17 June 1994.

———. "Something/Nothing." *Ironwood* 27 (Spring 1986): 170–75.

DeKoven, Marianne. *A Different Language: Gertrude Stein's Experimental Writing*. Madison: U of Wisconsin P, 1983.

Dembo, L. S. *Conceptions of Reality in Modern American Poetry*. Berkeley: U of California P, 1966.

Diamond, Irene, and Lee Quinby. Introduction. *Feminism and Foucault: Reflections on Resistance*. Ed. Diamond and Quinby. Boston: Northeastern UP, 1988. ix–xix.

H.D. *Bid Me to Live*. New York: Dial, 1960.

———. *Helen in Egypt*. Intro. Horace Gregory. New York: Grove, 1961.

———. *Hermetic Definitions*. West Newberry, MA: Frontier, 1971.

———. *Notes on Thought and Vision & The Wise Sappho*. San Francisco: City Lights, 1982.

———. *Palimpsest*. Carbondale and Edwardsville: Southern Illinois UP, 1968.

———. *Tribute to Freud*. Fore. Norman Holmes Pearson. Intro. Kenneth Fields. Boston: Godine, 1974.

———. *Collected Poems 1912–1944*. Ed. Louis L. Martz. New York: New Directions, 1983.

———. Rev. of *Goblins and Pagodas* by John Gould Fletcher. *Egoist* 3 (1916): 183.

Drucker, Johanna. "Women & Language." *Poetics Journal* 4 (May 1982): 56–68.

Dubnick, Randa. *The Structure of Obscurity: Gertrude Stein, Language, and Cubism*. Urbana: U of Illinois P, 1984.

Duncan, Robert. "H.D. Book: Book II, Chapter 6." *The Southern Review*. 21.2 (Winter 1985): 26–48.

DuPlessis, Rachel Blau. *H.D.: The Career of that Struggle*. Sussex, Great Britain: Harvester, 1986.

———. *The Pink Guitar: Writing as Feminist Practice*. New York: Routledge, 1990. 110– 22.

Dworkin, Craig Douglas. "Penelope Reworking the Twill: Patchwork, Writing, and Lyn Hejinian's *My Life*." *Contemporary Literature* 36.1 (Spring 1995): 58–81.

Ellis, Stephen. "Lock-Step Chaos: Leslie Scalapino's Multiples of Time." *Talisman* 8 (Spring 1992): 63–66.

Empson, William. *Seven Types of Ambiguity*. 3rd ed. Norfolk, CT: New Directions, 1968.

Fischer, Michael. Rev. of *Social Values and Poetic Acts*, by Jerome J. McGann. *Blake: An Illustrated Quarterly* (Summer 1989): 32–39.

Foucault, Michel. "The Discourse on Language." *The Archaeology of Knowledge and The Discourse on Language*. Trans. A. M. Sheridan Smith. New York: Pantheon, 1972. 215–37.

———. *The History of Sexuality, Vol. I: An Introduction*. Trans. Robert Hurley. New York: Pantheon, 1978.

———. "Nietzsche, Genealogy, History." *The Foucault Reader*. Ed. Paul Rabinow. New York: Pantheon, 1984. 76–100.

———. "Truth and Power." *Critical Theory Since Plato*. Ed. Hazard Adams. New York: Harcourt, 1992: 1135–45.

Fredman, Stephen. *Poet's Prose: The Crisis in American Verse*. Cambridge: Cambridge UP, 1983.

Friedlander, Ben. "Laura Riding/Some Difficulties." *Poetics Journal* 4 (May 1984): 35–42.

Friedman, Susan Stanford. "Creating a Women's Mythology: H.D's *Helen in Egypt*." Friedman and DuPlessis 373–405.

———. "Modernism of the 'Scattered Remnant': Race and Politics in the Development of H.D.'s Modernist Vision." *H.D.: Woman and Poet*. Ed. Michael King. Orono, Maine: National Poetry Foundation, 1986. 91–116.

Friedman, Susan Stanford, and Rachel Blau DuPlessis, eds. *Signets: Reading H.D.* Madison: U of Wisconsin P, 1990.

Frost, Elisabeth. "Breaking the Rules." Rev. of *Trimmings* by Haryette Mullen and *Crowd and not evening or light* by Leslie Scalapino. *The Women's Review of Books* 10.5 (February 1993): 11–12.

Goffman, Erving. *Frame Analysis*. Cambridge: Harvard UP, 1974.

Gray, Nancy. *Language Unbound: On Experimental Writing by Women*. Urbana: U of Illinois P, 1992.

Grosz, Elizabeth. *Volatile Bodies: Toward a Corporeal Feminism*. Bloomington: Indiana UP, 1994.

Gubar, Susan. "The Echoing Spell of H.D.'s *Trilogy*." Friedman and DuPlessis 297–317.

Hall, Catherine. *White, Male and Middle Class: Explorations in Feminism and History*. New York: Routledge, 1992.

Hanscombe, Gillian and Virginia L. Smyers. *Writing for their Lives: The Modernist Women 1910–1940*. London: Women's, 1987.

Haraway, Donna. "A Manifesto for Cyborgs: Science, Technology, and Socialist Feminism in the 1980s." *Feminism/Postmodernism*. Ed. Linda J. Nicholson. New York: Routledge, 1990. 190–233.

Harding, Sandra. "Rethinking Standpoint Epistemology: What Is 'Strong Objectivity'?" Harding and Hintikka, *Discovering Reality* 49–82.

Harding, Sandra, and Merrill B. Hintikka, eds. *Discovering Reality: Feminist Perspectives on Epistemology, Metaphysics, Methodology, and Philosophy of Science.* Boston: Reidel, 1983.

———. Introduction. Harding and Hintikka, *Discovering Reality* ix–xix.

Harryman, Carla. *Animal Instincts.* Oakland: This, 1989.

———. Interview. *A Suite of Poetic Voices: Interviews with Contemporary American Poets.* By Manuel Brito. Santa Brigida, Canary Islands: Kadle, 1992. 60–70.

———. "An Interview with Carla Harryman." By Megan Simpson. *Contemporary Literature* 37.4 (1996): 511–32.

———. *There Never Was a Rose without a Thorn.* San Francisco: City Lights, 1995.

———. *Vice.* Elmwood, CT: Potes & Poets, 1986.

——— and Lyn Hejinian. "A Comment on the Wide Road for O." *O* 4 (1993): 83–91.

——— and Lyn Hejinian. "from *The Wide Road.*" *Avec* 4 (1991): 26–30.

Hartley, George. *Textual Politics and the Language Poets.* Bloomington: Indiana UP, 1989.

Hartsock, Nancy C. M. "The Feminist Standpoint: Developing the Ground for a Specifically Feminist Historical Materialism." Harding and Hintikka, *Discovering Reality* 283–310.

Heidegger, Martin. *An Introduction to Metaphysics.* Trans. Ralph Manheim. New Haven, CT: Yale UP, 1959.

Hejinian, Lyn. "Barbarism." Unpublished essay.

———. *The Cell.* Los Angeles: Sun & Moon, 1992.

———. *The Cold of Poetry.* Los Angeles: Sun & Moon, 1994.

———. "La Faustienne." *Poetics Journal* 10 (July 1998): 10–29.

———. "Language and Realism." *Temblor* 3 (1986): 128–33.

———. Letter to the author. 22 January 1995.

———. Letter to the author. 25 January 1995.

———. Letter to the author. 4–5 August 1995.

———. *My Life.* Rev. ed. Los Angeles: Sun & Moon, 1987.

———. "The Person and Description." *Poetics Journal* 9 (June 1991): 166–70.

———. "The Poet and the World of Her Influences: Lyn Hejinian, Susan Howe, Myung Mi Kim." Talk. Mills College. Oakland, October 11, 1993.

———. "The Rejection of Closure." *Poetry/Talks.* Ed. Bob Perelman. Carbondale: Southern Illinois UP, 1985. 270–91.

———. "from *Sleeps.*" *Black Bread* 3 (1993): 37–44.

———. "Strangeness." *Poetics Journal* 8 (June 1989): 32–45.

Hoffman, Michael J. *The Development of Abstractionism in the Writings of Gertrude Stein.* Philadelphia: U of Pennsylvania P, 1965.

Homans, Margaret. *Women Writers and Poetic Identity.* Princeton, NJ: Princeton UP, 1980.

Howe, Susan. *The Birth-mark: unsettling the wilderness in American literary history.* Hanover: Wesleyan UP and UP of New England, 1993.

———. "*The Difficulties* Interview." By Tom Beckett. *The Difficulties* 3.2 (1989): 17–27.

————. *The Europe of Trusts*. Los Angeles: Sun & Moon, 1990.

————. "An Interview with Susan Howe." By Lynn Keller. *Contemporary Litera-ture* 36.1 (Spring 1995): 1–34.

————. *My Emily Dickinson*. Berkeley: North Atlantic, 1985.

————. *Frame Structures: Early Poems 1974–1979*. New York: New Directions, 1996.

————. *The Nonconformist's Memorial*. New York: New Directions, 1993.

————. "The Poet and the World of Her Influences: Lyn Hejinian, Susan Howe, Myung Mi Kim." Talk. Mills College. Oakland, October 11, 1993.

————. "Poetics Statement." *Poetic Statements for the New Poetics Colloquium, Au-gust 21–25*. Vancouver: Kootenay School of Writing, 1985. 12–15.

————. *Singularities*. Hanover, NH: Wesleyan UP and UP of New England, 1990.

————. "Speaking with Susan Howe." By Janet Ruth Falon. *The Difficulties* 3.2 (1989): 28–42.

Inde, Don. *Postphenomenology: Essays in the Postmodern Context*. Evanston, IL: Northwestern UP, 1993.

Jackson, Laura (Riding). "Engaging in the Impossible." *Sulfur* 10 (1984): 4–35.

————. "An Enquiry" *New Verse* (October 1934). 3–5.

————. *The Poems of Laura Riding*. New York: Persea, 1980.

————. "The Road to, in, and away from Poetry." *Chelsea* 35 (1976).

————. *The Telling*. New York: Harper, 1972.

————. *The Word "Woman" and Other Related Writings*. Ed. Elizabeth Friedmann and Alan J. Clark. New York: Persea, 1993.

————. "The Word-Play of Gertrude Stein." *Critical Essays on Gertrude Stein*. Ed. Michael J. Hoffman. Boston: Hall, 1986. 240–60.

———— and Christopher C. Norris. "An Exchange" *Language and Style* 19.2 (Spring 1986): 196–216.

———— and Graves, Robert. *A Survey of Modernist Poetry*. London: Heinemann, 1927.

Jarraway, David. R. "*My Life* through the Eighties: The Exemplary L=A=N=G=U=A=G=E of Lyn Hejinian." *Contemporary Literature* 33.2 (Summer 1992): 319–36.

Johnson, Barbara. *The Critical Difference: Essays in the Contemporary Rhetoric of Reading*. Baltimore: Johns Hopkins UP, 1980.

————. *A World of Difference*. Baltimore: Johns Hopkins UP, 1987.

Keller, Lynn. *Forms of Expansion: Recent Long Poems by Women*. Chicago: U Chicago P, 1997.

Kockelmans, Joseph J., ed. *Phenomenology: The Philosophy of Edmund Husserl and Its Interpretation*. Garden City, NY: Doubleday, 1967.

————. "Some Fundamental Themes of Husserl's Phenomenology." Kockel-mans, *Phenomenology* 24–36.

Koudis, Virginia M. *Mina Loy: American Modernist Poet*. Baton Rouge: Louisiana State UP, 1980.

Kristeva, Julia. *Desire in Language: A Semiotic Approach to Literature and Art*. Ed. Leon Roudiez. Trans. Thomas Gora, Alice Jardine, and Leon Roudiez. New York: Columbia UP, 1980.

Larsen, Jeanne. "Myth & Glyph in *Helen in Egypt.*" *San Jose Studies* 23.3 (Fall 1987): 88–101.

Lauter, Paul, ed. *The Heath Anthology of American Literature.* 2nd ed. Vol. 1. Lexington, MA: Heath, 1994.

Loy, Mina. *The Lost Lunar Baedeker: Poems of Mina Loy.* Ed. Roger L. Conover. NY: Noonday–Farrar, 1996.

Lubeski, Lori. *attractions cf distractions.* San Francisco: e.g., 1985. N. pag.

———. *Dissuasion Crowds the Slow Worker.* Oakland: O, 1988. N. pag.

———. *Flail.* Unpublished MSS.

———. "from *Shady Lane.*" *Chain* 2 (Spring 1995): 142–44.

———. "from *You Torture Me.*" *Abacus* 83 (July 1, 1994): 1–19.

———. *Obedient, A body. lift* 13 (September 1993): 25–48.

———. Personal interview. 6 August 1994.

———. *Stamina.* Buffalo, New York: Leave, 1994. N. pag.

———. *Sweet Land.* N.p.: Boron, n.d.

de Man, Paul. "Semiology and Rhetoric." *Critical Theory Since 1965.* Ed. Hazard Adams and Leroy Searle. Tallahassee: Florida State UP, 1986. 222–30.

McGann, Jerome J. *The Beauty of Inflections: Literary Investigations in Historical Method and Theory.* Oxford: Clarendon, 1985.

———. *Black Riders: The Visible Language of Modernism.* Princeton, NJ: Princeton UP, 1993.

———. "Introduction: A Point of Reference." *Historical Studies and Literary Criticism.* Ed. Jerome J. McGann. Madison: U of Wisconsin P, 1985. 3–21.

———. *Social Values and Poetic Acts.* Cambridge: Harvard UP, 1988.

———. *Towards a Literature of Knowledge.* Oxford: Clarendon, 1989.

McNay, Lois. *Foucault: A Critical Introduction.* New York: Continuum, 1994.

Meese, Elizabeth. *(Sem)erotics: Theorizing Lesbian : Writing.* New York: New York UP, 1992.

Merleau-Ponty, Maurice. *The Primacy of Perception and Other Essays on Phenomenological Psychology, the Philosophy of Art, History and Politics.* Ed. James M. Edie. Evanston, IL: Northwestern UP, 1964.

———. "What Is Phenomenology?" Kockelmans, *Phenomenology* 356–92.

Messerli, Douglas. *From the Other Side of the Century: A New American Poetry 1960–1990.* Los Angeles: Sun & Moon, 1994.

———. *"Language" Poetries.* Ed. by Messerli. New York: New Directions, 1987.

Meserole, Harrison T. Introduction. *American Poetry of the Seventeenth Century.* Ed. by Meserole. University Park, PA: Pennsylvania State UP, 1985. xvii–xxxi.

Metcalf, Paul. "The Real Susan Howe." *The Difficulties* 3.2 (1989): 52–53.

Moriarty, Laura. "Laura." *Avec* 4 (1991): 3–5.

———. "The Midnight Man." *Ink* 2 (1988): 114–15.

———. "The Modern Lyric." *Poetics Journal* 7 (September 1987): 133–39.

———. Personal interview. 14 October 1994.

———. *Symmetry.* Penngrove, CA: Avec, 1996.

———. *Rondeaux.* NY: Roof, 1990.

Morris, Adalaide. "The Concept of Projection: H.D.'s Visionary Powers." Friedman and DuPlessis 273–96.

Newman, Denise. "The Concretion of Emotion: An Analytic Lyric of Mei-mei Berssenbrugge's *Empathy*." *Talisman* 9 (Fall 1992): 119–24.

Olson, Charles. *Call Me Ishmael*. San Francisco: City Lights, 1947.

Oppenheim, Lois. "The Field of Poetic Constitution." Tymieniecka 47–59.

Ostriker, Alicia. "No Rule of Procedure: The Open Poetics of H.D." Friedman and DuPlessis 336–51.

———. *Stealing the Language: The Emergence of Women's Poetry in America*. Boston: Beacon, 1986.

Perelman, Bob. "Facing the Surface: Representations of Representation." *North Dakota Quarterly* 55.4 (Fall 1987): 301–11.

———. *The Marginalization of Poetry: Language Writing and Literary History*. Princeton: Princeton UP, 1996.

Perloff, Marjorie. *Radical Artifice: Writing Poetry in the Age of Media*. Chicago: Chicago UP, 1991.

Potter, Elizabeth. "Gender and Epistemic Negotiation." Alcoff and Potter 161–83.

Pound, Ezra. "Others." *Little Review* IV (March 1918).

Quartermain, Peter. *Disjunctive Poetics: From Gertrude Stein and Louis Zukofsky to Susan Howe*. New York: Cambridge UP, 1992.

Reinfeld, Linda. *Language Poetry: Writing as Rescue*. Baton Rouge: Louisiana State UP, 1992.

Riddel, Joseph N. "H.D. and the Poetics of Spiritual Mysticism." *Contemporary Literature* 10.4 (Autumn 1969): 447–536.

———. "H.D.'s Scene of Writing—Poetry as (and) Analysis." *Studies in the Literary Imagination* 12.1 (Spring 1979): 41–59.

Riley, Michael D. "The Truth of the Body: Merleau-Ponty on Perception, Language and Literature." Tymieniecka. 479–93.

Ruddick, Lisa. "A Rosy Charm: Gertrude Stein and the Repressed Feminine." *Critical Essays on Gertrude Stein*. Ed. Michael J. Hoffman. Boston: Hall, 1986. 225–40.

Scalapino, Leslie. "An Interview with Leslie Scalapino." By Edward Foster. *Talisman* 8 (Spring 1992): 32–41.

———. *Considering how exaggerated music is*. San Francisco: North Point, 1982.

———. *Crowd and not evening or light*. Oakland, CA: O Books, 1992.

———. *How Phenomena Appear to Unfold*. Elmwood, CT: Potes & Poets, 1989.

———. *The Return of Painting, The Pearl, and Orion*. San Francisco: North Point, 1991.

———. *that they were at the beach*. San Francisco: North Point, 1985.

———. "'Thinking Serially' in *For Love, Words* and *Pieces*." *Talisman* 8 (Spring 1992): 42–48.

———. "from *Waking Life*." *War* 0/3. Oakland: O, 1991. N. pag.

———. *way*. San Francisco: North Point, 1988.

————. Written exchange with the author. September 1994.

———— and Ron Silliman. "What/Person: From an Exchange." *Poetics Journal* 9 (1991): 51–68.

Schelling, Andrew. "Reading 'Thorow.'" *Talisman* 4 (Spring 1990): 115–18.

Schmitt, Richard. "Husserl's Transcendental-Phenomenological Reduction." Kockelmans, *Phenomenology* 58–68.

Schultz, Susan M. "Laura Riding's Essentialism and the Absent Muse." *Arizona Quarterly* 48.1 (Spring 1992): 1–24.

Scott, Bonnie Kime. *The Gender of Modernism: A Critical Anthology.* Bloomington: Indiana UP, 1990.

————. Introduction. Scott, B., *Gender* 1–18.

Scott, Joan W. *Gender and the Politics of History.* New York: Columbia UP, 1988.

Showalter, Elaine. "Women's Time, Women's Space: Writing the History of Feminist Criticism." Benstock, *Feminist Issues.*

Silliman, Ron. *In the American Tree.* Orono, ME: National Poetry Foundation, 1986.

————. *The New Sentence.* New York: Roof, 1987.

Smith, Paul. "H.D.'s Identity." *Women's Studies* 10.3 (1984): 321–37.

Spivak, Gayatri Chakravorty. *In Other Worlds: Essays in Cultural Politics.* New York: Methuen, 1987.

Stein, Gertrude. *The Autobiography of Alice B. Toklas.* New York: Random, 1960.

————. *How to Write.* Intro. Patricia Meyerowitz. New York: Dover, 1975.

————. *Lectures in America.* New York: Random, 1935.

————. "Narration: Lecture 2." *The Poetics of the New American Poetry.* Ed. Donald Allen and Warren Tallman. New York: Grove, 1973. 104–14.

————. *Selected Writings of Gertrude Stein.* Ed. and intro. Carl Van Vechten. New York: Vintage, 1990.

————. *Tender Buttons.* Los Angeles: Sun & Moon, 1991.

————. "A Transatlantic Interview 1946." *Gertrude Stein: A Primer for the Gradual Understanding of Gertrude Stein.* Ed. Robert Bartlett Haas. Los Angeles: Black Sparrow, 1971.

Stewart, Allegra. *Gertrude Stein and the Present.* Cambridge: Harvard UP, 1967.

Stimpson, Catherine. "Gertrude/Altrude: Stein, Toklas, and the Paradox of the Happy Marriage." *Mothering the Mind: Twelve Studies of Writers and Their Silent Partners.* Ed. Ruth Perry and Martine Watson Brownley. New York: Holmes & Meier, 1984. 123–39.

————. "Gertrude Stein and the Transposition of Gender." *The Poetics of Gender.* Ed. Nancy K. Miller. New York: Columbia UP, 1986. 1–18.

Tichi, Cecelia. "Spiritual Biography and the 'Lords Remembrancers.'" *The American Puritan Imagination: Essays in Revaluation.* Ed. Sacvan Bercovitch. Cambridge: Cambridge UP, 1974. 56–73.

Todd, Janet. *Feminist Literary History.* New York: Routledge, 1988.

Trinh, T. Minh-ha. *When the Moon Waxes Red: Representation, Gender, and Cultural Politics.* New York: Routledge, 1991.

Tymieniecka, Anna-Teresa, ed. *The Existential Coordinates of the Human Condition: Poetic-Epic-Tragic*. Boston: Reidel, 1984.

Watten, Barrett. "Political Economy and the Avant-Garde: A Note on Haim Steinbach and Leslie Scalapino." *Talisman* 8 (Spring 1992): 49–52.

Watts, Linda S. *Rapture Untold: Gender, Mysticism, and the "Moment of Recognition" in Works by Gertrude Stein*. New York: Lang, 1996.

Weedon, Chris. *Feminist Practice and Poststructuralist Theory*. Cambridge and Oxford, UK: Blackwell, 1987.

Weinberger, Eliot. *American Poetry Since 1950: Innovators and Outsiders*. New York: Marsilio, 1993.

Wellek, Rene, and Austin Warren. *Theory of Literature*. 3rd ed. New York: Harcourt, 1956.

Wexler, Joyce Piell. *Laura Riding's Pursuit of Truth*. Athens, OH: Ohio UP, 1979.

White, Hayden. *The Content of the Form: Narrative Discourse and Historical Representation*. Baltimore: Johns Hopkins UP, 1987.

———. *Metahistory: The Historical Imagination in Nineteenth-Century Europe*. Baltimore: Johns Hopkins UP, 1973.

———. *Tropics of Discourse: Essays in Cultural Criticism*. Baltimore: Johns Hopkins UP, 1978.

Young, Iris Marion. *Throwing Like a Girl and Other Essays in Feminist Philosophy and Social Theory*. Bloomington: Indiana UP, 1990.

Index